"As human beings seeking footing in our family, work and social worlds, we stand and walk on shifting sand. And so, as the authors of this remarkably lucid and insightful book argue, we need to find grounding in the secure bases provided across the course of a lifetime by people, pastimes, projects and professions that both provide a safe haven from life's inevitable storms and that challenge us to meet loss and opportunity with courage in the pursuit of greater meaning and calling. Rich in real-life illustrations, chock-full of practical strategies, and deeply wise in its integration of our unique histories as relational beings, The Craft of the Secure Base Coach offers a trove of principles and procedures for living with greater clarity and competence in our personal and professional lives. Read it for yourself and read it for the people and organizations you serve. I can guarantee that it will repay your investment."

Robert A. Neimeyer, *PhD, Author of Living Beyond Loss and Director, Portland Institute for Loss and Transition*

"In increasingly turbulent times, the ability to create the conditions where people can thrive is vital. To do this, one needs to cultivate secure base spaces where caring, daring and sharing is the norm. I highly recommend this book. It provides a powerful and practical guide to secure base work at both the personal and professional level, nurturing mind, body and spirit."

Dr. Susan Goldsworthy, *OLY, IMD Business School Professor and Co-author of award winning books: Care to Dare, Choosing Change and Where the Wild Things Were*

"This is an exceptional book that gets at the heart of coaching – learning how to be present and listen deeply, attuning to ourselves and others, and most importantly, focusing on our intention to walk alongside clients and provide them with a solid foundation as they navigate change and transition in their lives. Every section offers compelling examples, thoughtful reflections, and unique insights. This is a must-have volume that will prove invaluable to coaches and helpers from all backgrounds."

Darcy Harris, *RN, RSW, MEd(Couns), PhD, FT, Professor, Thanatology Department King's University College at Western University*

"An essence of the coaching profession is that it is about the love that we feel and the power of love to overcome fear and provide direction. Without that love, we lose curiosity about our clients' unruly inner world with its sun and shadow sides. Change takes place in a loving relationship. The craft of the secure-base coach provides profound and practical pointers to build truly loving relationships. This book makes your self-care as a coach as important as the care you offer your clients. A wonderful piece of work and guidance for the profession."

Erik de Haan, *Director of the Hult Ashridge Centre for Coaching and Professor of Organizational Development at the VU University Amsterdam*

"*The Craft of the Secure Base Coach* is an essential manual for coaches who aspire to facilitate transformational change within individuals, teams, and organizations. Through a masterful blend of theoretical insights, real-world case studies, and practical tools, this book empowers coaches to establish themselves as a 'secure base' – a pivotal source of inspiration and stability for clients navigating the complexities of personal and professional transitions. The authors guide readers through the nuanced layers of identity evolution, equipping them to support others in finding their anchor points amidst life's inevitable changes. Any coach committed to deepening their impact will find this book an invaluable resource for cultivating resilience and fostering growth in those they mentor."

Dr. Marshall Goldsmith, *The Thinkers50 #1 Executive Coach and New York Times bestselling author of* The Earned Life, Triggers, and What Got You Here Won't Get You There

"This is a very important and timely book. Intimacy is not a word you often hear in relation to coaching. But of course, as this book so eloquently and clearly explains, it is our earliest intimate relationships–our attachments–that create our inner map for all future relationships. We are finally beginning to grasp just how vital and foundational our capacity to bond with other humans and further, with our more-than-human world is to our thriving. This is the essence of interdependence, and without it we are lost. We will never find fulfilment, nor will we address the critical challenges facing us at a global level by going our separate and lonely ways. Indeed, the epidemic of loneliness in the world is the canary-in-the-coal mine: an indication that we have got things seriously wrong. The authors not only explain Attachment Theory, John Bowlby's brilliant addition to the psychological lexicon, with great clarity, but illuminate how it shows up in coaching, how it informs the client-coach relationship and therefore a successful coaching partnership. The authors bring in neuroscience and case studies to link the cognitive with the physical, the theoretical with lived example. A richly rewarding must-read for the coach who wishes to develop and deepen their art."

Hetty Einzig, *Leadership Coach, author, Association for Coaching Director of Publications Strategy and Executive Editor, Coaching Perspective global magazine*

"*The Craft of the Secure Base Coach* – Enabling Transition needs to be on the shelf of every counselor and life coach. This book offers sound suggestions in assisting counselors and coaches in helping clients not only cope with transitions, however painful they may be, but to even grow and learn from such life-experiences. As a grief counselor, this book will be one of my most valued resources."

Kenneth J. Doka, *PhD, Senior Vice-President, The Hospice Foundation of America, Professor Emeritus, The Graduate School, The College of New Rochelle*

"Transitions are part of life. Helping individuals and teams navigate change is often overlooked or done poorly. Van Wielink and colleagues demonstrate a thoughtful and detailed command of the subject. The writing style is engaging and the authors provide numerous exercises that readers could readily incorporate into their armamentarium of skills. The book is highly relevant to counsellors, coaches, psychotherapists, mentors, team leaders, and managers wishing to be more effective in their practice."

Lauren J. Breen, *PhD, FT, Professor of Psychology, Curtin University, Australia*

"This masterpiece has evidently been written based on authentic self-reflection and research by the authors. Throughout the whole book you feel the focus on 'walk the talk'. Throughout the book the loving, caring perspective combined at the same time with decisive daring questions for the secure base coach, form the basis of an abundantly clear message: all transitions, emotions and real, bold reflections form an opportunity to become more authentic and grow."

Dr. An Hooghe, *Professor of Psychology, Vrije Universiteit Brussel, Grief therapist, Marital and Family therapist*

"As I began reading this book, I noticed almost immediately that it evoked a visceral sense of bodily calm and wellbeing, as if affirming the truth of what is shared here. I am convinced this book represents an important and innovative contribution to coaching. Its integrative concepts and practices are an invitation to bring one's whole self to this relational work, and it will stimulate those in the field to work in ways that are courageous, creative, and ethical."

Dr. Reinekke Lengelle, *Associate Professor of Interdisciplinary Studies, Athabasca University; award-winning author of* Writing the self in Bereavement

"In a world marked by unexpected loss, change, and transition, the authors skillfully explore the concept of safe harbors – those restorative spaces for mind, body, and spirit. Their work thoughtfully underscores the importance of these havens as an essential component of effective leadership. Any reader who appreciates the value of mutual support and understanding in their professional and personal relationships will find this book engaging and insightful."

Phyllis Kosminsky, *PhD, LCSW, FT, Adjunct Professor of Social Work at Fordham University, member of the International Working Group on Death, Dying and Bereavement*

"Transition is fundamental and natural to the human experience, yet many of us have not learned the craft of supporting ourselves and others through life transitions in a way that fosters adaptation and growth while honoring the losses that come with change. The authors of this book have enabled readers to become mindful of the power of the secure base while learning how to coach themselves and others through life's transitions."

Dr. Jill A. Harrington, *DSW, LCSW, Creator & Lead Editor*, Superhero Grief: The Transformative Power of Loss

"*The Craft of the Secure Base Coach* is a transformative guide that transcends traditional coaching approaches, offering a holistic and profound perspective on coaching in times of transition. Whether you are a seasoned coach seeking new insights or a novice looking to deepen your practice, this book is a must-read for anyone committed to fostering growth, resilience, and transformation in themselves and others."

Sally Mounir, *APACS-certified psychotherapist and counsellor who has obtained a Graduate Diploma in Psychotherapy and Counselling from The School of Positive Psychology*

"At its beginning, this new book by Jakob van Wielink and colleagues sets the scene for the management of transition—'every new beginning of any kind starts with saying goodbye'. The challenge of life change is that we are not always responsible for its reasons and yet, must respond to its consequences. We find ourselves negotiating complex and sometimes traumatic transitions at times of loss, grief, and isolation. To embrace a new life, we need to let go of an old life that may no longer nourish us. Those who are fortunate realize that they cannot undertaken the transition journey alone and need the wisdom of coaching to formulate strategies for a healthy and sustainable life change.

This new book brings together the art and science of coaching practice. Using concrete case studies exemplars which will resonate with practitioners, as well as self-reflection exercises, the varied and stimulating content will provide a robust framework for the coaching practitioner to be secure in their own base, as they strive to reach out and support others. Given the real-world challenges that people face in contemporary life, this book is a welcome and vital resource for the professional coaching community, exploring our innate humanity through a carefully scripted and dynamic resource for daily practice.

Philip Larkin, *Chair, International workgroup on Death, Dying and Bereavement, Kristian Gerhard Jebsen Chair of Palliative Care Nursing, Palliative and Supportive Care Service, University Hospital of Lausanne, University of Lausanne, Switzerland*

"In *The Craft of the Secure Base Coach*, Van Wielink and his colleagues do a masterful job of synthesizing the literature on attachment, attunement, bonding, resilience, loss, grief, meaning and calling during times of transition to present a practical and compassionate book that will be invaluable. Integrating theory with numerous case studies, graphics, practical exercises, somatic integration, important points to take away and self-reflection for the reader in every chapter, these authors entice the practitioner to learn, reflect, integrate and develop new techniques in their practice. A Must-Read for coaches and therapists."

Mary L.S. Vachon, *RN, RP, PhD, Registered Psychotherapist in Private Practice, Adjunct Professor, Department of Psychiatry and Temerty Faculty of Medicine, University of Toronto*

"This seminal book recognizes change as inevitable, emphasizing the presence of loss in every transition. It offers practical tools to help establish secure and supportive relationships with clients navigating challenging times. By unpacking the losses they experience, it aims to facilitate a smoother transition process and foster resilience."

Dr. Heidi Horsley, *Executive Director – Open to Hope Foundation, Adjunct Professor – Columbia University*

"This remarkable group from the Netherlands recognizes that we live more or less wisely, not more or less scientifically. The craft of coaching of which they write is really grief counselling that both supports grievers as they experience the particular painful reactions that come over them in the wake of unwelcome changes in the world as they experience it and that aligns with grievers in seeking wisdom necessary for moving through transitions that require relearning how to live in response to those changes. Its combination of clear and compelling writing, substantial wisdom, wonderfully illustrative case studies, exercises for counselling settings, and self-reflections for counsellors makes it, on my view, must reading."

Thomas Attig, *author of* How We Grieve: Relearning the World *(Revised, 2011: Oxford University Press)*

The Craft of the Secure Base Coach

In *The Craft of the Secure Base Coach*, the authors take a new and combined approach to the professions of coaching and counseling to provide a guide for professionals wanting to better assist individuals and teams in periods of transition.

Based on up-to-date scientific insights, and grounded in concepts from attachment theory, this book explores the themes of life transition based on the authors' own Transition Cycle model, and how professional coaches and counselors can become a secure base for their clients during sometimes traumatic and transitional periods in their lives. Consisting of two parts, the first part of this book focuses on how to become a secure base coach, using case studies to illustrate how readers can affect real change with their clients when providing humanity and proximity to the professional relationship. The second part provides a more practical guide to working with individuals and groups, and how to apply the themes of the Transition Cycle to help with guiding transition.

This will be a valuable resource for coaches, counselors, and therapists, as well as those currently in training. It will also be of use to leaders wishing to learn more about their coaching skills, as well as social workers and grief counsellors/therapists.

Jakob van Wielink is a partner at The School for Transition, an international leadership coach and trainer and associated with the Portland Institute for Loss and Transition.

Klaartje van Gasteren is a partner at The School for Transition, an international leadership coach and trainer.

Marnix Reijmerink is a partner at The School for Transition, an international leadership coach and trainer.

Anne Verbokkem-Oerlemans is a leadership coach and the Head of Training at The School for Transition.

Leo Wilhelm is an executive in the Dutch central government, a leadership coach and an affiliate of The School for Transition.

Riet Fiddelaers-Jaspers, PhD, is a leadership coach and grief therapist at the Expert Centre Coping with Loss and a mentor of The School for Transition.

The Craft of the Secure Base Coach

Enabling Transition

Jakob van Wielink, Klaartje van Gasteren, Marnix Reijmerink, Anne Verbokkem-Oerlemans, Leo Wilhelm and Riet Fiddelaers-Jaspers

Routledge
Taylor & Francis Group

LONDON AND NEW YORK

Designed cover image: The image on the front cover was designed by Douwe
Hoendervanger, www.douwehoendervanger.nl.

First published 2025
by Routledge
4 Park Square, Milton Park, Abingdon, Oxon OX14 4RN

and by Routledge
605 Third Avenue, New York, NY 10158

Routledge is an imprint of the Taylor & Francis Group, an informa business

Translated by James Campbell. James can be found at www.thelastword.eu

British Library Cataloguing in Publication Data
A catalogue record for this book is available from the British Library

Library of Congress Cataloging-in-Publication Data
A catalog record has been requested for this book

ISBN: 9781032730226 (hbk)
ISBN: 9781032701233 (pbk)
ISBN: 9781003424178 (ebk)

DOI: 10.4324/9781003424178

Typeset in Times New Roman
by Taylor & Francis Books

Contents

Figures

Tables

The inn

What came your way in the course of your life
it wasn't all happiness that happened to you
How can you make sense of your setbacks
Try sharing them, too long alone wears you out

Where do you find the strength not to turn sour
Even when nothing stays the same as before.
Who says it won't get better behind your walls.
And no longer closed–off, means no longer alone

I'm happy to walk with you awhile
Then you'll feel a little less weight for a while
Uphill is easier with the two of us
And the higher we get, the more we can see

"What are you doing" is a question you heard so many times
"Who are you" you never hear, when that's what really matters
You need a solid base, not empty words
You can move forward, if you know where you stand

Everything in life you looked forward to
Faith and hope and love, you've tasted them all
Where is your happiness now, your lust for life
But the moment you start moving, you remember who you are

I'm happy to walk with you awhile
Then you'll feel a little less weight for a while
Uphill is easier with the two of us
And the higher we get, the more we can see

Look the inn is open for you
Let's celebrate our joys, share our sorrows
There is a place for us here and we'll take our time
So that you will soon feel and see again outside

The song *The Inn* was written by Henk Pool and Paul Passchier for the occasion of the fifth anniversary of The School for Transition.

Contributors

Jakob van Wielink (1974) is a pioneer in the application of secure base thinking to coaching, therapy, and counseling. He is a partner in The School for Transition in Huissen (Netherlands). He is also a faculty mentor at the Portland Institute for Loss and Transition (USA) and a member of the International Work Group on Death, Dying and Bereavement. In 2022, Jakob was the *Ira Nerken International Keynote Speaker* at the annual conference of the Association for Death Education and Counseling, of which he is also a member. Jakob works internationally as an executive coach for leaders and their teams and is an educator and trainer of professional coaches. He has contributed to many books about coaching, therapy, and transition and is a member of the Advisory Board of the *Journal of Coaching*. *The Craft of the Secure Base Coach* is Jakob's ninth book about the process of transition. He previously co-authored, among others, *The Language of Transition in Leadership*. In 2019 he published *Loss, Grief, and Attachment in Life Transitions* in the Routledge series *Death, Dying, and Bereavement*.

Klaartje van Gasteren (1980) is a partner in The School for Transition. She brings her experience as an international consultant and business expert to her work as a secure base trainer and coach. She coaches organizations, (management) teams, and professionals in leadership development. Together with colleagues and peers, Klaartje has published articles on (personal) leadership and transition. She has contributed to *The Language of Transition in Leadership* and co-translated *Leading from Purpose* by Nick Craig. In her work in The School for Transition, Klaartje's particular focus is on working with the theme of female leadership.

Marnix Reijmerink (1978) is a partner in The School for Transition. He coaches teams, organizations, and their leaders at home and abroad in their (leadership) development. Marnix is chief trainer of the *Secure Base Team Coaching* course, where he trains peers to work with teams, organizations, and their leaders. He also works with a particular focus around the theme of male leadership. Marnix publishes on (personal) leadership, transition, and team development. He contributed to the book *Language of Transition in Leadership* and is co-translator of the books *Hostage at the table* by George Kohlrieser, *Care to Dare* by George Kohlrieser, Susan Goldsworthy, and Duncan Coombe, *The Father Factor* by Stephan Poulter, and *Leading from Purpose* by Nick Craig in Dutch.

Anne Verbokkem-Oerlemans (1974) is Head of Training at The School for Transition. Together with Jakob van Wielink, she delivers the year training *Secure Base Coaching: Professional Coaching in Transition* and delivers several other training courses at the School. Anne focuses her coaching in particular on body-centered work. Anne previously co-authored articles for the *Journal of Coaching* around female leadership, and leadership in high risk situations. In The School for Transition, Anne, together with Klaartje, has a particular focus on working with the theme of female leadership. Before her work at The School for Transition, Anne was an organizational coach in the Royal Netherlands Army. She supported commanders in shaping transition within the organization and contributed to social safety within teams.

Leo Wilhelm (1966) is a consultant with The School for Transition. He is a grief coach, secure base coach, and author and works as an executive in the Dutch government. Leo has been a longtime volunteer at a hospice. Leo has contributed, together with Jakob van Wielink and Riet Fiddelaers-Jaspers, writing about counseling around loss and grief, and about transition. He has co-authored several books and articles and contributed to compilations edited by Robert Neimeyer and Johan Maes, among others.

Dr Riet Fiddelaers-Jaspers (1953) is an inspirational force at The School for Transition. She is founder of the Expert Centre Coping with Loss, in Heeze (Netherlands) and co-founder of Opleidingen Land van Rouw (Professional Education: The Land of Grief). In her private practice, she coaches professionals, from the systemic perspective, in the fields of attachment, grief, and trauma. She is a sought-after speaker, chairperson/moderator, and delivers training courses. She developed the Masterclass *Systemic Working with Traumatic Loss* for the Expert Centre Coping with Loss and participates as a trainer. Riet's oeuvre is vast. She has written dozens of books in Dutch about loss and grief, attachment, and trauma. Riet is also co-author of *The Language of Transition in Leadership*. Together with Hanneke Fiddelaers, she has a presence in the digital world via their Dutch podcast *De verliescirkel* (The Cycle of Loss).

De School voor Transitie | The School for Transition

The School for Transition is a secure base for people and organizations who want to shape transition. The School offers courses, workshops, coaching, and supervision for senior leaders and professional coaches, such as the Secure Base Coaching and Secure Base Team Coaching courses. In addition, the School provides personal leadership programs for professionals.

Expertisecentrum Omgaan met Verlies | Expert Centre Coping with Loss

The Expert Centre Coping with Loss was founded in 2005 by Riet Fiddelaers-Jaspers, PhD. The centre works with loss in a broad context, supporting people and professionals through serious illness, death, divorce, adoption, out-of-home placement, and radical change of residence or work. The centre also supports in terms of loss of safety, attachment, and belonging. The training courses offered by the Expert Centre reflect this broad perspective.

Acknowledgments

Some things happen to us. They happen or occur without our actively seeking them, or doing anything for them. So it seems with this book too ... or not, perhaps.

In 2015 the first group completed *Secure Base Coaching: Professional Coaching in Transition,* in Huissen (Netherlands). That course arose, in part, from the retreats *Personal loss in perspective*, where participants learn how to relate to profound life-events from the perspective of their life-line. The framework of those retreats was the Transition Cycle, 'our' window on human development. A window that seeks to acknowledge the connection of past, present, and future, where loss is a part, but not the end.

In 2017 the first *Secure Base Team Coaching: Professional coaching of teams in transition* took place. By developing this course alongside *Secure Base Coaching,* we were able to link the themes of transition to the challenge of group dynamics. We encourage supervisors of teams and organizations to shape transition and challenge them to also shape the specific focus it requires. In doing so, we see a clear difference between working with individuals and working with groups (teams and organizations).

Thus, during the initial and ongoing development of these courses, the craft of the secure base coach began to ask for our attention. Both training courses invite participants into a personal exploration of the craft, leading to deep capability.

As it is with many things in life, this book began as an idea, a dream to take this craft and all its rich facets much further than just training courses in Huissen. A dream that came true when Marloes van Beersum of Boom publishers told us they were interested in publishing a book in the Netherlands about the craft. Because, according to Boom, the time was ripe for a standard work that zooms in on the process of transition through the identity of the coach and the practice of transition-coaching. Heartfelt thanks to Marloes and Boom. And special thanks to Lilian Eefting, our Dutch editor. Thanks to her sharp eye for detail, the text gained clarity and elegance.

It was inspiring for the five of us to write this book and to be inspired and assisted by Riet Fiddelaers-Jaspers. While writing, we were confronted with how the themes of the Transition Cycle impact our own lives. This book gave us the chance to write down what we actually do every day that we are working with our clients, teams and organizations and, turned out to be a great joy for all of us. It makes our work accessible to a large group of professionals around us.

Needless to say, we cannot do our work, and could not write this book, without the shoulders on which we stand. They are many and broad, and in reading this book you will have come met many of them. We would like to mention few in particular.

George Kohlrieser has been influential in teaching us the importance of secure bases in the context of organizations and leadership. This makes him a source of inspiration for us to make the themes of the Transition Cycle the tool of choice for human development in the professional context.

Robert Neimeyer shows us that loss is always to be found in human stories. The work he does around meaning-making in major life transitions feeds and supports our work. He teaches us that every major event is an invitation to give meaning, through trial and error, to your own life story.

Wibe Veenbaas, together with Piet Weisfelt, introduced George Kohlrieser's *Bonding Cycle* to the Netherlands, renaming it *The Attachment Cycle*.[1] Their initiative – which spurred the development of *The Loss Cycle* by Riet Fiddelaers-Jaspers and Sabine Noten – inspired Leo Wilhelm and Jakob van Wielink to develop the perspective we know as The Transition Cycle today.

Martijn van Lanen and Jorien Ouweneel know the language of transition. Their love for people and the craft makes them a valuable and critical resource for us. Thanks to their keen proof reading, the manuscript became more solid and resilient.

The examples and stories in this book, that illustrate the work we do, could not have come about without the many clients and participants in our education and training programs. They were always willing to share with us their lives and experiences around transition. We are incredibly grateful to them. Without their willingness, and courage, to begin that journey, we would not be able to practice and develop our craft.

A special tribute to a special colleague, Michiel Soeters. He has been an associate of The School for Transition for many years, and is the face of GeenManOverboord.nl (No man overboard). He took the initiative to publish Stephan Poulter's books *The Father Factor, The Mother Factor and The Shame Factor*. From his experience and knowledge, he has made an important contribution to the body of work around the influence of our parents on our identity.

We owe so much to our partners and our families. Without their support and the space they gave us to write, this book would not have been possible. Writing a book requires many sacrifices; theirs perhaps the greatest.

Finally, a word of thanks to all the people who, over the years, from their bonds with us, have been a source of inspiration for us personally and for the practice of our craft.

Jakob, Klaartje, Marnix, Anne, Leo and Riet

Note

1 Veenbaas, W., Hjort, M., Broekhuizen, M. and Dirkx, M. (2019). *Passe-partout. Vensters op leren. Kaders (Passe–partout. Windows on learning. Frameworks).* Utrecht: Phoenix Opleidingen.

Introduction: It will happen, but it will take time

Caroline arrives at the coach's office with a concern about a protracted conflict in her team; it's her fourth session. Previously they explored her life-line and the presence – or lack – of secure bases in her life. A painful and overwhelming memory is the moment she and her father were taking her mother to rehab after years of alcohol abuse. The coach sits opposite her, as he always does. He sits in the chair, Caroline opposite him on a bench. After a few moments she says to him, as if out of the blue, "That stuff about secure bases doesn't work at all in practice. It's just theory". He is thrown off guard; feels the urge to come up with a response. Maybe he does mumble something.

Then he takes a breath and is silent. He notices what is happening within himself. Something like panic and restlessness. A tendency to withdraw. Taking another breath he makes eye contact with Caroline. Two images arise in him: a young girl, left alone by her mother, and the young woman opposite him, struggling to take her place in the team. "Might I come and sit next to you for a moment?", he asks. She nods silently. He moves across.

He sits beside her in silence for several minutes. He notices how her loneliness touches him. Like his own loneliness that he knows all too well. Caroline's breathing calms and soon tears are flowing. "May I ask you what your tears are about?", he asks. She takes a deep breath and looks him straight in the eye. "The experience of someone coming and sitting next to me, looking from my perspective. That's really new. It gives me some relief."

For years, this encounter with Caroline stayed with him. In that session, so much about attachment fell into place for him. And he still often hears an inner voice saying: "Just cross over (to the client's side)" when a session is tense or stuck.

The era we live in is very focused on celebrating individualism, self-expression, self-confidence and self-development. The craft of the professional coach also aims to develop healthy autonomy and resilience. The coach does

DOI: 10.4324/9781003424178-1

this in a world where change and uncertainty are the daily currency. A world where one crisis seems to follow another.

This aspect of the coach's work, focusing on 'staying present' and 'being or remaining yourself' is a strong quality. However, to tap into autonomy and make it fruitful, we will have to look with our clients for the context in which they learned to trust themselves, when things get really tense and life confronts them with unforeseen challenges.

In examining that context and how it permeates the here-and-now, the paradox we find is that the presence or absence of others plays a crucial role in our resilience. Resilience – the ability to bounce back in the face of disappointment and setbacks – does not develop in isolation. On the contrary. It is our intimate relationships (or lack of them) that shape our lives and our resilience. Autonomy and bonding are two poles that simultaneously attract and repel each other. The combination of healthy autonomy and resilience is only possible when we are bonded.

In the last century in particular, there have been numerous concepts and schools of thought that help us understand how human bonds are woven and maintained. The concept that has received the most scientific study is, at the same time, the one least known to those outside traditional (clinical) psychology and psychiatry. It is called *attachment theory*. And it is precisely our attachment(s) that determines if and how we make real bonds. The kind that give life its shine.

The miraculous world of attachment

About 70 years ago, a British psychoanalyst called John Bowlby laid the foundations for what at that time was a groundbreaking (attachment) theory. In his anthology *A secure base*, [1] Bowlby recounts how his work was so new that the famous and influential report he wrote for the World Health Organization had only just enough supporting data to be accepted.[2] He passionately appealed for ongoing research: "It is for workers in the coming half-century to refine perceptions, to elucidate complexities, and to give the power to prevent mental illness." His colleague Mary Ainsworth – who introduced the concept of *secure bases* – would go on to play a leading role in the validation of Bowlby's attachment theory.

Our relationships with others are the source of our greatest support and joy, but also cause our deepest wounds. We cannot avoid this paradox; after all, to avoid pain is to avoid life. From our first breath, the human system, guided by our brain, is primarily focused on seeking proximity with available others. Attachment is therefore not a choice, it is an instinctive movement fundamental to survival. Attachment is a survival strategy: authors such as Mario Mikulincer and Philip Shaver show how much it carries over into our adult lives.[3] Our brain is pre-programmed for bonding. If we have good fortune on our side, attachment leads to protection and nourishment in childhood, comfort as we get older and, throughout our lives, gives us the experience of being known, and of belonging to somewhere and to someone.

Human beings are not made to be alone. Our attachment system is designed to be able to experience security, to discharge and recharge and live life. We could say that our attachments provide the fundamental mechanism for developing resilience. Attachment prepares us for the great letting go that is always waiting for us and makes it possible to live a full life.[4]

A stubborn challenge in practice

Secure attachment is the beginning of all growth and the ability to cope with adversity. The latest studies show that the security of that attachment is not actually 'fairly' distributed. Indeed, it is not so great if you belong to the 40 percent–50 percent of people who are (predominantly) insecurely attached because their early experiences were not optimal. For example, their caregivers were insufficiently available, dismissive, unreliable, absent or perhaps even threatening. It is a misconception to think that this only refers only to severely inappropriate behavior and traumatic experiences.

Another misconception is that if there is enough love, the attachment will be secure. The presence or absence of love has only a limited effect on attachment security. In counseling and coaching practice, this is one of the most difficult areas to research. Most coaches, therapists and coaches did not previously look at their parents or caregivers through the lens of secure or insecure attachment. Indeed, most are quick to say: "At my home, I was safe and secure. My parents loved me. Things happened from time to time, but nothing really serious." Yet there is much more to be said about this.

Azim was 35 when he was fired. He was accused of being passive. This passivity led, among other things, to carelessness in his work. Passivity and Azim go hand in hand in his marriage, causing a tremendous strain on the relationship.

When his coach asks him about his experiences of being encouraged, Azim recounts how he was given all the space he needed to take the initiative: "I was not given any challenges. There was actually hardly any criticism if something didn't work out, so I never felt I had to perform." When asked how exam results and school choices were handled, Azim says it was never really important. "My mother was a kind, sociable woman. She was interested in what I was doing, but she didn't ask much. I think it was, at times, a bit too much for her. She was often very tired. My father was fond of repeating that 'good is good enough' and encouraged me to go to college in the nearby city instead of university, although I actually would have much preferred the latter. It enabled me to continue living at home. I liked that, but I think I also did it to satisfy him. I guess that, in a way, I gave in to him."

Azim discovered – through being a loved child – the insecure aspects of attachment he'd been exposed to in his life, namely a lack of genuinely involved proximity and encouragement. In the process of counseling, he learns to actively trust himself with new attachment figures with whom he looks at the painful episodes of his life, especially the consequences of being fired. Gradually, what has come to be called *acquired secure attachment* develops: new internal models that enable Azim to allow himself to feel vulnerable and, in this state, to take emotional risks that lead to new feelings of safety.

Actually, it's all between the ears

Developments in attachment research and the latest scientific insights into how our brain works are inextricably linked. Secure attachment allows our brain to remain calm in situations of stress and danger (experiences triggered, for example, when we are faced with the pain of loss), so that we can explore what can bring us healing, growth and meaning. In other words, secure attachment ensures that our *mind's eye* – the part of our brain that determines our focus – can be and remain focused on learning, rather than on survival and danger. This neurological development takes place in the context of our relationships with others. It starts at birth and continues into adulthood, with the people with whom we build intimate relationships based on the bonds we form with them.

The scientific discipline that studies this development is part of what we call interpersonal neurobiology. It makes connections between development in the brain, the impact of loss and trauma on the structure of the brain, and how these mechanisms carry over into the client–coach relationship.

No model or theory alone enables change. How our brains function and how attachment works are not what heals our clients. What heals is the nature and security of the therapeutic relationship. John Norcross put it this way: "The question for coaches is no longer 'what is the theoretical starting point?' but rather 'what relationship, adjustment and approach will prove most effective for this client in particular'."[5] It is fascinating how current research is revealing the basic principles that enable healing in the client–coach relationship.

Healing in this context does not mean the absence of triggers, or eliminating the possibility of being touched by old experiences. What it does mean is that the physical memory of these experiences no longer hinders us from bonding with ourselves and our surroundings and maintaining these bonds. Healing means being able to build bridges to others and to the world around you, with healthy self-esteem, in a way that is sustainably fulfilling.

Nobel laureate Eric Kandel showed that when clients actually experience changes in their situation as a result of coaching (or counseling), the brain is also changed.[6] What is fascinating, is that the mechanism making this change possible is precisely the client–coach relationship. In that relationship, emotional processes occur in the right brain that are of a completely different nature from the emotional development of our brain when we are young. Effective coaching focuses on developing language that our right brain understands. Such language allows the client to feel more able to manage emotions. No longer is the client held hostage by emotions at defining or critical moments. The client has emotions, but the emotions don't have the client.

It happens in proximity

We will see in this book how coaching through transition (change at the identity level) does not go without loss. Every new beginning of any kind starts with saying goodbye. Every new beginning of any kind starts with separation. When clients face loss, it triggers old attachment experiences of dealing with separation, what Bowlby named *separation anxiety*. It triggers positive or negative experiences a person had in past attachments. We can interpret 'past' as meaning the entire childhood. Based on those experiences, one develops a behavioral repertoire of responses that might or might not be helpful and appropriate.

If a child has enough positive experiences of an attachment figure, a secure base who remains present and available during disappointment, frustration and (temporary) separation, it develops a healthy behavioral pattern that leads to resilience. The child experiences that emotions can be expressed and explored without running the risk of not belonging. If that attachment figure was not, or temporarily not, present during those same experiences, separation anxiety and protest behavior develops that will persist until the (or another) attachment figure becomes available. Such behavior can easily continue for decades, and also arise during the coaching session.

Those of our clients struggling with change – and the losses that come with it – and actively searching for paths to healing are always looking for new answers to old questions. As we make our way through life, our neurons grow in present bonds. Our brain has an almost absurd plasticity; neurons that are actively used produce new proteins that in turn strengthen those neurons. This mechanism was made famous by Donald Hebb's statement that "neurons that fire together, wire together."[7] The close proximity of the professional coach who is also a secure base for his client is what stimulates neurons to do their work.

This necessary proximity is also physical. Attachment experiences store themselves in our bodies. The body 'remembers' how it previously reacted to breaks and separations in attachment, and it always responds very directly and in the same way it reacted back then. Learning to perceive and understand the body – our temple – and our reactions is, therefore, inextricably linked to the journey that is transition. The body never lies. Our brain does.

As neurons, in proximity to another, do their work, step by step they over-write old attachment experiences in our brain, creating new pathways. *That's where the healing kicks in.*

From rescuer to enabling transition

Getting to know yourself as a person and as a coach is a prerequisite for doing the precious work you are being called to do. And however much this wisdom is taught in most counseling courses, the practice of coaching can be much more gritty. Getting to know yourself also happens in the encounters with your clients. They will constantly activate triggers that bring you back to your personal story. Or to the part of the story that you, as a coach have created about yourself, and with which you are able, at times, to skillfully circumvent the truth of certain events and experiences in your own life.

A coach is not a robot, but neither is she neutral. Nevertheless, she should be able to know herself and manage her own inner world in a way that prevents her from displaying unhealthy and obstructive behavior towards her client. Knowing your own existential – fulfilled and unfulfilled – needs and desires, facing your wounds and traumas, noticing your reactions and responses, helps avoid getting into situations of (blind) transference and counter-transference.

The demon that will overcome most coaches at some point in their career is *rescuer behavior*. We all like to help; few would openly claim that they do not like to help. If we haven't done sufficient work to reveal our own attachment and loss issues, however, it can lead us to believe we are helping others when we are actually trying to get what we ourselves need. Thus, we are essentially more focused on being reassured by our client – as long as he finds me good, kind, professional, successful, experienced... enough – than we are focused on taking risks that might truly deepen the client–coach relationship. A risk that will undoubtedly also reveal conflicts.

Just as every addiction finds its ground in elements of insecure attachment, so too is rescue behavior a kind of addiction. An addiction that, for the coach, will ultimately lead to forms of exhaustion, unfulfillment, and stunted professional growth. In the end, rescuers – like perfectionists – are unable to tackle their own problems and challenges, be they emotional, physical, cognitive or spiritual in nature. It's persistent.

Good education in the craft of coaching must include a deep examination of where our own rescuer dynamics surface. In its re-acknowledgement and recognition, we become Superman with a torn cape; wounded healers. For it is only when we can bow to the reality of our own wounds that we become truly human in our coaching. Human first, then professional.

The negative effects of 'professional' first are visible everywhere in society. And this points us again to the essence of attachment: proximity. Clients don't just drop in to see a coach to pass the time of day. For one reason or another, they are no longer succeeding on their own, or in the ways they used to. Healing only becomes possible when a client meets a flesh and blood person who knows how to, and regularly, manifests real proximity. Translating that knowledge into concrete action enables a radically different, counterintuitive experience of proximity.

In close proximity, our neurons are actively used and this happens precisely in the client–coach relationship in which, through careful empathic attunement, the deepest emotions can be explored. In this attunement, the client experiences new feelings of security that allow him to navigate the edges of the abyss, belayed by a new kind of confidence. There, and there alone, a new belief arises, hope is experienced and love becomes possible. There, new answers to old questions are found.

Yes, guiding through coaching is an act of love. With that love for clients and curiosity about what makes us human, the coach is able to create a situation where the other is more important than himself. Not out of heroic altruism or megalomaniac self-denial. But because the healing he is finding in his own life is at the service of the person opposite him; the person inviting him to cross over to closeness, to close proximity.

Shaping the craft of the secure base coach

The publication of this book is the confluence of a wonderful request from Marloes van Beersum, at Boom Publishers, and our common wish. In the courses offered by The School for Transition, such as *Secure Base Coaching* and *Secure Base Team Coaching*, participants gain a profound understanding of the wonderful world of the themes on the Transition Cycle, all of which originate in the attachment approach. We dreamed of a book that would further unlock the wealth of knowledge and experience we have accumulated through training, the craft of professional coaching and working with clients and coachees. *The Craft of the Secure Base Coach: Enabling Transition* is the result. This touches on an even bigger shared dream: to help make a world where more people feel safe. Not for the sake of security itself, but for the extraordinary growth that becomes possible as a result.

Whatever question the client comes to you with, you can always apply secure base coaching. There is no contraindication to this approach. The only contraindication is whether you feel you are the appropriate coach for the client at that moment. For example, when you are too affected by the client's story in your own story, and you find that you can no longer be fully caring and at the same time daring, it is advisable to refer. The same applies when you notice that you cannot be unconditionally present because of your own triggers, or you no longer have insight into projection and transference mechanisms. This says nothing about whether or not you can safely and meaningfully apply the secure base approach in relation to the client or the coaching question, but it does say something about whether or not you yourself can be the right instrument for the client at that moment.

So it is right and important to ask yourself what you can handle as a coach. The existential question is about your ability and your will to come close, be close, and stay close. So this question is not primarily about the other person and the nature of the problem with whatever possible 'label', 'diagnosis', or 'pathology', but about ourselves. About our part in the contact, our possible inability or resistance to deal with pain, fear or rigidity in the other, touching something in ourselves. Each must first become aware of his own limits in order to observe them.

This book is structured in two parts. In the first part – *Being a secure base coach* – we reflect on the main building blocks of the craft and explore with you the roots of your coaching approach. How has your coaching been shaped by your inner landscape? How have you explored that hinterland, worked on it, integrated it and made it fertile so that it feeds the growth of others? We discover what transition is and how working in proximity makes change possible.

In the second part – *The practice of secure base coaching* – we follow the themes of the Transition Cycle. This opens into the recurring existential themes of coaching: making contact and welcoming, experiencing attachment and resilience, bonding and shaping intimacy, suffering loss and saying goodbye, grieving and putting the pieces of the puzzle of life back together again, experiencing meaning, and living your calling. We explore these themes at both individual and organizational levels. We provide you with concrete methods you can use in your coaching practice.

For the sake of readability, we choose to use the 'he/him' form in this book, which of course also means 'she/her'. We use the terms secure base coach, coach and counselor alternately, always referring to the secure base coach.

"It will happen, but it takes time", said John Bowlby. Developing and refining a craft is a journey of practice, discovery, practice and … practice. Above all, it is the adventure of getting to know yourself, enjoying that there is always so much left to discover. Examining your attachments, as well as those of the people who turn to you in exquisite trust, remains something of an enigma. And that's how it should be. For the human being who is no longer curious about the unknown in himself and others, although alive, is already, slowly leaving that life.

On your journey with this book we wish you good travelling companions, extraordinary (in)sights and fun along the way. You are worth it. And so is your client.

Huissen, Spring 2024
Jakob, Klaartje, Marnix, Anne, Leo and Riet

Notes

1 Bowlby, J. (1988). *A secure base. Parent–child attachment and healthy human development.* London: Routledge.
2 Bowlby, J. (1951). Maternal care and mental health. A report prepared on behalf of the World Health Organization as a contribution to the United Nations program for the welfare of homeless children. *Bulletin of the World Health Organization,* 3: 355–533.
3 Mikulincer, M. and Shaver, P. (2017). *Attachment in Adulthood. Structure, Dynamics, and Change.* New York/London: Guilford Press.
4 Wielink, J. van, Wilhelm, L., and Geelen-Merks, D. van (2020). *Loss, Grief, and Attachment in Life Transitions. A Clinician's Guide to Secure Base Counselling.* New York: Routledge.
5 Norcross, J. and Lambert, M. (2011). *Psychotherapy relationships that work. Evidence-Based Responsiveness.* New York: Oxford University Press.
6 Kandel, E. (1998). A new intellectual framework for psychiatry. *American Journal of Psychiatry,* 155(4): 457–469.
7 O'Connor, M. (2022). *The Grieving Brain. The surprising Science of How We Learn from Love and Loss.* New York: Harper One.

Glossary

In our work, and therefore also in this book, the language we use has evolved to suit the specific therapeutic needs. Certain words have thereby a meaning beyond their original mere functional meaning. In the text, we aim to clarify these special meanings. In this glossary, we bring together the words we feel are most important to clarify beforehand.

Attachment	The subconscious act – and neurobiological necessity – of seeking close proximity with an available other, who is supposed to be better able to deal with life's challenges
Attunement	The responsiveness to someone's needs and moods, both emotionally, physically, mentally, and spiritually
Available	Not only being accessible, but also consciously present, emotionally and mentally, with your full attention and an open heart
Belonging	Being welcome in and being part of a larger group or system
Bonding	The conscious and deliberate act and choice to connect with others on a level of vulnerability and intimacy. We will use the term bonding consistently, where we feel that (mere) connecting to others misses the intended layer of intimacy
Boundary	The personal boundary refers to the intangible, dynamic, and fluid, yet personally very important and strict space or confine, both physically and emotionally; we also use the word boundary to refer to events and experiences that mark a clear demarcation on one's life-line, between before and after the event or the experience
Conflict/battle	Conflict is about being able to disagree about something openly, while staying curious and

DOI: 10.4324/9781003424178-2

	bonded, with your heart open; battle is the escalated level where the bond is broken and the hearts are closed
Fruit (response)	Our wounds (both physical and emotional) cannot only heal, they can even bear fruit when we are able to move from 'despite' to 'thanks to'. That response is the fruit of our wound
Genogram	The schematics of your family system, but containing more info than a family tree about relationships, both 'above water' and in the undercurrent
Grief	The total palette of emotional, physical, cognitive and spiritual reactions that can occur when you are faced with losing someone or something meaningful to you. Grief then is not restricted to when a loved one dies. That is why we consistently use the word grief, since we also cover non-death losses. In case of a death related loss the words mourning or bereavement could also be used

Specific types of grief

Anticipatory grief	When the loss can be seen coming; anticipatory grief contains all the elements of grief, while the loss has not manifested definitively
Complex grief	Severe grief resulting from a loss where many of the indicators of complex grief are at play all at once
Disenfranchised grief	When a loss is not (re)acknowledged by others, grief is very present but neither 'seen' nor acknowledged. When the (meaning of the) relationship was not visible or overt, or when events were not (allowed to be) public, the loss remains hidden, causing disenfranchised grief
Hidden grief	see Disenfranchised grief
Pre-grief	Synonym of anticipatory grief
Secondary grief	The grief over a secondary loss (see Loss and Secondary loss)
Solidified grief	When unaddressed grief is never attended to, the grief reactions can solidify
Unaddressed grief	When denying or not recognizing a loss for yourself, and not properly saying goodbye, grief will still ensue, but will not easily be recognized as such

Life-line	The representation of life events on a time axis, running from birth until now, symbolizing one's lived life so far
Loss	Is missing definitively who or what was meaningful to you, or could have been meaningful to you; loss then can also refer to what never came your way

Specific types of loss

Cumulative losses	Losses that occur in a short period of time, stacking one on the other
Diffuse loss	Losses that are less tangible, that lack clarity; they are perhaps unresolved in some way. The loss is often hard to pinpoint specifically on your life-line. Examples are unwanted childlessness, or a parent with dementia
Hidden loss	A loss that is not acknowledged by or cannot be shared with others; hidden loss can cause hidden or disenfranchised grief
Primary loss	The apparent loss, what is most important in the loss
Secondary loss(es)	Loss(es) attached to the primary loss, but less visible or tangible at first hand. Secondary loss(es) can become apparent over time. When losing a job for instance, the loss of coworkers, structure and self-esteem can be secondary losses presenting themselves over time
Unaddressed loss	When denying or not recognizing a loss, and not properly saying goodbye
Mind's eye	The selective filter in our brain that determines our focus. By nature, the mind's eye is focused on the negative, on danger and on avoiding fear, shame and pain. In the presence of external secure bases, this preprogrammed tendency of the brain can be overridden, ensuring that all emotions – of any kind – are welcome without judgment
Movement/motion	Not only physically, bodily, but also emotionally, mentally, and spiritually; being willing and capable to be moved empathically, and to sense your inner movements
Presence	Not only being bodily present, but also accessible and emotionally and mentally available
Proximity (professional)	As opposed to (professional) distance; not only geographically, or physically, but especially

	emotionally close and near; professional proximity in that sense, for us, is at the base of the therapeutic relationship
System (family system)	Firstly the family that you are born into, consisting not only of your relatives, but also of the codes and behaviors by which the system is characterized and defined and the history preceding the system. The system has boundaries to determine who is in and who is not. Your place in the system is dependent on your birth, relative to your siblings. Shifts can happen though and cause confusion, for instance when a son who is not the oldest sibling gets responsibilities that are denied the oldest girl. After your family of origin, any group can be seen as a system, being governed by similar rules of place in the group and dynamics of inclusion and exclusion
Touch	Not only physical, but also emotional
Transition	The emotional, cognitive, physical and spiritual process that people go through when facing profound change, chosen or not chosen. It is change at the identity level
Welcome	Refers to the level of positive response with which the system indicates acceptance of your presence; learning being welcome with your first (family) system, you can also learn what is needed to welcome yourself in other – possibly stressful – situations and systems
Wound	Not only physical, but also socially and emotionally; an attachment wound then is an experience of having being rejected by an attachment figure; this experience does not have to be a conscious memory, since we experience things from the moment of our birth, before we have language at our disposal
Wound response	The typical defensive survival reaction where the wound would not be touched again, or you would not be wounded again; as opposed to fruit response

Part I

Being a secure base coach

In the introduction, you learned that this book is made up of two parts. You are now about to start Part I. In this part, we first reflect on what transition is, and what role it plays in your life. You will discover how transition is evoked by change, that every change contains loss, and how transition is also, essentially, not the same as change. We pay attention to the background to your attitude as a secure base coach. You can think of this as the being energy of the craft. After all, as a coach, you yourself are the instrument you deploy.

In this first part, we lay a foundation for working from proximity in counseling. We discover how to work in this way at the layer of identity. Through working with the signaling function of emotions in the learning through new experiences, we come to the body and nervous system and how they form their own portal to what wants to be learned. Finally, we reflect on dialogue as a vehicle for guiding individuals and teams.

We conclude each chapter with self-reflection questions for you as a coach. This is how we help you make the journey from inside to outside.

DOI: 10.4324/9781003424178-3

Chapter 1

Life is shaping transition

For two years, Maria was employed by a company, putting heart and soul into her job. She worked hard and was proud to be part of a this successful company. She really saw herself as a part of it. Until one day, her director accused her of breaking internal rules and creating an insecure atmosphere in her department. Several months of intensive talks followed, eventually leading to her dismissal. It was an emotional and confusing period for Maria. What had she missed, done wrong, what wasn't right? The feedback she received was: you don't tune in, you don't involve others and you do it all your own way.

Change requires recognition of what was lost

Maria has to face a change at work that affects more than just her work. It seems to involve her whole being. Change is a constant in life. Change is observable around us and in our lives. We change homes, cities, friends, partners, work, country, faith and beliefs. And in every change, explicit, vague or hidden, something is lost. To give meaning to change, you must contemplate what is or will be lost.

> **Definition:** Transition is identity-level growth evoked by change.[1]

Recognizing and acknowledging the loss and exploring what has been lost,[2] is the starting point of any real transition. *What does this change mean to me, who have I become because of that which I have lost or that which was lost?* And then to be able to truly say goodbye to who or what is no longer there. For a person at such crossroads of life you, as a secure base coach, can be meaningful to them. By your presence, availability, and willingness to be your client's companion along these paths of transition.

It happens to us, it is unavoidable. As we bond, the time inevitably comes when we lose also. Loss is necessary for growth and development through all

DOI: 10.4324/9781003424178-4

the years of our lives.[3] We lose some of our deepest attachments to others. We lose some of our most cherished parts of ourselves. We must also, both in the dreams we dream and in our most intimate relationships, relate to everything we will never have or be. The deeper the bond, the more it leaves us vulnerable to loss. And we grow in the letting go and the leaving behind. That is exactly where you, as a secure base coach, are present in your client's life.

> *"It's time for me to really do things differently," are Martin's opening words to his coach. He talks about how his intimate relationship is under a lot of stress. It is palpable in the room as he talks about it. "Sometimes I think I'll just quit. Sometimes I think I'm completely done with it." Then he falls silent, looking at the coach. "Somewhere, I can also feel, Martin, that you are tired', the coach says. Martin lowers his head into his hands and a deep sigh escapes. "Yes" … agrees Martin. "And I don't want to quit, I just don't know what to do to change it anymore. So that it gets a bit lighter again."*

We reflect in this chapter on the impact and effects of experiences of loss – especially when they have not yet been grieved: possibly because the losses have not been recognized or acknowledged, or because the grief at the moment of loss was too great to let it into the heart. We call this disenfranchised grief.[4] Grief goes underground, so to speak, but does not disappear. It solidifies, you might say, and forms a protective layer around the loss so that the burden becomes manageable.

But because of that layer, integrating the loss into the life story gets put on hold. In the case study, Martin seems to want to end his relationship. The coach guides him to old loss that has not yet been grieved, where it has become 'dark', obstructing his intimacy and vulnerability with his partner. That is where the work necessary to grieve and to enable transition starts ("So that it gets lighter again").

So there is a price to pay for not allowing – at a certain conscious level – the emotions, experiences and thoughts associated with the loss. To avoid the pain of the loss, a certain part of the self is – unconsciously – closed off; in Martin's example his vulnerable part where he feels powerless. The pain thus remains under lock and key. However, avoiding the pain and not grieving the loss also leaves potential untapped. We show how, by working on the levels of emotions, identity and the body, you bring this not-lived potential – that is rattling at the gate of the clients request for help so to speak – into being.

We introduce in this chapter the themes and concepts that we will elaborate on in the rest of the book. We briefly describe them in this chapter and will indicate why they are important for anyone planning to work as a secure base coach. Among other things, this will introduce you to the themes of the Transition Cycle, the stages of transition, and secure bases.[5]

Shaping transition

Transition is somewhat different from change and at the same time is intimately related to it.[6] Change is about concrete, visible things or situations in the outside world. In the work context, at organizational level you can think of a move to a different building, a merger of two companies resulting in a new logo on the building or a reorganization which, along with the new organizational chart, also creates a new hierarchy. At team level, it could be about changes in team composition, setting new goals or getting a new assignment. Individually, you might have to respond to these changes at organizational or team level, as well as the possibility of redundancy or dismissal. In the private sphere, changes such as moving house fall into this category, as do the beginning and ending of personal relationships, the arrival of new family members, or the death of loved ones. Changes take place in what we also call the 'upper' (or surface) stream': visible, discussable, measurable. Changes mainly take place on the outside.

Transition is the emotional, cognitive, physical and spiritual process that people go through when facing profound change, chosen or not chosen. It is change at the identity level. How do I endure feelings of powerlessness, of helplessness? How do I respond to 'if only' thinking. Can I allow myself to be physically touched and comforted. In phases of intense grief, how can I put my trust in something greater, numinous. You can feel that these questions and the answers that go with them are accompanied by a process *within* the human being. Transition takes place in the 'undercurrent' of change: often vague or invisible, intangible. It doesn't lend itself to business or performance metrics. Transition takes place more on the inside, within and between people.

Undercurrent

The phenomenon of undercurrent can be encountered in nature in full force on the coast. On certain beaches, as you approach the water you will see warning signs on the groynes: Dangerous Current. The ebb and flow of the sea has a driving and pulling effect, which you can already feel when you are just ankle-deep in the water. Around breakwaters and sandbanks, this motion causes a powerful current (a.k.a. a rip tide or undertow) that can quickly pull an unsuspecting swimmer far out to sea.

The water finds its way back to the sea through the deeper sections, the gullies, which are perpendicular to the beach. Even trained swimmers can be no match for this current. *Going against the tide*, as the proverb attests, is utterly futile. Going with the flow until it loses momentum, and then breaking out sideways to return to the beach, is what lifeguards learn. Surfers actually use these currents to get more easily behind the surf to wait for good waves.

> Where water is in motion, there is always an undercurrent. Flowing water, then, has a visible and an invisible current. When navigating – another timeless leadership metaphor – you will have to account for both of these currents.

The fact that change affects people radically is because, first of all, change means the end of an old, but familiar situation. Every change, desired or not, starts with losing something or someone. Humans prefer to avoid the pain associated with loss. Our brain does not like pain, according to research by Elizabeth Carter and Kevin Pelphrey.[7]

Shaping transition requires making a counterintuitive movement to, as it were, give an answer to the newly created situation. In order to be able to say goodbye, you will first have to move towards the pain and discomfort, so you will be able to leave the old behind.

Our brain is set up to predict our world based on previous experiences. When the world around us changes, the brain has a model of reality that no longer fits. It takes time and mental capacity to bring these two 'worlds' back together.[8]

Loss and goodbye elicit a sense of discomfort, where the question is whether that discomfort can be allowed. Particularly in a business context, where change is often presented as an opportunity and an improvement, it is common for little attention to be given to that which is lost. Is there room for the discomfort that can accompany loss and parting? Is there recognition of the losses people suffer? Is there time to pause and is there time for the brain to adjust? In your personal life, too, you initially move away from the pain associated with loss and change; this is the brain's biological response. When your mother dies, you might be inclined not to dwell too long on the pain you experience. To reflect on the distress, the upheaval, the intense loss, and grief is a challenge.

The brain hates pain

In a world where change is a constant, it can be helpful to better understand how our brain is structured and how it, sometimes, supports us in shaping and, sometimes, not shaping transition.

Let's start with an example. If a child meets a snarling dog, it is likely the child will react with fear. The amygdala – the part of the brain responsible for emotions, emotional behavior, and motivation – activates *direct-arousal* centers in the brain-stem and forebrain. This activation creates a state of heightened excitability by producing substances such as noradrenaline in the brain and adrenaline in the body. The child becomes hyperalert and ready to respond to 'danger'. In Chapter 2, we describe what Stephen Porges calls *neuroception*. This involves activation of our fight, flight or freeze systems. The specific mental representations (collections of images in the brain) that are active during this *arousal*, become associated with this experience of danger and recorded in the brain. The neurons activated simultaneously become intertwined. A coupling has now been created where 'dog' equals danger and can cause amygdala activation and a brainstem response. And so, on a subconscious level, *self-fulfilling prophecies* are being created in the brain.

Even when seeking contact with others, our brain appears to be more focused on signals of anger than on signals of joy. Research by Elizabeth Carter and Kevin Pelphrey shows that in addition to the already known responses of specific brain areas (amygdala, brain stem and forebrain), two other areas of the *social brain*, namely the lateral fusiform ventricle and an area central to the middle temporal ventricle, also respond more strongly to signals of anger than to signals of joy. The social brain is the part that interprets the intentions of others during social contact, such as linking facial expression to emotion and personality.

Previous experiences, therefore, focus the brain on predicting what is coming so that it can put the 'right' systems in place to survive. Gaining different experiences actually means you are choosing to go against the brain's initial movement, against its own self-fulfilling prophecy. And so we are able to rewrite our own mental representations. This can feel counterintuitive, both for the client and for you as the coach.

What often makes it extra difficult to say goodbye to the old, familiar situation is that the new situation is usually still partly unknown. There is usually an image, a dot on the horizon that needs or wants to be reached. To get there, however, there is still an intermediate stage you have to go through. The old is not quite over, the new has not yet arrived. In the in-between period, there can be ambiguity, uncertainty. For some, this is a threatening period, because there is no grip, no control. For others, though, it can be a period of opportunities and possibilities: to use this space by undertaking something new. People have to move through this at their own pace. Some let go more easily than others. Not everyone takes on something new in the same way.

At a personal level, but also at the level of a team or organization, transition can involve growth when you can see change as a source of learning and development. In part by asking people questions, about what the change is like for them, what they need and by exploring what it means for them, growth can occur. Transition can take shape when there is recognition and acknowledgement from the organization, the environment and from yourself that something was lost. When you are actually allowed to say goodbye, you become free to bond with the new. And you can also renew yourself and your team in stepping forward.

Saying goodbye thus starts with the recognition and acknowledgement that something has been lost. Saying goodbye is then a matter of doing. Doing means actually saying goodbye on a cognitive, emotional, physical, and spiritual level to that which was lost. For instance, by speaking it out or by designing rituals that enable a client or a team to actually say goodbye.

By being consciously engaged with transition, through saying goodbye and bonding again, you are likely to benefit from a different perspective about yourself. You might discover qualities or parts of yourself that were not previously visible or used.

Every time Vera wants to share something in the group, she feels her emotions coming to the surface, yet she holds back; she dare not let them show. In several sessions with coaches and participants, she starts to see the mechanisms by which she does not allow her 'real' self to show. Her foot is, as it were, always on the brake; a brake she does not seem to be operating herself. She feels insecure and anxious, she says, afraid of "falling through the cracks." The coach suggests to Vera that the next time she feels her emotions rising, not to close her eyes, but to look around the group, to make eye contact.

It isn't long before her emotions are visible. Vera's whole body starts shaking and she starts crying. "Can you tell me what happens to you when you look around the group, looking everyone in the eyes," the coach asks. "I'm so scared," Vera says. Guided by the coach Vera explores the fear she's feeling. Soon she arrives at a profound event in her life: "I lost my sister in a car accident. I was driving. It's been ten years and every night the same nightmare where I keep crashing into the other car."

"What would it be like, Vera, to move forward in this by going back and saying goodbye to your sister?" the coach asks.

In the approach that follows, a participant sits opposite Vera, representing her sister. Vera feels into the moment of the accident again. She gives words to her guilt, that she feels she should atone in some way. Mentions the cramp and fear she still experiences. The coach invites Vera to switch seats with the representative; to take her sister's position and experience what it is like for her sister to see Vera like this. Vera discovers how calm she becomes when she sits on this chair, takes her sister's position. As her sister, she speaks words of love; of regret that she was not able to have more adventures with Vera. She speaks of how strongly she feels their bond with each other.

Vera is back in her own chair, and the coach asks her what it is like to make these discoveries and hear her sister's words. Vera tells how her guilt for surviving the accident also sometimes stops her from feeling joy; in friendships and with her partner. The coach then asks, "What was your favorite activity together?" Vera smiles as her answer bursts out: "Road trips!" She then starts to weep uncontrollably: "I suddenly realize that since the accident, I haven't had an adventure, a road trip. The only reason I drive the car now is purely practical. My sister and I used the car to go on adventures, usually without a plan. I lost my free spirit."

In the concluding dialogue, the coach asks Vera if she can commit to choosing a day and asking a friend to go on a 'road trip', the way she did with her sister. Then the coach asks her: "What have you just learned about yourself?" After a few moments silence, Vera replies: "That I no longer have to hold my breath because I survived the accident. And that I may discover my free spirit again."

Every change means saying goodbye to the old, while the new is not always quite there. Perhaps you think you are not yet ready to let go of the old, or you are not yet able to accept the new. Between the old that is not-yet-gone and the new that has not-yet-arrived, there is an in-between space where most of the transition process takes place. We also use the word liminality, derived from the Latin word for threshold. This in-between space can be seen as a liminal phase, a period similar to rites of passage such as birth, coming of age, marriage, and funerals.[9]

In crossing boundaries, entering and eventually leaving the in-between space, you have boundary experiences. In the in-between space, most of the work takes place in the saying of goodbye, grieving the loss and (re)orienting to who you now are. Your brain receives signals that do not reflect the reality as it was registered. It still assumes the bond with who or what, which in reality no longer exists. The brain does not yet 'know' the new, partly unknown, situation. Your brain has new neural pathways to build and use, new representations of reality to make.

Exactly where the conflict arises between the two streams of information in the brain is where learning starts.[10] This phase becomes a learning experience when the brain is able to create new pathways. This means learning new habits. Inevitably, one's sense of identity is also adjusted; we are confronted with the question: "Who am I without this or that significant other. This process is an emotional, and therefore neural and biochemical, process that requires time, and feedback through experience. As a coach, you are significant in being present during your client's boundary experience so that she can turn a loss experience into a learning experience. You take the time, in connection with your client, to connect his new reality to his identity. You help the brain adapt to the newly created situation. So you are present, as it were, in the 'conflict' that has arisen in your client between old and new.

Here, the closer the bond, the greater the impact of the loss can be. This means there is more work for the client in living through these boundary experiences.

Boundary experiences

During radical change, dealing with the in-between space often feels like stumbling through the proverbial desert. In the Old Testament, to escape slavery in Egypt, the people of Israel travelled through the desert for 40 years before they got to the Promised Land.[11] Early in the journey, as they stand before the Red Sea, with Pharaoh's army close behind, the people complain that they would have preferred to stay in Egypt. The parting, and crossing of the boundary into the desert, already proves difficult, despite being delivered from slavery. The forty year period eventually proved necessary, even though the people first arrived in the Promised Land earlier. But then they reacted ungrateful for the opportunity, as their scouts indicated there were dangers in the 'Promised' Land. The people preferred to return to the old familiar situation of slavery in Egypt rather than surrender to the new unknown. For punishment, they were then sent into the desert for 40 years.

Forty is symbolic, in the Bible, of a period of reflection and repentance, of preparation and trial. Sometimes forty days – think of Lent – sometimes forty years. The desert, with its silence and seclusion, is without parallel as the place for reflection away from the hustle and bustle of life.

Some people consciously seek that silence and isolation. However, consciously choosing for it can make the ordeal even harder. Lost in the vast space, looking for water, deceived by mirages, confronting questions arise. What worked before, doesn't work now. It made the Israelites long to return to the old days, even though they had to return to a life of slavery.

Nobody can know how long their transition will need. It cannot simply be planned or engineered. It might take much longer than imagined or, during the process, desirable. Time passes irrespective of how you spend it. While in that time, you have your own desert to endure, manifesting as the way you deal with the uncertainty. Temptations to give up and fall back lurk. Every boundary you have to cross demands something of you.

Leaving the old behind and moving into the limbo of the desert requires making choices. Just as moving across the desert and finally leaving the desert behind does. Should I stay or should I go? Do you go now, or perhaps later? What do you take with you and what do you leave behind? You have several boundaries to cross. In making those choices, you cannot rely totally on previous experience. Because something has changed. That change is precisely why you are in the desert. Old answers are often no longer sufficient. New answers dpo not simply present themselves. You will have to experiment with new ways of moving, in new directions, to reach towards new sources of support. To seek answers from people who came before you in the desert.

You find yourself in a place of learning. Learning to say goodbye, learning to grieve, learning to allow abandoning and feeling abandoned. Because, if we don't … we will have to do it all over again, suffering even more loss.

Maria tells the coach that, since she has been stuck at home after being laid off, she feels uneasy. She is not panicking, she says, but there is an incredible restlessness inside her that, no matter what she does, she is unable to feel settled. This surprises her, partly because she does not have to worry so much financially at the moment, because she received a generous redundancy package. The restlessness is so distracting that often, when she is walking around her village, she has to think hard about where she is supposed to be going.

The coach says to Maria: "When I listen to you and see how you move your hands, you seem to feel like you've lost your way. Am I right?"

"Yes!," she says, turning and staring intently at the coach. "I'm totally, damn lost."

"I see it makes you emotional. Is it true that this brings back a very old experience?" As they continue this exploration, Maria says she had to leave home at a young age because of her parents' divorce, which caused a lot of confusion and feelings of insecurity. While at university, those feelings faded somewhat into the background. In her first job, where she worked for 12 years, she experienced a strong sense of security and of feeling at home there.

Her redundancy makes her feel disoriented and she notices those old feelings of confusion and insecurity have returned. "When we explore this together in this way, it seems we are discovering together a chapter on your life-line that merits a closer look. Do you agree?" the coach asks. Maria nods a silent yes.

With every boundary you cross, old losses can resurface. When goodbyes have not been properly said, the strength of your reaction to a goodbye in the present can surprise you. For instance, in the session, Maria discovers that the loss of her job has surfaced an earlier loss of security and home when her parents divorced. Together with the coach she starts to remember what she experienced during and after their divorce. Earlier in this chapter, we wrote about the solidification of unabsorbed grief and the resulting stalling of its integration into your life. The pain of the old loss remains locked away until a new goodbye, as in Maria's example, brings it all up again. The coach has to encourage his client to explore this old pain, despite the fear it may evoke, and support her through whatever arises.

Working with a 'Mary' around these themes, or working with a team, also shines a light on you as a professional. You might 'guide' your clients from a willingness to research your own life line. How do you respond to your own boundary experiences? And do you know what has and has not helped you in doing so? You might not know in advance the way into the liminality of the other, but you do know that you must spend some time in between the boundaries of old and new. And you are willing to travel with them and be present from your own experience. In the next chapter, we will elaborate further on how guiding from professional proximity can might look.

In Chapter 10, we take an even deeper look at working around loss and separation. Saying goodbye urges you to give up your hope for a different history and to really grieve for what was (not) there. In this way, you uncover deeper layers in yourself that, in some way, have been lost. You learn *to land (again) in life*. And there you discover that very little can shape your identity more profoundly than that which you truly grieve.

Themes of transition

The Transition Cycle helps you to gain insight into the boundary experiences on your life-line. It is a lens through which you examine experiences; in your own life and that of your client. The themes on the Transition Cycle are recurring; they come into play when people start and end relationships – with other people, but also with things material and immaterial: objects or places with special meaning, that for us carry beliefs, dreams, and ideals.

The Transition Cycle has six pairs of strongly interconnected themes: in the order of time they are important in the ongoing cycles of entering into and ending relationships. The themes are not only connected around the circle, but also across it via the spokes. During almost any kind of coaching or counseling, exploring the themes on the Transition Cycle delivers much, often unexpected, insight.

In Part II, we explore these theme pairs and their interrelationships in more detail. Below, we provide a brief explanation. From Chapter 7 onwards, the themes of the Transition Cycle and how to work with them at individual and team level are described in more detail.

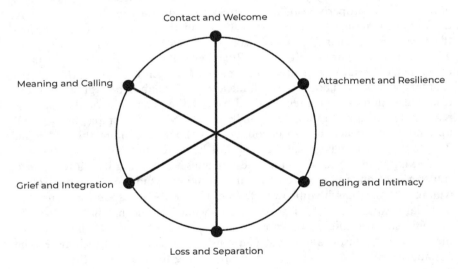

Figure 1.1 The Transition Cycle

Contact and Welcome

Who you are deeply, at the level of your identity, is about the place you are allowed to take. At birth, you already have a place in this world: your place in your family of origin. Your place in the row of children, if there were sisters or brothers, or alone. Your place in relation to your parent(s): in a foster family, with a stepparent or in a blended family, or adoptive parents. Your first place in life you carry with you forever.

This place is always part of a bigger picture, of a family history of people who came before you. A history from which and into which you were born, with generations before you that you also carry within you and that have meaning.

Your place and first welcome recur every day in every new meeting. In each new 'small' daily contact and welcome at school, work or sport, with friends, in-laws, colleagues, the theme of your first and deepest contact and welcome, to some degree, resonates.

Attachment and Resilience

Where you are first welcomed into the world is where you learn to attach: you seek proximity to others as a natural survival strategy. Attachment is not a choice, it is a condition of life. It is the natural (instinctive) and unconscious behavior by which proximity of an available other is sought. The way you learn to attach depends on the availability of – initially – your parent/caregiver as attachment figures.

Availability is more than just being present, it requires emotional presence and accessibility. When our attachment figures are not only sufficiently and reliably present, physically and emotionally, but are also sufficiently reliable and predictably reachable, and respond appropriately to our needs, we can learn to attach safely. When attachment figures – no matter how good their intentions – are unable to fully meet our needs, we run the risk of learning to attach *insecurely*.

In the development of our attachment style, our resilience also develops. How we deal with setbacks and disappointment is directly linked to how we react – also neurologically – to stress such as drastic change. Resilience is thus linked both mentally and physically to how we have learned to attach. How did you learn to regain physical and emotional balance after a stressful event? How did you respond when emotions like sadness or anger were triggered by something you experienced? In a secure attachment, you learn not only that you are intrinsically worthwhile, but also that you are self-reliant and can get stuff done on your own. How our attachment figures respond to us makes neural connections that influence our attachment style and, thus, our resilience.

When attachment figures are sufficiently available to you and you learn to attach securely, your attachment figures can become *secure bases* for you. Even where it seems that your attachment figures were there for you and you seem predominantly securely attached, exploring this period of one's life can unearth less-positive images. These might include sub-optimal or no availability of your attachment figures, insufficient encouragement, and insufficient physical contact, perhaps offering a different perspective on your development and thus your attachment.

> **Definition:** A secure base is a resource that makes you feel welcome and inspires and encourages you to face life's challenges, trusting in that bond.[12]

Peter tells the team, during the morning training session, that he had a "good childhood" and that he felt loved by his parents. In the second day of the team training, he says that while talking with a colleague, he suddenly recalled a memory from his childhood about how, under pressure from his father, he continued basketball training at the national level, even though he no longer enjoyed it.

When the coach asks what it was like to remember this, Peter replies, "It's confusing, also kind of painful, uncomfortable." After a short pause, he says, "And I realize, with everything I'm learning here about attachment, that it wasn't all peaches and cream at home. That sometimes my high standards for myself and my colleagues might have something to do with this."

Bonding and Intimacy

Bonding is the conscious act of approaching others, the choice to come closer – in vulnerability – in order to deepen the relationship. Your attachment style forms the blueprint of your ability to bond with others. Where, as a baby, a small child, you had no choice in your attachment, when you bond as an adult, you do have a choice. However free this choice might seem, it is, to a very large extent, determined by your attachment style. With a secure attachment style, you experience more freedom of choice than with an insecure attachment style. In bonding with someone else your vulnerability gives form to your intimacy.

Your ability to allow intimacy also depends on your attachment style. An insecure attachment style will either lead to avoidance of intimacy, because disappointment in the attempt to bond would have too much impact, or to dependent and claiming behavior, in which the other person does not experience freedom of choice.

Vulnerability

Vulnerability does not appear as an independent theme on the Transition Cycle. On the one hand, it is inseparable from Bonding and Intimacy; on the other hand, it plays a significant role in all the themes on the Transition Cycle. You could say that vulnerability is on the periphery of the Transition Cycle, never far away.

Brené Brown, with her research on vulnerability and shame, is seen by many as the founder of this concept.[13] Her 2010 TEDx Talk in Houston on *The Power of*

Vulnerability, had a massive impact on millions of people, particularly because – alongside the scientific research she presented – she used herself as an example: a human being, with all her imperfections.

Vulnerability is about your willingness and ability to let yourself be touched (emotionally) and share that with those around you. Vulnerability carries the risk of rejection because, without any guarantees, you are reaching out and standing for what you need. On the one hand, vulnerability implies a conscious choice – an attitude to life even, to take the risk of being rejected again and again – to want to be touched. On the other hand, vulnerability is a quality, a sensitivity you can develop. And developing your vulnerability allows you to deepen your bond with others.

Of course the opposite to vulnerability is invulnerability. Then you are not – anymore – willing to be touched, affected. A common error is to confuse vulnerability with weakness. Weakness is something else, it's a lack of determination, of the ability to stand on your own two feet and for what you believe. With weakness, you allow your freedom of choice to be limited by circumstances outside yourself, and you surrender autonomy. Vulnerability is a free choice to take responsibility and whatever comes with it.

Vulnerability is also about *the extent* to which you are willing and able to let yourself be touched. In developing your vulnerability, you will surely run into situations or experiences that might ask too much of you at that time. Moments when the pain just feels too great. Moments when the choice to withdraw, to escape the pain, seems more attractive than reaching out and risking rejection. Vulnerability demands reaching out anyway, through the pain. Trusting that you will get the support you need. The extraordinary thing is that the very act of allowing all your vulnerability to grow actually diminishes the pain, because the bond is restored.

Loss and Separation

Loss is about the termination of the attachment you had or wanted to have to someone or something. Saying goodbye and separating involves the emotional, physical, cognitive, and spiritual actions you take to acknowledge and reflect on loss.

Every bond in this life, irrevocably and inevitably, comes to an end sometime. Your ability to acknowledge loss and to give form to separation shapes you more than anything else. Big and small disappointments, moments of failure, every ending or unfulfilled need, results in a loss that can be experienced fully, a loss that invites you to say goodbye.

Loss cannot be undone. Loss and separation can be about people, but equally about material things we are attached to in some way, and intangibles such as ideals, dreams or beliefs.[14] Conscious separation is the bridge to grief, which only becomes possible after saying goodbye.

Grief and Integration

Grieving a loss is about the total palette of emotional, physical, cognitive and spiritual reactions that can occur when you are faced with losing someone or something meaningful to you. Grieving asks you to integrate the loss into your life story, to weave it together as it were. To mend the torn fabric of your life, to close the gap. Integration does not mean agreeing with it, it means accepting it as it is and ceasing to fight. It means giving up thinking you can change it or fix it.

Grief comes in all degrees of intensity, depending mostly on the significance of the relationship that was lost, on your own resilience and the quality and amount of social support you have. The more meaningful the relationship, the more intense the grief will be, where resilience and social support help you to bear the effects of grief.

Grief often does not take a straightforward course. Time does nothing for you if you do nothing during that time. Grief can come in waves[15], in alternating emotions of sadness, loss, anger, gratitude, and relief. Waves of thinking about what you should or would have done differently, where you keep playing out the same scenarios in your head. (often called rumination). Waves in which your body reacts differently than you are used to, your energy fluctuates, your appetite changes, concentration, and focus are lost. Waves in which existential or spiritual questions and doubts arise. Grief, in times of profound loss, can swing like a pendulum between dealing with loss and recovering from it.[16] You can be overwhelmed by the loss or, on the contrary, so completely absorbed by what daily life demands of you. Sometimes your focus seems, finally, to be returning and then grief overwhelms you again.

Healing

At the beginning of this chapter, we wrote about healing, your ability to choose your own response in the present, regardless of the wounds from your past. Just as a scar can continue to pull after healing, so too can an inner wound. Old wounds can remain sensitive to new events or experiences.

Just as you don't want love to end, grieving the loss doesn't have to stop completely. However, the intensity of grief and the extent to which it can overwhelm you should diminish. We are therefore reluctant to use words like 'passing' or 'processing'. We consciously choose to 'integrate' the loss into your life. Integrating is about the merging of parts into a new unity and is thus a 're-making whole' of what was torn apart by the loss. Different from before, admittedly. By healing we also mean, that despite the loss, you can live life fully again, allowing joy and experiencing beauty. And there is even the possibility of 'growth after loss'. Like a broken bone is actually stronger where it has healed. So, perhaps, you might be able to experience deeper joy than before.

Meaning and Calling

By integrating loss into your life story, you can give it meaning.[17] Here we don't mean labelling the loss as meaningful in itself. The loss has no intrinsic meaning. How you respond to the loss gives the event meaning in your life. You connect it to who you are, as it were. The loss challenges you to rewrite a part of your life story and find out who you are without that meaningful person or element that you lost.

Meaning-making is about actively choosing how you relate to events – especially incidences of loss, setbacks and failure. Through the choices made, you take leadership, as it were, over the events on your life-line. In feeling into and weighing up experiences and trials, you can create space by moving from "This is what happened to me," to "This is what shaped me." Loss experiences are, at their core, learning experiences; you move from "I got here *in spite of,*" to "I got here *because of.*" A movement in which not everything is 'solved' or made easy, but one which enables you to experience joy and beauty again alongside the memories that are there, to imagine and look forward to the future, and to make new bonds and deepen existing ones. Elements that enable us as human beings to experience joy in life.

In this way, you can also come to (deepen) your calling.[18] So, what do we mean by *your calling*? It is a combination of who you are and what you want to achieve or bring about in this life, bonded with others. By giving new meaning to a loss, there can be growth at the identity level. From this developing of your identity and from a reorientation to what you want to put into motion in this life, your calling can become clear(er).

In exploring the themes on the Transition Cycle with her coach, Maria comes to realize that she does not bond with others because she is always focused on working hard and getting results. "I thought I was doing people a favor; now I see that I am alienating people by not showing interest in how they are doing."

The coach is silent for a few moments and then says: "As you are speaking, I see your chest rises and your chin and neck tighten."

"Yes, that's right, I want so much to do things well. And when that doesn't seem to work out, I start to panic. It's a familiar scenario."

The coach guides Maria towards revealing where she knows this from. In dialogue with each other, she arrives at a memory from the past where Maria was fiercely criticized by her father if she achieved (only) average results at school. If she got a 'C' for math, her father sent her to her room and told her to "think about how you are going to do this better next time!" During the exploration with her coach she realizes this left her with a strong feeling of insecurity. "I am beginning to realize that I work hard from this sense of insecurity and, actually, not because it makes me so happy, as I always believed," Maria says with tears in her eyes.

By working round the Transition Cycle, theme by theme, you eventually complete the circle, so to speak. In dialogue with the client, we often move from the here-and-now to the past; we recognize certain themes there and then return to the here-and-now to help the client say goodbye to that which no longer serves her. Maria notices that how she behaves in the here-and-now has its origins in her relationship with her father. Doing these explorations might sound like an easy route to follow, but in many cases it is not. It is a very personal journey in which, in the case study, Maria examines her relationship with her father based on the Circle themes. This offers Maria a deeper knowing of herself as she learns to understand the dynamics of how she starts and ends relationships.

The importance of secure bases during transition

When shaping transition, we need secure bases. Secure bases support you when you are confronted by profound changes that bring new challenges and invite you to shape transition.[19] Changes or new experiences often offer you no choice but to experiment with new behavior or a new method of engagement, especially when your familiar ways and responses are no longer sufficient. As a result, you might find yourself on the edge of your comfort zone. Right on the edge of where you still feel comfortable, have some feeling of being in control and not too much stress or anxiety. In the discomfort that trying out things on the edge of your comfort zone can bring, it helps to feel the support of your secure bases, and how they encourage you to take risks.

The risk of experimenting with any new behavior or approach is that you will fail or you are rejected by people who know you because you are behaving differently. This risk creates stress in your brain, as it prefers to stay on its well-trodden (neural) pathways. Fear of the unknown and uncertainty about your new behavior can make you avoid getting too close to the edge of your comfort zone. Curiosity and enjoying experimentation, on the other hand, can help you to push the boundaries.[20]

No matter how important edge-of-the-zone experiences can be, real learning based on new experiences takes place inside your comfort zone. There, from calmness and security – essential for your brain, which needs to be in a calm state to evaluate experiences properly – reflection and analysis of experiences is possible. In the presence of secure bases, the comfort zone provides a *sense of belonging*, where you can anchor the learning outcome via dialogue with your secure bases. Your brain makes new connections and learns to forge new paths. Giving meaning to experiences, while in your comfort zone, can be a motor for personal growth. This allows you to expand your comfort zone, consciously engaging in more-different behaviors than before.[21] We will discuss the comfort zone in more detail in Chapter 2, which examines professional proximity.

Peter is a young man of 25, recognized as being very talented. At the company where he works, there is a relaxation room and every week you will find him there, playing table football. He is added to a challenging project as a second consultant. The primary consultant, Jan, who has worked for the company for over 15 years, chooses to play a game of table football with Peter every week. They are evenly matched; sometimes Peter wins, sometimes Jan. Always, after the match, they sit down. Peter shares where he feels challenged, what he is uncertain about. Jan listens to him, asks him questions, encourages and affirms him, and challenges him to keep taking risks, even in such an important project as this.

The craft of the secure base coach

Craft is the timeless name for the capabilities that you learn mainly through practice so that you can apply them in your profession. In the days of guilds, when a young person mastered the basic skills, he could become an apprentice. Learning by doing, under the supervision of a master craftsman, to whom they would be *apprenticed*. Work as practice, practice as work; becoming proficient, gaining flying hours. Compare it with the 10,000 hours of practice guideline: to develop a talent, a minimum number of hours would be needed.[22] While the number of hours themselves are important, according to Anders Ericsson's it is mainly about practicing correctly – and receiving feedback on that – and doing so with the support of a secure base.[23]

That is how we see it for the secure base coach. Although, as a coach, you can learn a lot from all the textbooks of the masters who have gone before you, you will have to spend your hours mainly in practice. Putting what you learned from your master(s) into practice, getting feedback on it, in order to learn what works for you. To do what works more and more. To be continually developing and refining your craft.

Experience is an important teacher. Learning from your own experience certainly applies to the exercises and approaches you use. This book contains many exercises and methods to accompany the chapters in Part II. Above all, we suggest you start by doing them yourself. You can share the results with colleagues and peer groups. This way, you can apply the exercise, method, or approach in guidance.

Code of ethics

Shaping your craft requires a broader context where it can develop and take on its own particular form. As a coach, you might have or feel a strong connection with colleagues who are shaping the craft of leadership coaching in their own unique way. You will stand on the shoulders of masters who have gone before you, and you might, in turn, lend others your shoulders. This is how the impact of working with the Transition Cycle themes grows in the world.

To feel connected within a bigger picture that guides your actions as a coach, it is valuable to (explore how you will) commit to a code of ethics and conduct. Such codes recognize and reinforce basic values and ethical principles. The code meets our need to know how to act ethically. It is a shared framework that guides our behavior and that of our peers, a compass guiding us in the direction of right behavior.

The School for Transition has its own code of ethics and conduct that includes the basic values of love, autonomy, balance, support and leadership and seven elements of associated behaviors that belong in our code of conduct. These reflect important elements of being a secure base, such as caring-and-daring and dialogue. And in this way, The School for Transition gives form and substance to what it is doing in the world. "We do the right thing even when no one is looking."[24]

The ethics and code of conduct of The School for Transition is attached as an appendix at the back of this book.

To be able, in proximity, to lead your client in the right direction, your own responses at transition moments in your life can also be (re)examined and lived through again and again. In each new self-examination, you find new or supplemental answers to old hurts and losses. You are able to further heal parts of yourself. We call it healing when such situations from the past no longer determine your reactions in the present. When you have regained the freedom to choose your own response in the present. This assumes that you have the willingness to keep doing this research about your own life line. *What were the major turning points in my life and what does the way I responded to them mean for who I am now as a coach?*

Important points to take away

- Loss is inevitable because as soon as we create bonds we will also suffer losses. Loss is necessary for growth and development.
- Change and transition go hand in hand. Change is about concrete situations in the outside world. Transition is about the emotional, cognitive, physical and spiritual process people go through in change.
- Every change starts with an end and ends with a new beginning. In between is a neutral zone where the old is not quite over and the new has not yet arrived.
- Change requires saying goodbye to what is lost. We grow as human beings in letting go and saying goodbye.
- Grief as a reaction to a loss encompasses all reactions: emotional, physical, cognitive and spiritual.
- Transition takes place in the undercurrent of a change and brings growth at the identity level.
- By actually saying goodbye, we shape transition and it becomes a source of learning and development.

- Our brain hates pain and is focused on signals of danger and predicting what is to come. Thus, our brain does not automatically help us to enable transition. This requires a choice.
- We are not defined by what we have experienced, but by the choices we make as a result.
- To shape transition, we need secure bases that support and challenge us in shaping transition.
- Craft requires on-the-job practice, becoming proficient and acquiring 'flying hours'.

Self-reflection for the coach

- What transitions did you experience on your life-line and how have those transitions shaped who you are today and what you do now?
- What losses have you had in your life and how have you learned to reflect on them?
- What painful events on your life-line still require exploration?
- What was an impactful loss and how does it affect your work as a coach?
- How is your connection with your body? What blockage(s) do you still notice and how does this affect your work with clients?
- What transition is currently playing out in your life and to what or whom must you say goodbye?
- How well do you know that liminal place in your life, the phase between the old that is not yet over and the new that has not yet arrived? And what have you been able to learn from being in it?
- What have you learned about showing your vulnerability and how willing are you to use this in your work?
- Who was available to you at key transition moments in your life and how did these secure bases help shape those transitions?
- Who (were) are your important teachers when it comes to your profession and what have you learned from them?

Notes

1 Wielink, J. van, Fiddelaers-Jaspers, R., and Wilhelm, L. (2023). *Language of Transition in Leadership. Your Calling as a Leader in a World of Change.* New York: Routledge.
2 The three–part 'recognize, acknowledge and explore' is taken from Fiddelaers-Jaspers, R. (2019). *Een rugzak vol verdriet. Kwetsbaarheid en kracht van rouwende jonge mensen (A rucksack full of grief. Vulnerability and strength of grieving young people).* Utrecht: Ten Have.
3 Viorst, J. (1998). *Necessary Losses. The Loves, Illusions, Dependencies, and Impossible Expectations That All of Us Have to Give Up in Order to Grow.* Upper Saddle River: Prentice Hall.
4 Doka, K. (1989). *Disenfranchised Grief. Recognizing Hidden Sorrow.* Lanham: Lexington Books; Doka, K. (2002). *Disenfranchised Grief. New Directions, Challenges, and Strategies for Practice.* Champaign: Research Press Inc.
5 Van Wielink, J. and Wilhelm, L. (2022). Coachen bij verlies. In gesprek over het verlies achter de coachvraag (Coaching loss. In conversation about the loss behind the coaching question). In: Donders, W. and Ruijs, L. (Ed.). *Coachende gespreksvoering (Conversational techniques in coaching).* Amsterdam: Boom.
6 Bridges, W. (2009). *Managing Transitions: Making the Most of Change.* Boston: Da Capo Lifelong Books.
7 Carter, E. and Pelphrey, K. (2008). Friend or foe? Brain systems involved in the perception of dynamic signals of menacing and friendly social approaches. *Social Neuroscience*, 3(2): 151–163.
8 O'Connor, M. (2022). *The Grieving Brain. The surprising Science of How We Learn from Love and Loss.* New York: Harper One.
9 Van Gennep, A. (1909). *Les rites de passage. Étude systématique des rites de la porte et du seuil, de l'hospitalité, de l'adoption, de la grossesse et de l'accouchement, de la naissance, de l'enfance, de la puberté, de l'initiation, de l'ordination, du couronnement, des fiançailles et du mariage, des funérailles, des saisons, etc.* Paris: Emile Nourry.
10 O'Connor, M. and Seeley, S. (2022). Grieving as a form of learning. Insights from neuroscience applied to grief and loss. *Current Opinion in Psychology*, 43: 317–322.
11 The Bible book *Exodus* tells about the exodus from Egypt; the Bible book *Numbers* about the initial arrival and return to the desert; the Bible book *Deuteronomy* tells about the final entry into the Promised Land.
12 Wielink, J. van, Fiddelaers-Jaspers, R., and Wilhelm, L. (2023). *The Language of Transition in Leadership. Your Calling as a Leader in a World of Change.* New York: Routledge.
13 Brown, B. (2015). *Daring Greatly. How the Courage to Be Vulnerable Transforms the Way We Live, Love, Parent, and Lead.* New York: Penguin.
14 Harris, D. (2019). *Non-Death Loss and Grief. Context and Clinical Implications.* New York: Routledge.
15 There are various views and models of grief, going back to the work of Sigmund Freud. For an overview, see: Wielink, J. van, Wilhelm, L. and van Geelen-Merks, D. (2020). *Loss, Grief, and Attachment in Life Transitions. A Clinician's Guide to Secure Base Counseling.* New York: Routledge. Grieving as a wave motion occurs as early as Bowlby, J. (1988). *Attachment and Loss, Volume 1–3.* London: Random House.
16 Stroebe, M. and Schut, H. (1999). The Dual Process Model of Coping with Bereavement. Rationale and Description. *Death Studies*, 23: 197–224; Stroebe, M. and Schut, H. (2010). The Dual Process Model of Coping with Bereavement. A Decade On. *Omega*, 61(4): 273–289.

17 Neimeyer, R. (2006). Bereavement And The Quest For Meaning. Rewriting Stories Of Loss And Grief. *Hellenic Journal of Psychology*, 3: 181–188; Neimeyer, R. (2019). Meaning reconstruction in bereavement. Development of a research programme. *Death Studies*, 43(2): 79–91.

18 Wielink, J. van, Fiddelaers-Jaspers, R., and Wilhelm, L. (2023). *The Language of Transition in Leadership. Your Calling as a Leader in a World of Change.* New York: Routledge; van Wielink, J. and Wilhelm, L. (2020). (Re)discovering Calling in the Wake of Loss through Secure Bases. *AI Practitioner*, 22(2): 13–18.

19 For more background, see, for example, 'The power of secure bases' chapter in Kohlrieser, G. (2006). *Hostage At The Table. How Leaders Can Overcome Conflict, Influence Others, and Raise Performance.* San Francisco: Jossey-Bass.

20 Ali, F. and Tan, S. (2022). Emotions and lifelong learning. Synergies between neuroscience research and transformative learning theory. *International Journal of Lifelong Education*, 41(1): 76–90.

21 Wielink, J. van, Fiddelaers-Jaspers, R., and Wilhelm, L. (2023). *The Language of Transition in Leadership. Your Calling as a Leader in a World of Change.* New York: Routledge.

22 Gladwell, M. (2009). *Outliers: The Story of Success.* Penguin Books.

23 Ericsson, A., Prietula, M. and Cokely, E. (2007). The Making of an Expert. *Harvard Business Review*, July/August: 115–121.

24 Ethics and code of conduct of The School for Transition.

Chapter 2

Guiding from professional proximity

Professional proximity

> Jane asks to have personal coaching, giving the reason that she recently lost her brother. In the beginning of the first session, she sits a bit defensively in her chair, as if it was not her that asked for this session. "Do you want to tell me what is going on in this moment?" the coach asks. For a long time Jane says nothing; the coach waits patiently as a heavy silence fills the room.
> "I'm embarrassed," Jane says, without looking up, in a monotone, her voice bearing the faintest hint cracking.
> "You're embarrassed," repeats the coach, "Do you want to tell me more about that?"
> Again silence. "Yes, well, I don't quite know what to say, but shouldn't I be able to handle this myself? Surely it's me that needs to get my life back in order." More silence. "He wasn't supposed to die," she says in a whisper.

With the heart open, without knowing where the journey is going, curious. This is how you can be present as a coach. Human: vulnerable, touchable and close to be a secure base for your client. This approach might be radically different for you as a coach to what you learned so far in your career. Perhaps you learned that guiding people necessitates taking professional distance. We invite you to do the opposite. To explore what it is like for you when, in your coaching, you are your client's trusted companion on this journey, in proximity. Your proximity makes it gradually possible for the client to utter words of shame, to go into what is painful, to take similar steps as Jane does in the story above.

Professional proximity creates a mindset from which you want to create a bond in order to offer real safety to the other person. From that safety, you can challenge the other person to do what is necessary to answer the coaching question – and also make new discoveries yourself. You don't know the

DOI: 10.4324/9781003424178-5

answers in advance. Professional proximity requires *presence*, the dynamic act of *being present*, of giving the other your full attention, without losing touch with yourself. Being present with nothing but an open heart and open hands, without wanting to solve anything – that is the basic attitude of presence. It is about your willingness and ability to be so present that you are actually a secure base in your relationship with the other person.[1]

Imagine that the next time a client enters your office or a team enters the training room, you connect with that other person/team fully and openly with your body and consciousness – with the desire to get closer more and more, to seek the intimacy of personal contact. What does it look like when you do this? What kind of eye contact, how are you present in your body, how do you breathe, how do you stand, sit in your chair? And what do you reveal about yourself in the encounter, what of the other person do you allow into your heart?

The importance of proximity in the counseling relationship comes from your client's need for attunement. Attunement is necessary for experiencing security so that the client's brain can feel peaceful enough to be open to new experiences.[2] From allowing those new experiences, learning arises.

Attunement

Attunement describes your degree of receptivity to another person's emotional needs and state of being. When you are attuned to someone, you respond with language and behavior appropriate to the state of being of the other person. You recognize the mood and emotions of another person and tailor your own response accordingly.[3]

If we look at attunement through the lens of a concert orchestra, we see they not only tune their own instruments before they start playing, they tune them based on a shared note. This vital process starts by the oboe sharing the note with the exact vibration. This note is picked up by the first violinist, who passes it subsequently on to the other string instruments, then to the brass section, and finally to the remaining wood instruments. This tuning – the ability to listen to the transmitted tone and replicate this frequency in one's own instrument – is vital to any successful symphony.

If you still have an old radio, you will be familiar with the need to tune it into the frequency of the station you want to listen to. Around the frequency at which the program is broadcast, there is often unwanted noise, or another station close by broadcasting a different program. To listen to your favorite program, it is necessary to tune in to exactly the right frequency.

This is also how we see the need for attunement in the counseling relationship. It's about finding a common frequency that both of you can tune into. In this context, we also talk about resonance or sympathetic vibration. When both coach and client are attuned to each other, it is often the case that the vibration of one reinforces the other: the energy between the two of you increases.

Attunement can already be found in how mothers and fathers respond to their newborn child's emotional and physical needs. This can range from matching facial expressions, adjusting intonation, picking up the child when it cries, feeding or changing. We see that attunement is directly linked to early childhood experiences of welcome and attachment. How you are present and respond to your client's emotional needs form the basis for contact.

Attunement touches directly on the basic human need to be welcomed and bonded, to belong, to feel you have a place – *a sense of belonging*. This experience of belonging helps build and maintain the client's comfort zone, from where it is possible to experiment and practice on the edge of or even outside this zone.

The encounter as a source of learning

To enable learning, we need secure bases. As you read in Chapter 1, a secure base is a resource that makes us feel welcome and inspires and encourages us to face the challenges that life presents. When we talk about secure bases, we are always talking about *caring* and *daring*. A secure base offers security, bonding and trust (caring), and encourages and challenges risk-taking (daring). This seems like a contradiction in terms. However, both are needed to tap into a person's untapped potential and thus enable growth.

In the contact and bond between coach and client, what enables the dance between caring and daring? Your greatest tool is how you meet someone, the encounter. Both the encounter with the other, and the encounter with yourself, while in contact with the other. Bonding is about energy being exchanged, cognitively, emotionally, physically, and spiritually. In the eyes of the other you meet yourself, you see your own light and your own dark, your own shadow. The other person's story touches on your own life story as a coach. As a human being, you are neurally equipped to empathize with the other person and empathize with their situation.[4] The other person's discomfort requires you to endure your own discomfort, to accept being touched.

We are all made to bond and empathize with others. *Our brains are hardwired for connection.* Out of shame and fear (separation anxiety), people unfortunately often do the opposite.[5] As a coach, you can't escape this either. No matter how experienced you are, you'll already have felt the fear of rejection. Your desire to belong (sense of belonging) comes into the session with you. Sensing this and yet bridging the gap with the other – reaching out, welcoming and truly bonding with the other – is part of your task as a coach.

Drama triangle

The drama triangle is always lurking close by, doing your work with an individual or doing team work. We want to mean something to the other person, perhaps being hyper-sensitive to what the other person might need. In proximity, there is a chance of falling into the position of the *rescuer*. The rescuer is one of three parts of the dynamic known as the drama triangle: the *rescuer*, the *victim* and the *persecutor*; these positions reinforce each other in a negative sense. Despite the (apparent) helping intentions of the rescuer, his behavior might put the other person in the position of, or reinforce the sense of being, the victim or the persecutor. This is because underneath the rescuer's behavior, he has no connection to the other person's need. The rescuer wants to 'fix' the other person, to be seen and recognized in his rescuer role. In doing so, however, the rescuer ignores the autonomy of the other person. By attuning – aligning your willingness to want to help with the other person's needs – you address their autonomy.[6]

At a deeper level, rescuer energy is an attachment movement. It is a response to insecure attachment, a way of masking the pain of not being seen or avoiding the fear of losing connection. You can imagine that if you include this kind of attachment movement in contact you're unlikely to open into a process of discovery and learning. At its core, 'rescuing' is a lack of daring and an excess of caring, even if it might feel or look like something else.

If you would only provide security and protection, you would be a source of great comfort to someone. However, if you did not encourage risk-taking, discovery and challenge, you would be too protective (*rescuing*) and inhibit their growth. When you push someone into risk-taking while offering insufficient protection and security, a person will feel insecure, exposed to danger. When vulnerability is magnified, someone might instinctively start defending or protecting themselves, closing themselves off to learning.[7] The experience of risk-without-protection mainly appeals to the neurological systems that ensure survival; systems that, to a large degree, simply repeat what you already know to do, and are not programmed for learning and development. Too much safety or unsafety both prevent you from entering into the state essential for learning, that of receptivity and curiosity.

Eight participants are sitting in a group with the coach. The coach is guiding a group discussion with the participants around transgressive behavior. One of the participants shares such an experience with the group, vulnerable. Another participant reacts rather loudly: "That's not transgressive, is it? That should be possible, right? I think what you said is absurd!" The coach is shocked, loses her curiosity and says: "That's not for you to judge. He clearly feels vulnerable sharing his experience."

During the break, the participant who shared his experience comes up to the coach: "I really appreciate that you stood up for me, and I would have liked to have had the chance to respond myself, to say how I felt about it." Immediately the coach realizes she reacted too quickly, from an automatic desire to protect and rescue the participant. She apologizes.

After the break, the coach explores with the group if they have similar experiences of trying to rescue someone and what emotions that action helps them avoid or minimize in themselves. She also apologizes to the 'second' participant. "I reacted too strongly when I said, 'It's not up to you'. I realized in the break how I was triggered. It was like my father saying, 'Don't get above yourself.' Shall we continue looking at this issue?"

Transference and countertransference

Johan comes home after a long day at the office. When he comes in, the table is set and his wife, Irene, is sitting at it with a half-empty glass of wine. She looks at him and says, "You're so late." Johan immediately feels himself tense-up and responds in a slightly louder voice than he would really like: "I'm ten damn minutes later than we agreed because I've been stuck in traffic! I'm tired of you always getting at me for being late. I'm sick of your criticism!"

Meanwhile, Irene has begun clearing the table and stops in front of him with a plate in each hand: "Why are you getting so aggressive right now!"

"I'm not getting aggressive at all, I'm irritated at what I just said. I work my ass off to earn enough for us to live comfortable, and then I get this 'welcome', when I'm ten minutes late because of the traffic."

This goes on for several minutes until Irene closes the kitchen door and shouts that she is going to do the dishes. Johan is left alone in the room.

When Johan and Irene engage in conversation about this altercation, later in the evening, when both have calmed down, they discover how small words or movements are triggering responses to earlier experiences. For example, Irene feels disrespected by Johan, because he doesn't call her to say he'll be late. When Irene mentions this, Johan feels criticized. Irene says she experiences Johan as aggressive immediately his body tightens, his chin tips slightly upwards and he starts looking at her sternly.

In every contact you make, you are confronted by the root of your old attachment movements, just like Johan and Irene. Whether in our marriage, in friendships, in teams, whenever we meet another person, we repeat past movements. Even being close to your client, your presence might trigger, in your client an old attachment experience, which can be positive or negative. When your client reacts to a situation in the present based on feelings, thoughts and beliefs from past experiences, this is called *transference*. At the moment of counseling, you might notice the transference reaction as inappropriate to the current context. But, in the context where the response originated, it was.

However, not only can your client be *transferring* (old triggers) to you, it can also happen to you as a the coach. Transference can then trigger *countertransference*, with both parties reacting from old, usually painful and negative experiences. The question is not so much whether counter-transference happens, but much more whether you are able to notice it, and how you then deal with it. Countertransference is a natural phenomenon. The root cause lies in your emotional reaction to – and how you are affected by – your contact with others. In Chapter 4, which takes a deep dive into emotions, you will see that these actually have a signaling function, they initiate action. You will see that when you have the courage to bring your feelings and your own vulnerability (when this best serves that instance of guiding the client) into the contact, this opens doors that might have remained closed. In this way, transference and countertransference are not just a strong risk that should be overcome but, above all, a source of learning and growth.[8]

A specific form of transmission is *projection*. You then unconsciously project feelings or thoughts you are having onto the other person, so that in a self-fulfilling prophecy your perception is colored by your projections on the other. In many cases, you are a mirror for the client, who projects his own patterns onto you without realizing it. Feelings of anger, infatuation, feeling rejected, panic when you are not immediately available – these are all feelings that can be triggered when working in proximity. Sometimes, for your client, if they see even a momentary sternness in your eyes, they find themselves back sitting opposite their father or mother again. Working in close proximity requires the coach to be willing and able to bring these patterns out into the open where they can be safely examined. As a secure base coach, you are a safe place where looking into these patterns becomes possible. It is at these boundaries, working at the cutting edge, where the promise of a new perspective for the client is found; a new experience and another step on the road to healing.

The coach is giving feedback to a member of the group. The recipient is visibly distressed to hear that she appears to show no interest whatsoever in trying out an exercise. The coach has a brief conversation with her. A nervous twitch in her face reveals how much she is struggling to control her emotions.

Shortly afterwards, in the break, the participant approaches the coach, saying that she doesn't quite understand what it is she isn't doing right, and that, anyway, the exercise doesn't really suit her. The coach repeats the previous feedback, more or less exactly.

The woman becomes clearly irritated and looks away. The coach says: "You seem to be moving away. Am I right?" She responds that she does not feel listened to and that she experiences the coach as having a judgment about her. In a dialogue, with the coach helping her to look into her process, she discovers that she frequently felt judged by her father. Often when she expressed her opinion, she was often told that she was too young to understand. Realizing this enables her to deal with feedback in a different and more positive way.

Later, during a supervision session, the coach is asked to look back at the situation. She realizes that when she was giving the feedback, her heart was a bit closed. This was even stronger the second time, during the break, and came at the expense of caring.

Close proximity and presence

When being close and working in intimacy, your body – as much as your words – is a critical tool. Unconsciously you send signals, and in return tune in to the other via the signals you receive. Your body is the first to 'speak', as it were, even before you open your mouth. You can see this *responsiveness* as 'dancing' in the moment, doing the dance of mutual attunement. Each synchronizes and adapts to what seems – tacitly – desirable or acceptable to them, in that moment.[9] Thus, through your body you give an unconscious and non-verbal response, an unspoken statement of how you are experiencing the other's presence.

Your physical presence requires you to be as aware as possible of how you are present in that moment. Your embodied presence can help you create an atmosphere in which you can work effectively with your client.[10] You create a learning environment by being wakeful and relaxed. In addition you can show yourself in. the contact as vulnerable, with emotions, feeling and sensing. You allow yourself be touched by your client's vulnerability. By using your own intimate physical awareness to perceive signals and sensations in your body – *interoception* – you can be professionally close. It is precisely by using your 'way of being' to complement your 'way of doing' that your coaching becomes effective.[11]

In Chapters 4 and 5, we will go deeper into the role your neural system plays in presence and contact.

Proximity beyond your workplace

Although coaching contracts are temporary and exist within a professional relationship, your secure-base relationship with the client can continue after the conclusion of the coaching process. The client can internalize the relationship, carrying you as a secure base with him after the coaching. Dennis Klass uses the term *continuing bonds* for this: the internalized memory of what was learned becomes a constant source of resilience.[12]

Letter from Seval Sönmez, coach and trainer in the psychiatric context:

"I have to share this with you. I dreamt about you last night. You came to visit my house for a special occasion, I don't know what. A little later, my family joined us. And I introduced you to my father. But it was very strange. I said to you: 'This is not possible at all, because my father is dead.' And you said, 'No way. Look, he's still alive, he's always with you.'

I woke up with such a nice feeling inside me. You see, my father passed away ten days ago and I am struggling with my loss because he was very dear to me. But this morning, after my dream, I was suddenly reminded of what you said at our first meeting. That your mother was always with you, that you felt her everywhere.

It was so nice to hear that from you in my dream. I also feel that my father is with me everywhere and this dream makes that even more real. Your dream visit really lifted my spirits."

Your own journey and self-disclosure

Life stories and situations are, of course, unique. They differ from client to client and are in turn different from your personal story. However, the themes on the Transition Cycle are universal. *'What is most personal is most universal', to speak with* Henri Nouwen.[13] Through these themes, stories affect each other, bringing forth the recognition and acknowledgement of compassion.

Because your client's life story and yours can also run along parallel lines, it serves your client if, as a coach, you perform appropriate self-disclosure with your story and share your most important life experiences. As Virginia Satir stated: *'Can we take it as a given that the coach's self is an essential part of the therapeutic process?'.* [14] As you share your own moments of learning and choices with your client, he feels he is not alone, although he will still have to live his life himself. This is one of the ways, as a coach, you can be a source of inspiration for your client.

In the field of coaching, from the outset there have been very different theories and views about the value of sharing your own life experiences during coaching sessions. In short, there used to be great reluctance to use 'yourself' and examples from your own life. The concern was that the risk of (counter)transference was too high; it was thought that with the right methods and techniques, the 'person' of the coach did not matter. There is now agreement that – regardless of specific techniques and models – it is precisely the nature of the coaching relationship that determines how successful a coaching process will be.[15] Deploying your 'self' in the here-and-now of the encounter with your client, taking into account the role that (counter)transference can play, is precisely what makes you, as a coach, both personally and professionally important for your client and contributes to healing and growth.[16]

As a secure base coach, you might become skilled in using your own experiences to serve the other person's journey. You can do this by bringing in such an experience, for example, but it can also be seen in the nature of your questions and your interventions. Your own wisdom has a place in the coaching. You become visible – as a companion – in your shared humanity, without taking over the other person's story. That last part, that is the art and the craft. You learn how to do that along the journey. In that learning, you might experience a difference between the conscious use of self-disclosure and spontaneous self-disclosure. The question of whether and how your personal stories contribute to your client's process should always be your compass.[17]

> *"Jane, may I share something with you?"*
>
> *"Yes," Jane says, looking at the coach with surprise and curiosity.*
>
> *"Several years ago, I suddenly lost my best friend died, A period of heaviness and withdrawal descended upon me. I lost my lust for life, locked myself up in my own world and didn't believe anyone could understand how I felt. So I didn't share it, because I assumed there was nobody out there who cared or wanted to hear my story.*
>
> *My line manager at the time called me in one day. He shared with me how he had seen me change recently, that I had gone from being a very promising employee to almost invisible in the department.*
>
> *Unexpectedly, as we spoke, I broke down. I couldn't control my emotions. It was as if they were controlling me. I spent half an hour in the room with my manager talking, crying and sitting silently. Until at one point I said to him, 'It can't go on like this, I need help.' Through my work I found a counsellor with whom I had regular sessions. Slowly I started to piece together what was happening to me.*
>
> *And you know, as I speak, I can still feel the release that came in that first conversation with my line manager. And the frightening moment when I thought it might totally swamp me and I would disappear forever into my grief."*
>
> *Jane's body shakes, releasing a deep, anguished sob. "That's exactly what's happening to me. I'm so afraid of falling apart."*

Being a secure base means being fully there with the other, with your vulnerability, and with your total attention and presence. We call it *watchful presence*: being attentively present, ready and willing to explore. Looking to the other, yet not distracted by them; aware of your own thoughts or feelings, in shared presence with the other person. Although you do not know where the client is going or what they will discover, you are honestly curious about what is unfolding. What matters is your ability to slow down, to follow the other person, to walk just a step behind your client, present and welcoming whatever is and might be.

An important tool for coaches is dialogue. Dialogue is characterized by exchange on every level: cognitive, emotional, physical and spiritual. This means being present in these areas in that moment, willing to step into the arena of encounter, open to whatever emerges. Sometimes sharing your own experience can be an act of service; sometimes you can reflect back to the client what he tells you, colored by your wisdom: "When you talk about it like that, it sounds like you feel kind of lonely and abandoned." Bringing in your own wisdom does not mean that you are presuming you know better. It means trying to connect the other person's experiences to a larger system, as it were. So you tap into your own experiences and knowledge as well as the experience and knowledge of others to underscore what you seem to observe. You could also say that you connect the micro-narrative of your client with a macro-narrative. This allows your client (and you) to land in a larger story that provides support and possibly a new direction.

Unconditional acceptance

Professional proximity is about being present to your clients' thoughts and feelings: positively, supportively, unconditionally. Carl Rogers, one of the founders of humanistic psychology, called this *unconditional positive regard*.[18] You are then present to the client's story and experience without judgment. You respect the value the client gets from it.

Unconditional positive regard, according to Rogers, is unconditional acceptance of the client. You are and remain a supportive and appreciative presence while your client speaks out and allows himself to be 'seen'. The client remains independent and responsible for himself; you do not attempt to rescue the client or approach him as a victim. The quality of your presence gives the client permission, as it were, to have and safely share their own feelings and beliefs.

People need this to develop a positive self-image. In addition, they can also develop a positive image of others and therefore positive expectations. People with a positive self-image and self-esteem benefit from greater confidence and motivation to achieve their personal and professional development goals, and to work on self-actualization, because they believe they do this.[19]

Humanly speaking, it is impossible even for a secure base coach to manifest full unconditional positive regard at all times and with everyone. However, that does not absolve us from trying, and learn from self-reflection when we fail. Unconditional positive regard is not about always agreeing or approving of your client. It does not give the client license to behave however they wish. While thoughts and beliefs can be limitless, behavior cannot. There will always be boundaries which determine how you act as a coach and what you will accept. With a code of ethics and conduct you can make those boundaries explicit in advance and refer to them when necessary.

The creative power of hope

As a secure base coach, you might be hopeful that there'll be development and growth in your client, knowing that emotional and attachment wounds can heal. In your guidance you may serve as a source of unconditional hope through creative attention.[20] In your language, too, you might invite your client to keep hope. This needs language that keeps open, that does not shut down, that is positive towards the future, that inspires: "I cannot" becomes "I am working on it, I am practicing"; "It looks really difficult" becomes "I have every confidence I can do it.".This is where your own themes inevitably become tangible and visible. As coaches, we might guide our clients by believing in a new future that holds all the self-doubt and pain that presents itself. Or, to speak with Vaclav Havel: hope is not the conviction that something will turn out well, but the certainty that something makes sense, regardless of how it turns out.[21] We guide by showing that we, too, always have the choice to answer, and shape our lives, from the desire to find and follow our calling.[22]

As coaches, we can explore how to be a resource from which clients can draw. We can start by being a mirror for the client who might be searching for opportunities to integrate the different strands of life, hoping to integrate his losses into the changes he is facing. Invite your clients to tell their stories and listen to them with creative attention. This invites a new perspective for and with your client, often the start of a new movement. You are a coach, but first you are one human being meeting other human being.

Hope is expressed within counseling both in the expectation that the client has the skills – or knows how to develop them – to achieve his goals and that the process itself is contributing to achieving those goals. Hope is also expressed in a deep trust in your client's autonomy, even if your client doubts himself. You might think that clients who themselves express hope at the start of and during their sessions are more likely to have a successful overall outcome. Yet research suggests this is not so. However, it does show that the level of hope of the *coach* during the work makes a positive difference and that its impact can affect the client directly and indirectly. The direct impact is noticeable in the relationship during counseling sessions, when the coach's hope permeates the quality of the encounter. Indirectly, hope can filter through to the client after the completion of coaching. When the client has been able to internalize the coach's hope that the results will be sustained, it works as a continuing bond.[23]

Increasing safety

To work in close proximity and safety, you have to deal with the paradox that safety can only be tested if you are willing, when it feels unsafe, to take an emotional risk (as much daring as caring). Only by testing the tension does it become clear whether it is safe.

The virtuous upward spiral in which more openness leads to more trust, fueled by experiencing that one's trust is not betrayed, has to start somewhere. If you wait to connect with your feelings until there is proof that your trust is justified and it is safe enough for you, the circle will never become the upward spiral. You can start small: opening up a little more than the psychological contract might seem to allow at the time. Thus, the circle can start in which the trust given in advance turns out to be justified. Then, based on reciprocity, the spiral of increasing openness and trust can be shaped together.[24]

Many marriages have to deal with this big challenge: "I find it challenging to say, but you are so often looking at your phone, that I don't feel seen or appreciated. Apparently whatever is on there is more important to you than us. The other day you even did it during our dinner date at our favorite restaurant."

His wife looks at him and is silent for a moment. Then she takes his hand and says: "Phew, that's tough to hear. I didn't realize at all that it has this effect on you. To me, it always seems such an ordinary thing. I'm really sorry I did it at the restaurant. And promise you'll tell me if I start doing it too much again."

Caring and daring go hand in hand. You cannot have one without the other. But they must be in the right order. Caring always precedes daring. We have to show love first and, only then, set our boundaries: first the love, then the limits. This order is fundamental to the message being heard, which allows learning to take place. A secure base is 100 percent caring and 100 percent daring at the same time.

You might be familiar with this situation. Your client starts talking, and he can't stop talking and you notice yourself drifting off, losing focus. You have to immediately interrupt him: "I am interrupting you for a moment, because I want to be sure I hear and understand you correctly. Is it right that you said …?"

You bring tension into the exchange, but the result is increased safety. You'll probably also know the situation when a question or thought bubbles up in you during the dialogue, which increases the tension for you as a coach. For example, the question: "And exactly how are you avoiding intimacy here and now in your contact with me?". You can assume that if you are willing to take the risk to challenge him this way, your client will feel invited and seen and, above all, will make new discoveries.

Not only is it unwise to avoid tension, it is beneficial, at times, to consciously seek it out. Your client has, as yet, not found an answer to the question which brought him to you. Whatever work your client has done so far, hasn't been enough to answer his question fully. That is why the client came to you. You try to look beyond the question and listen to what is showing itself behind the question.

Secure base versus safe haven

A *safe haven* – a refuge, sanctuary – is a necessary, but not sufficient, component of a secure base. Necessary because the road will be bumpy at times and we might need to pull over and take a break, to gather strength. But it is not enough. The secure base simultaneously makes it possible to leave the safe haven, and to take risks. It supports us to move beyond our comfort zone, while still feeling 'comfortable' (safe), and challenges us to explore and stretch the boundaries of the familiar, of our comfort zone.

A secure base coach makes the encounter safe by being dependably present, but does not choose for it to be easy or only comfortable. In Bowlby's words, being bonded to secure bases makes you feel secure in world that is not safe.

Clients might talk poignantly in a session about how they have experienced disapproval and rejection whenever they dared to show their vulnerability. People seeking a sense of belonging (everyone) will often have felt disappointed and damaged in their lives. To survive they make themselves hyper-careful about allowing their vulnerability to show. It has to feel completely 'safe' for them.

When we say "decided", it sounds like an active decision. Far from it. Stored deep in our brain, our unconscious responses persistently confirm our primary programming. The only way off this spiral is to cross the bridge again; showing your vulnerability is the key to creating and sustaining real bonding. This is one of the ways you encourage your clients, who might not have felt completely safe so far, again to risk, to be vulnerable. To share whatever they are feeling that needs to be shared, even if they didn't get the response they hoped for before. Although they might find the courage to take the risk, there is no guarantee they'll get a positive response. What you can do, is suggest to your client that they see this experience as part of their own learning process. What might change in their self-image after taking the risk? What is important is that the client becomes aware of how he uses his agency to shape the contact and that, by doing so, he can overcome his own unease.

(In)security and the nervous system

Your nervous system constantly scans for security and for danger; thus it determines your response to events in the external world. At the subconscious level it is constantly looking for internal, external and relational signals of danger and security. This process, known as neuroception[25], is active at every point in the coaching session, even before the client (or anyone else) arrives. You can increase trust between you and your client by making this process explicit.

Clients often bring with them situations from their work or private life where they felt uncomfortable without knowing exactly why. By making (their) unconscious scanning explicit, they start to acquire a better understanding of what, for them, are the signals that trigger feelings of insecurity and thus why they react as they do. Experiences or situations typically trigger insecurity include, the feeling of not being seen or not being heard; being ignored; treated with contempt. Something as simple as an angry face, a shrill voice, someone coming too close, standing over you, making you feel like you don't belong or that you are stupid. The list is endless.

By the way, you might think that you consciously create a safe setting because you ensure you are friendly and welcome a client warmly. But it is the client who determines if this is actual or not. If clients have prior experience with people who appeared, initially, to be friendly, but then turned out to be untrustworthy or treated them poorly in some way, then your friendliness might, to them, be a signal of danger.

To explore how safe your client feels, try the following questions:

- *Do you feel safe?*
- *How do you know you feel safe?*
- *Is the distance between you and me okay for you?*
- *What happens if I sit closer to you? (And move closer while asking.)*
- *What happens if I stand a little further away? (And do what you suggest).*

Our nervous system is totally and constantly interconnected. This means that we might believe we are hiding our feelings of anger, irritation or fear, but the nervous systems of the people around us, as they unconsciously scan for security and danger, pick up what we are really feeling. We've all had the experience of feeling in some way a bit disturbed after meeting someone, without being able to put our finger on why. Nervous systems read each other and react to each other. It's up to you (as coach) to learn to notice when this is happening and to enter into the dance of emotional regulation, with the client, in ways that increase security.

During a session, the coach invites Annemarie to lie, face up, on the floor, close her eyes and bring awareness to her breathing. The coach then places her hands on the client's abdomen and chest and asks the client to breathe in a circular way, with no break between inhalation and exhalation. After a few minutes, the client's body slowly starts to tremble. The client opens her eyes and looks worriedly at the coach. Looking into her eyes, the coach says, in a soft voice, "It's OK, trust your body, it knows what it is doing." As the coach repeats these words, the client's trembling grows into shaking. After a few minutes, the client calms down naturally, her breath becomes quiet and steady and the trembling eventually stops.

The coach sits with her on the floor for some time while the client looks at her. Occasionally, the coach nods.

Later, in a short conversation, the client tells how she repeatedly wakes up at night because of tension in her body. She says she has learned, through doing this breathing exercise in the security created and held by the coach, that she can discharge the tension that builds up in her system and feel more spaciousness in her body.

The contemporary scientific focus on the brain goes hand in hand with understanding the working of the nervous system. The vagus nerve[26], the 'wanderer' travels through your whole body connecting brain to lungs, heart, stomach, and intestines. The focus of our attention here is on the functioning of the autonomic nervous system and the insight it provides into how people experience stress and deal with tension, and some useful tools if offers coaches.

Fight, flight, or freeze

We could call this a hierarchy of responses: how the autonomic nervous system responds to danger.[27] The oldest and first response uses immobility and freezing in the face of (perceived) danger. We see this in the animal world, where the best option in the face of danger is often to play dead. If this doesn't work, the second response comes in, fight or flight. Not freezing but moving, usually as fast as possible. This is the defense system of mammals. It is notable that most animals seek a sheltered, protected place when in danger. Beginning at birth, many mammals – and especially humans – look for an adult when they need protection and safety. This brings us to the third response, that of seeking safety through active bonding and social engagement: the seeking of a *secure base*.

it is safe;
bonded;
socially engaged;

imminent danger
fight or flight;
mobilisation;

persistent danger;
freeze;

Figure 2.1 Hierarchy of responses

These different responses to (un)safety occur in a specific order. Imagine them as a ladder. The top rung is the social engagement system. When danger threatens, this drives you to make contact with another person, someone you perceive as a secure base. If this step brings you back into equilibrium, calmness returns. If you cannot find or contact anybody, and the danger persists, you descend a few rungs to where fight or flee is the choice you must make. If neither of these is possible, you find yourself at the bottom of the ladder. Here, there are no options, no possibilities for defence; you fall silent, you cannot make a movement, you feel disconnected and so you freeze. The way back is to climb up the ladder. It is through you, the coach, as the client's secure base, that he or she can slowly but surely climb back up into the social engagement system. Through conscious breathing and movement, supported by your calming presence, the client is able to start moving again.

> *Inge had an insecure childhood. Although she has been successful in her career, she is constantly on her guard. Her internal radar never rests. If I tend to get too close, even when first greeting her, she feels impelled to run back out of the door (flight). By exploring this together she gets some insight into her primary tendency, her first response. Instead of fleeing, which was her normal behavior (find another job, terminate a friendship, stop any shared activities), she says she wants to flee without taking any action. She has now reached a point where she recently said to her manager: "I would rather just run away right now", without actually doing so. Speaking this out allowed Inge to stay and discuss the issue with her manager.*
>
> *I have to be very attentive to what is happening with her, when we are working on the edge. She so easily can flee down to the bottom of the ladder and out of connection. She might still be sitting opposite me, but inside she has checked out. She is sitting like a statue, her eyes blurred, open but seeing nothing. This has happened with us so often, that she notices it before me: "You know I'm not here anymore. You're speaking but nothing is getting in."*

It is important for your client to learn to recognize, at any moment, where they are on the ladder. When we find ourselves in one of the fight, flight, or freeze states, our body and brain are held hostage by survival responses. It is only in the social engagement system that bonding and change are possible. It is also important for you as a coach to recognize and acknowledge the signals emanating from your client so that you can explore them later together.

Try working with your client to find words or images that symbolize these different systems. "What images come to mind when you feel bonded to others and to the world?" "When I was gliding over the ice with my friend, feeling the biting wind and hearing the ice crackling under our skates." Each response will have its own words and images. At the bottom rung, it is often the feeling of being cut off, falling into darkness, being disconnected from everything and everyone, unable even to utter a word.

Important points to take away

- Professional proximity is a mindset that ensures you avoid the self-fulfilling prophecy that is professional distance. Professional proximity is about your willingness and ability to actually be present as a secure base in your relationship with the other person.
- Being present with your client requires aligning with them and finding a shared wavelength to which both parties can tune in and resonate.
- In the encounter, learning becomes possible by caring and daring being simultaneously present in the bond.
- In coaching, old attachment patterns can be triggered that might lead to transference and countertransference, in both client and coach.
- Humans are neurologically equipped to respond empathically.
- The conscious physical presence (embodied presence) of you as a coach creates a field for learning and development. Via awareness of your body, you can be professionally close.
- The secure-base relationship with the client can be a continuing bond that endures beyond the conclusion of the coaching process.
- In sharing your own life experiences with your client, you can be their inspiration. As a companion, you become visible in your common humanity without overriding the other person's story.
- Unconditional positive regard is the basic attitude towards your client in which you are without judgment, even if you do not agree with everything.
- Every encounter is a source of learning, for yourself as much as for the other person.
- As a secure base coach, you work with unconditional hope through creative attention.
- As a secure base coach, you are a hope provider. You have and display a deep faith in your client's autonomy, even when they doubt it themselves.
- Being present with your vulnerability and full attention is the *watchfull presence*.
- Conversely, security can arise by taking an emotional risk when it feels insecure. It is only by testing the tension that it becomes clear whether it is safe.
- Your nervous system is constantly scanning for security and danger. It is the director of your response to events outside of yourself. The autonomic nervous system has three responses: fight, flight, and freeze.

Self-reflection for the coach

- How do you shape your professional proximity? How close do you dare to be?
- As a coach, how do you bring yourself into the state where alignment with the client is possible?
- In your family of origin, what did you learn about caring and daring and how has that shaped your craft?

- In what ways are you a secure base? What do you still have to learn when it comes to 100 percent caring and 100 percent daring?
- In what situations are you sensitive to transference and counter-transference and how do you use these experiences for your personal and professional development?
- How are you in touch with your own body and how do you use this in coaching?
- How do you show yourself in the encounter? What do you allow to be seen, what do you hide?
- How do you experience unconditional positive regard in your life and how are you confronted by it in your work?
- How do you give hope to others?
- Are you willing to take risks in your coaching? What does this ask of you?
- When have you allowed others to see that you have been emotionally affected by something, also when it didn't seem safe? What did you learn from this?
- When did another person's sensitivity arise in contact with you, when it did not seem safe for that other person? What could be discovered there?
- How do you encounter personal responses of fight, flight, and freeze in your craft? And do you incorporate these situations into your work with the client?

Notes

1 Compare also Baart, A. (2004). *Een theorie van de presentie (A theory of presence)*. The Hague: Boom Lemma.
2 Siegel, D. (2007). *The Mindful Brain. Reflection and Attunement In The Cultivation Of Well-Being*. New York: W.W. Norton & Company.
3 Cf. Hooghe, A. (2019). *It's a matter of attunement. Exploring couple communication in times of child loss and child cancer*. Dissertation offered to obtain the degree of Doctor of Biomedical Sciences. Catholic University of Leuven.
4 Keysers, C. (2011). *The Empathic Brain. How the Discovery of Mirror Neurons Changes Our Understanding of Human Nature*. Amsterdam: Social Brain Press.
5 Ongenae, C. (2013). Interview with Brené Brown: ' Als we met hart en ziel willen leven, moeten we onze angst voor de donkere kant van het leven loslaten (If we want to live with heart and soul, we must let go of our fear of the dark side of life)'. *De Morgen*.
6 The drama triangle is also known as Karpman triangle, after its founder: Karpman, S. (1968). Fairy tales and script drama analysis. *Transactional Analysis Bulletin*, 7(26): 39–43. Supplement by Choy, A. and Lee, A. in McKimm, J. and Forrest, K. (2010). Using transactional analysis to improve clinical and educational supervision. The drama and winners' triangles. *Postgraduate Medical Journal*. May: 86(1015): 261–265.
7 Kohlrieser, G., Goldsworthy, S., and Coombe, D. (2012). *Care To Dare. Unleashing Astonishing Potential Through Secure Base Leadership*. San Francisco: Jossey-Bass.
8 Katz, R. and Johnson, T. (Ed.) (2016). *When Professionals Weep. Emotional and Countertransference Responses in Palliative and End-of-Life Care*. New York: Routledge.

9 Chartrand, T. and Lakin, J. (2013). The antecedents and consequences of human behavioral mimicry. *Annual Review of Psychology*, 64: 285–308.

10 Kolthoff, P. (2021). *Standing firm in intense situations. Balancing your leadership with Embodied Learning*. Amsterdam: Boom.

11 Erdős, T. (2021). *Coaching Presence. Understanding the power of non-verbal relationship*. Maidenhead: Open University Press.

12 Klass, D., Silverman, P. and Nickman, S. (2014). *Continuing bonds. New understandings of grief*. London: Taylor & Francis.

13 Nouwen, H. (2017). *You Are the Beloved: 365 Daily Readings and Meditations for Spiritual Living: A Devotional*. Veghel: Image.

14 Satir, V. (2013). The therapist story. In Baldwin, M. (Ed.) *The use of self in therapy*. New York: Routledge.

15 Norcross, J. and Lambert, M. (2011). *Psychotherapy relationships that work. Evidence-Based Responsiveness*. New York: Oxford University Press; Blow, A., Sprenkle, D., and Davis, S. (2007). Is who delivers the treatment more important than the treatment itself? The role of the therapist in common factors. *Journal of Marital and Family Therapy*, 33(3): 298–317.

16 Aponte, H. (2022). The Soul of Therapy. The Therapist's Use of Self in the Therapeutic Relationship. Contemporary Family Therapy, 44(1): 1–8.

17 D'Aniello, C. and Nguyen, H. (2017). Considerations for Intentional Use of Self-Disclosure for Family Therapists. *Journal of Family Psychotherapy*, 28(1):23–37; Katz, R. and Johnson, T. (Ed.) (2016). *When Professionals Weep. Emotional and Countertransference Responses in Palliative and End-of-Life Care*. New York: Routledge.

18 Rogers, C. (1951). *Client-centred Therapy. Its Current Practice, Implications and Theory*. Boston: Houghton Mifflin.

19 Bozarth, J. (2013). Unconditional positive regard. In Cooper, M., O'Hara, M., Schmid, P., and Bohart, A. (Ed.) *The Handbook of Person-Centred Psychotherapy and Counselling*. New York: Palgrave Macmillan – Springer Nature.

20 Weil, S. (2009). *Waiting for God*. New York: Harper Perennial.

21 Havel, V. (1990). *Disturbing the Peace: A Conversation with Karel Hvížďala*. New York: Alfred A. Knopf.

22 Reijmerink, M., van Gasteren, K., van Wielink, J., and Wilhelm, L. (2018). Geloof je dat het ooit nog goed met me komt? De coach als bron van onvoorwaardelijke hoop door scheppende aandacht (Do you believe I'll ever be okay? The coach as a source of unconditional hope through creative attention). *Tijdschrift voor Coaching*, (3): 30–35.

23 Coppock, T., Owen, J., Zagarskas, E., and Schmidt, M. (2010). The relationship between therapist and client hope with therapy outcomes. *Psychotherapy Research*, 20(6): 619–626.

24 Covey, S. and Merrill, R. (2008). *The Speed of Trust. The One Thing that Changes Everything*. New York: Simon & Schuster.

25 Porges, S. (2011). *The Polyvagal Theory: Neurophysiological Foundations of Emotions, Attachment, Communication, and Self-Regulation*. New York: W.W. Norton & Company.

26 Swinnen, L. (2021). *Activeer je nervus vagus. Een revolutionair antwoord op stress- en angstklachten, trauma en een verminderde immuniteit (Activate your vagus nerve. A revolutionary response to stress and anxiety symptoms, trauma and impaired immunity)*. Tielt: Lannoo.

27 Porges, S. (2011). *The Polyvagal Theory: Neurophysiological Foundations of Emotions, Attachment, Communication, and Self-Regulation*. New York: W.W. Norton & Company. Dana, D. (2018). *The Polyvagal Theory in Therapy: Engaging the Rhythm of Regulation*. New York: W.W. Norton & Company.

Chapter 3

Real change takes place at the level of identity

In Chapter 1 we say that transition is growth at the identity level, evoked by some kind of fundamental change. Transition takes place both visibly and invisibly, in the undercurrent as it were, within people and between people. What turns change into transition? When something different starts moving at the level of *who I am*.

> *Jane is a successful entrepreneur who built her business up from scratch and it continues to grow and thrive. Clients love coming to her. However, sitting beside the coach, head bowed, she stares at the floor. "I Looking at what I have achieved and how other people see me, I should be really happy with who I am. People see me as always smiling and friendly but, deep inside, everything's in turmoil: I'd rather lie on the sofa all day under a blanket."*
>
> *Jane poignantly shows there is no simple answer to the question "Who am I?" This question is always lying in wait, beneath the surface, waiting to be answered. In the secure zone of the coach, what she allows to come to the surface – to be seen – is the turmoil inside and her need to withdraw.*

In search of your identity

Your client – Jane in the case study – comes to you with a coaching question. It concerns a change she wants to happen, or a change that has happened and she wants to better understand and learn how to live with. The key question seems to be, "Who do I want to be or become?" Change also involves losing something, or letting something go. In a way, your client's question is also about saying goodbye. With certain kinds of loss, it is clear to your client, and to you as coach, what will be lost. It could be a job, a relationship or a loved one (primary losses).

With many of the events on one's life-line however, it is less obvious what, or when, something was lost. These might include loss of a sense of security, loss of trust, loss of a familiar place, or loss of health. These, less tangible, less visible losses often occur as a side effect of primary losses. Job loss often

DOI: 10.4324/9781003424178-6

leads to loss of self-confidence, loss of belief in the value of one's career, or a real or perceived feeling of a loss of fairness, of justice. These so called secondary losses play, as it were, in the background of the primary loss.[1] All losses require recognition and acknowledgement, because their effect can be profound on your client's presenting question. Examining losses on the life-line and the ways in which goodbyes were or were not said, gives a new perspective on the question: "Who am I?" This question then becomes: "Who am I without whatever (or whoever) I have lost?"

> (Back to Jane.) In the first few sessions – working along her life-line – a number of impactful life events are revealed: her parents' divorce; her trip to New Zealand – and the love-of-her-life she meets there and has to leave behind, because he does not want to emigrate and she wants to return home – and the sexually transgressive behavior of her ex-partner. In all of these cases, the conversations reveal that she has not allowed herself to feel the pain surrounding these losses: of security, of love and of trust.

Looking at the impact on your client of the loss, the questions are about who your client was until the moment of loss, and how the loss shapes her now: "Who am I with this loss and who can, might, or do I want to become now that this loss has happened to me?" In working with "Who am I?", you are working with the client at the level of their identity. This brings together everything you and your client have learned in your journey together within the themes of the Transition Cycle. All the events, so far, on the life-line, all the secure bases that were (not) there, all the choices that someone made and were made for them, have shaped someone into the person they are today.

The question "Who am I?" cannot be separated from "Who have I become so far?". The question of one's identity has multiple layers. It is an examination, revisited through working on the life-line, of what the client has formed around his or her self, in response to and often as protection against life experiences.

> Through a number of sessions, where Jane and the coach explore her most profound life events, she sees that she developed a shell of untouchability around herself. What she projects, her smiles, focus on others and hard work have made her the successful and respected entrepreneur she is today. "When I go back to those events, I can still feel the pain and the impact they had on me. I didn't think about it that much at the time. I had no space for it, it was too painful. Anyway, there was no one to ask about it." Jane says in one of the sessions.

Identity layers are created over time by your experiences and how you respond to them. From an early age, you develop your identity in relation to others. As a child you depend on others for your welfare and survival. In your younger identity, you naturally adapt to others in order to belong. When no newer experience takes the place of adapting, it becomes your default mode.

When you realize this, however, you also realize that who you have become as your response to particular events, says very little about who you are at the deepest layer. When the environment does not match your needs, you put a layer around your core to protect your *being* from harm. This is how, layer by layer, you build your 'shell'. In Jane's example, her layers include being untouchable, being smiling and cheerful, caring for others, and working hard. However, the more layers you build, the harder it becomes to know and live from your core. As coach, you help the client to acknowledge, examine, and explore the layers from the knowledge that beneath the fragmentation caused by our experiences we remain, at our core, whole and undamaged. When we are prepared to engage with the question "Who am I?" our wholeness becomes visible.

Rewriting your own story

You come to know yourself in terms of how you responded to life experiences. You can, as it were, tell a story about yourself that was true in a particular time and place. However, that story might no longer be true, no matter how attached you are to it. It might hinder your ability to be who you really are, now, and to bond with the world from there. You began living the story you tell, because that's what your *body* was living. You formed your identity around the wound, layering these stories around yourself in order to stay whole.

Looking for an answer to the question "Who am I?" requires an honest and courageous examination of "Who do I think I am?". Working at the level of identity means that you might challenge your client to explore the story they tell themselves and others. When you inevitably uncover the damage and the pain, you will have to guide your client to breathe through the pain to the other side, where a new story can emerge.

Is it really true that he is *introverted*, or *always there for others*? Does that story still serve him? Or might he discover the threads of a different story today? Is your client really a man *who doesn't need anybody else*, is the woman in the chair opposite you really a woman who *stands up for what she believes* or *finds it hard to set boundaries*? Or are they people who, on seeing what happens when they do things differently, challenge themselves to follow that impulse, because they believe this could get them closer to who they truly are? The coach is there to encourage them to begin telling a different story, a story with its origins revealed in the transition moments on the lifeline. A story that creates the space and freedom to learn and to live fully.

In Jane's case study, the conversations take her back to childhood memories of how much she loved horse riding. The coach suggests going to the local riding school and taking a walk around. Two days after the session, Jane apps a photo to the coach of her sitting on a horse. "My first ride in years. I had so much fun!"

Your identity consists of the responses you give to events in a particular period. They are time-bound and from your capacities then. So your identity can also shift over time; it can change, enabling you to respond differently. When you are able to *choose* different responses to events, you will, in turn, trigger different reactions from those around you, get different feedback, different responses. So we see that you can interrupt this circle, in which you and your identity are constantly reforming each other to what was. When you begin thinking differently about yourself, you can begin behaving differently. When you begin behaving differently, you get different responses from your environment, which you can use to enrich and/or change the way you think about yourself.

Being open to feedback allows you to test your self-image and align it with how you come across to others. Then you can make choices. "Do I want to come across this way?" Do I want to have that effect on others?" When you want to regulate how you influence others, feedback lets you know if you are succeeding in influencing others in the way you want to. Good feedback helps you behave more authentically. That might sound contradictory. Can a person become more authentic?

Growing in authenticity

Authenticity is for us about being genuine, about integrity, the degree to which you come across as credible and trustworthy. You could put it as *the degree that the intention of your behavior or message matches the perception of the receiver*. This means your behavior or message must be congruent and consistent, that you *walk your talk* in every aspect of your communication, verbal and non-verbal. When your 'message' comes across, perhaps unconsciously, as other than what you intend, the recipient doubts the veracity of what he sees and/or hears. Imagine saying yes while shaking your head from side to side. How can the other person know what you mean? Should he trust what you say? Or what you do? So there can be various elements of your behavior or communication that diverge from your message. These range from intonation and emphasis, to body posture, obscure words, unconscious use of filler words or clichés, the timing of when you say or do something, even down to a disconnect between your clothing and your message. This is why feedback is so important: it helps you increase congruence and consistency in your behavior and communication, which increases your authenticity.

Continuous authentic originates in self-knowledge at the deepest layers, from where you can act and react consistently and congruently. This self-knowing comes into play, for example, when old themes in your undercurrent are triggered. You could put it this way: if you let yourself be seen without your mask, how recognizable would you be to the other person.

Authenticity is experienced – by yourself and others – when your core behavior remains the same whatever roles you are fulfilling in your life. What kind of person are you at work and at home? At the tennis club or in a public role? In all these roles, you can choose to show who you are at your core, by being authentic. This increases feelings of security for everyone involved. In Chapter 12, on Meaning and Calling, we'll continue exploring how being authentic in all your life roles supports awareness of who you are and what you want to bring into the world.

Finally, authenticity is not fixed: in parallel with identity, it is always evolving.

The pull of the past

In the personal development our clients long for, they are often held back by limiting beliefs from the past. As much as a person wants to break free of these, they are attached as if with powerful elastic – to the beliefs – from their own history and family of origin. When changes occur, when they begin to contravene these 'old' beliefs, the elastic stretches as far as *loyalty* allows, before pulling them sharply back. They feel the conflict-of-loyalty between how they are behaving now and what they learned was acceptable in their family of origin. This usually causes discomfort with the change they are going through now. An inner 'voice' saying "This is wrong." or "This is not allowed." Or up pops a belief like "I can't do it", which is often an echo of messages from their past.

To have survived in their family of origin, a person will have had to adapt; in that context, at that development stage, there is no choice. It is where these *loyalties* developed, became the elastic band that still holds them to their past. They have internalized their family's values (they carry "the smell of the nest" with them) and cannot go against them (they cannot "soil the nest").[2]

The way his parents carried out their roles significantly affects the answers your client has given – at least so far – in shaping the layers of his identity.[3] Children are dependent on their caregivers during their upbringing, and that dependence means they experienced whatever their caregivers said or did as not only 'normal' but 'right'. Children must believe that their parents know what they are doing, otherwise the uncertainty would be unbearable.

Examining the layers of belief around self-identity necessitates digging-out the origins of our limiting beliefs and identifying who they actually belong to. Your client might have adopted them while growing up, but they don't really belong to him. No matter how long a client might have been living independently, this is, emotionally, a *leaving home again*. In peeling off these layers, the client cannot escape the letting go of (some of) his past.

Prompted by the life-line work, Jane and the coach explore her relation-
ship with her father. She realizes that she was taught by her father that
"You can do anything and you should never give up". This 'command' also
governed Jane's participation in intense high-level sports, where her father
constantly demanded more from her. "What did you miss in how he 'sup-
ported' you?" the coach asks her. Jane has a lot of trouble answering this
question. "He did it with so much love and I know he had my best interests
at heart!" When the coach asks the question again, Jane finds a different
answer: "I would have liked so much just to sit on his lap and know, deep
down, that everything was okay. And that we had gone skiing for fun,
instead of always having to be better than everyone else."

Together they travel back through time and complete Jane's story. It seems
her father wasn't just a man who wanted what was best for her, he was also a
man who did not sufficiently show his daughter that she was okay and loved.
So Jane gains a different perspective on her story, allowing feelings to arise of
sadness and perhaps anger for what she didn't get. The journey continues
with her discovering that she is a woman who needs reassurance ("I just
wanted to sit on his lap for a while.") and a woman who enjoys sports.

So Jane travels with her coach from past to present, arriving ultimately at
who she wants to be, finally answering the question she first brought to the
coach. From origin to destination.

Layers have also formed in your identity through responses that originated
generations earlier and are passed on as 'rules' from generation to generation: "This is the way we do things here." They might be based on events
from family history that still have great impact in the present. Were these
things to be proud of, or to be ashamed of? Did one of your ancestors amass
a fortune, or lose everything? Was a family member a resistance hero or a
collaborator? Were your ancestors slaves, refugees perhaps? Impactful events
from the past shape one's identity.

Epigenetic research shows, increasingly clearly, how negative circumstances
during pregnancy can cause genes to be switched on or off. This affects the
life of the baby and later the growing child. The environment of the womb
can alter gene expression. The same research shows that your thinking, feeling and choice of words have an impact on how your genes develop. Your
thoughts can switch genes on and off; those same thoughts are responses to
the way you see and interpret your life experiences.[4]

Safiya fled to the Netherlands with her mother at a young age, to escape a
coup in her homeland. In a small Dutch town she grew up, went to school
and found a nice job at a startup, some distance away. While at university,
she continued to live at home, but now wants to live closer to her work-
place. Many of her friends have already left home and she sees it as the
logical next step. Loyalty to authority was instilled in her mother, and she

wanted her daughter to work for the government. Safiya is critical of current politics and often this leads to clashes with her mother. As Safiya does not want to leave home with ill feelings between them, she engages in conversation, hoping to better understand her. Mother explains how their family had worked for the government for generations, right up until the coup. Out of loyalty and gratitude to the new country, where she feels safe, her mother would have liked Safiya to continue that tradition.

The unique journeys of woman and man

Jechiel is in his early fifties and grew up in an Orthodox religious community. Together with his wife, he has four boys and one girl. His 'princess', he called her at birth. Now, thirty or so years later, father and daughter are seeing the coach together for a special session. Jechiel is following a training course which requires him to engage with his family members about the impact of his parenting and the bonding they experience with him. It is painful for him to realize that – especially in the first 15 years after the children were born – he stuck so rigidly to his picture of what family life should look like. His sons have told him how they did feel loved by him, but what made the strongest impression was his sternness. And how that – in their words – has made them feel a bit distant from him, that they don't feel relaxed around him. The conversation with Sifra, his daughter, doesn't even begin; she is clearly holding back. Jechiel feels that something isn't right. He asks her if she would be willing to meet with him and his coach. During the session, Jechiel talks about how he wanted all his children to be safe, especially Sifra. How he was afraid she might be hurt by men. That was his fear, and he tried to do something about it by stimulating contact between Sifra and her mother, especially when Sifra was a bit older. When the coach asks what has been most painful for Sifra as she grew up in the family, she is a little quiet at first. She finds it stressful to speak and "doesn't want to hurt papa". She tells of how her father cuddled her a lot until she was eleven years old and almost always was the one who took her to bed. When she got her period, this suddenly ended. Jechiel holds his breath a little as he says softly to Sifra: "Yes, I wanted to show respect for the fact that you were becoming a woman". The coach asks Sifra what the effect was on her. Sifra says it confused her. She couldn't understand why her father stopped, and she was afraid to ask. Why did the hugs and cuddles stop?" She felt rejected and believed her father was less interested in her and loved her less. "I no longer felt quite so safe with you", she says. Fighting back his tears, Jechiel takes a deep breath and asks her, "Please could you tell me what the effect has been on you as the adult woman you are now?" Sifra reacts very emotionally. She explains that she has not been able to really love herself as a woman and, in her marriage, has struggled with intimacy. She keeps all men at a distance, even her husband, and this is putting a lot of pressure on their relationship. Her father's rejection had another painful effect, it made Sifra distrustful of other women. " I didn't go to mother about it either because I thought she and papa had decided, together, that was how it should be. But I can't say anything other than that whole period, together with the ridicule of my brothers towards me, has had a negative impact on my self-image as a woman.

There are similarities in how women and men grow up into adulthood, and unique differences. In the example of Jechiel and Sifra, you can sense how subtle and defining what you learn, growing up and maturing as a woman, can be. The same applies to men. Did the mother encourage her sons to go out into the world and take risks and explore, or did she, under the 'pressure' of her love, *keep them on a short leash*?

Our female caregiver (mother, stepmother, adoptive mother or other female mother figure) is our first fundamental secure base. The extent to which you were able to trust yourself to her as a child, and how much she welcomed you, has a tremendous influence on how you later interact with women, how you learn to give and take in loving bonds with women. This applies equally to men and women. In most cases, the father is the second secure base in your life. It is with your father, grandfather, stepfather or father figure that you first learn to give and take in a loving bond with men.[5]

The influence of your father and/or mother extends far beyond their physical presence or absence. There is nothing more present than an absent parent. Through their parenting style and their physical and emotional presence or absence, they lay the foundation for our personal attachment style and our survival strategies (coping mechanisms). In our earliest childhood, we interpret their explicit and implicit messages in relation to our survival and well-being. We adapt to them to maximize our chances of love and survival. And we internalize the beliefs. Beliefs that give us a 'book of rules' for our adolescent and adult lives. This 'book of rules' is anchored in our limbic brain and subconsciously guides our behavior in relationships, our self-regard and how we perceive ourselves. In fact, these rules shape our 'father factor' and 'mother factor'.[6]

The rules deal with themes such as money, relationships, status, ethics, conflict, love, and sexuality and are the ways we answer this question, "How can I fit in so that I belong and matter and am *good enough?*". One can imagine that the degree of attachment-security strongly determines the extent the child has learned to adapt and how much the feeling of being 'not good enough' (shame) has developed. As Stephan Poulter point out: '*Your shame factor is a mix of your mother factor and your father factor*'.[7] Although the workings of these three 'factors' – father, mother, and shame – are the same for men and women, the effects on each gender's development are different. Men and women each walk their own developmental path, which reflects the different influences of additional early male and female role models on each gender, such as siblings, uncles and aunts, teachers, and friends.

The socialization of males occurs in the company of other males. The man learns to express emotions around men, first with the father or father figure, later around other men. Growing up in a healthy environment, a boy mirrors his father (figure) who gives a positive example, of how men behave, by being emotionally available. A *group* of men acts as a mirror, an "identification model" to share, to learn, to express; an image of how to be when you step back into the world from there.[8]

For some boys, the pain, fear and anger around the absence of an emotionally available father (figure) casts a long shadow, and often leads to them acting out their anger in society and in relationships. Antisocial behavior, aggression, and addiction are manifestations of abandonment, rejection and neglect, fed by the underlying feeling of being "not good enough".[9]

Cardiovascular disease kills 50 percent more men than women. Worldwide – excluding deaths from war and hunger – men live an average of seven years less than women. Many studies show that some of the critical contributing factors are that they bond less, are more likely to take unhealthy risks and they are less likely to share their feelings. Although women are more prone to depression, the vast majority of suicides worldwide are committed by men.[10] For men, the mother is usually the essential factor in the separation process; she helps him leave the family home.

Women socialize with women: they learn to express themselves, express their emotions and to tap into their unique strengths as women. The mother is the ever-present model of *how I want to be when I grow up*. In every woman's journey, at whatever life stage, it is nourishing to be inspired and encouraged by other women. At the same time, the father figure's emotional involvement is essential for her to develop self-esteem and self-confidence. More than men, women have to learn how to engage in conflict by maintaining an open dialogue, and to summon the courage to push back and set limits where necessary. It is mostly in contact with their fathers and in their presence, that daughters learn how to deal with conflict. Fathers teach and encourage their daughters to express themselves, negotiate, and, when necessary, to confront.[11] In the story of Jechiel and Sifra, we see what happens when the father fails to give his daughter what she needs.

In women, the anger and shameful beliefs ("I don't matter", "I'm not good enough", "I'm not worth it") that arise in the face of rejection, neglect and abandonment often hit home. The effect on self-esteem and the ability to bond and be intimate is often profound. With George Vaillant: '*Children who do not learn at home about basic trust and love, have a limited ability in later life to be assertive, take the initiative and experience autonomy: all are capabilities that underpin successful adulthood*'.[12]

So when working on the identity level with clients, we cannot escape paying attention to the client's unique journey to becoming an adult man or woman. What was the influence of your mother and female, what was the influence of your father and male role models on your development? As a child, did you see your parents being loving and intimate, touching, hugging, and kissing each other? Did you see your parents entering into conflict with each other in your presence and also bringing it to resolution? Did you see your father honor your mother in her femininity and your mother honor your father in his masculinity? To what extent could you ask questions about (your) sexuality? How did your family of origin deal with nudity, disclosure and shame? Was there room for your sexual development, your doubts, your fears, your experimenting, and was there respect for your boundaries? Was there intimacy, support, conflict and security between you and your siblings? How have the answers to these questions affected who you have become as a woman, as a man? These are questions that you as a counselor and your client may need to investigate when working with the lifeline and working on the level of identity. This kind of courageous (daring) dialogue encourages learning, experimentation and different experiences in encounters with men and women.

It's a group session and Jarno stands facing one of the female participants. The coach placed her opposite him, and she is representing his wife. Jarno said, a moment earlier, that he feels inadequate and that this feeling so overwhelms him that it puts a cloud over his and his wife's relationship. In this small constellation, it is immediately apparent from the postures of Jarno and his 'wife' that there's a heaviness around them: both stand, facing each other, heads bowed. When the coach asks Jarno's 'wife' to share what is going on for her, she says she feels nailed to the floor and cannot move. She feels minimal contact with Jarno. This affects Jarno, who looks down and says: "Yes, that's exactly how it is. And I don't want it to be like this!". The coach asks another male participant to stand close beside Jarno. The coach asks Jarno to look at this man standing beside him. After a while, some signs of relaxation appear in Jarno's body and the coach invites him to share what he's feeling. Jarno speaks of his feelings of inadequacy, that stop him feeling free and happy. The man puts his arm around Jarno's shoulder. This makes Jarno emotional and he moves away from the contact. The coach invites him to speak out what is happening. Jarno says the man's arm on his shoulder pulled him back into his family of origin, where he felt so inadequate amongst his brothers. The coach tells him to look at the man again and tell this directly to him. The man responds by hugging Jarno and saying "It's OK, man". Jarno stays in the hug. Tears flow and his body visibly shakes and discharges. After a few minutes, the coach asks Jarno to turn around and look at his wife. As he does so, Jarno's expression changes. The coach asks Jarno's 'wife' what she sees and what she feels. She says: "He looks clearer, brighter; there's a light in his eyes and he seems to have become more of a man. It makes him attractive!" Jarno smiles and takes a firm step towards her. "I would like to dance with you. Would you like to dance with me?" asks Jarno, somewhat cautiously. The woman accepts his invitation. When the coach finally asks Jarno what he has learned, he says: "I realize that I don't have any men around me with whom I can share this stuff, and I need to do something about that sooner rather than later."

Moving from *in spite of* to *thanks to*

Just as a lobster grows out of its armor shell and has to shed it to continue developing (a process called molting) – and is then totally unprotected until its new shell is formed – it can feel just as uncomfortable and vulnerable trying to fit with your new identity. Especially when this asks you to distance yourself from familiar, limiting beliefs from your family history.

The terms 'person' and 'personality' are derived from the Latin word *persona*, meaning mask. In classical antiquity, actors with fixed masks portrayed characters on stage. Owing to the distance between audience and stage in large theatres, actors' facial expressions were lost. Stage masks with fixed and magnified expressions made it easier for audiences to recognize the roles actors played and the characters they portrayed.

Derived from the concept of stage masks of antiquity, we say that someone who comes across as inauthentic is *hiding behind a mask*. However, we can also see the layers of identity as a stack of masks. Each mask results from a particular response to events in your life, displays an adaptation that was necessary to survive in the social context of that moment, at the fundamental level to continue to belong. Or, as a minimum, to feel accepted and not excluded. You needed these masks to survive. The question now is what does it take to allow yourself and others to see behind your mask(s).[13]

When an individual or a team comes to us seeking our guidance, we rarely begin with identity and masks. However, if we really want a deep-level transition – change at the identity level – questions about who we really are and the masks we have adopted will inevitably surface in the relationship between client and coach. Who am I, and how do I know how to express this self? Who am I at the deepest level and is this 'me' the person I manifest in the world? Jane, the successful entrepreneur from our example at the beginning of the Chapter, finds out that she does not reveal her authentic self to the world. This creates tension. Feeling this tension, working with the masks that she has come to 'know' as herself, she sets to work.

The final transition – desired by the client – occurs when a movement becomes possible in which he is no longer able to plough on by ignoring his life-line as much as possible. The necessary movement becomes doable when, with his coach, he revisits the painful events on his life-line. Looking back, however far is needed, from this safe place, he can discover how these events shaped him and which masks they created. The deeper he goes the closer the client gets to answering the question "Who am I really, in my essence?" And the place to start looking is where there are wounds on the life-line. By exploring them and giving them meaning, the client can move from *in spite of* to *thanks to*. Back to Jane's example for a moment: by acknowledging the pain of her relationship with her father, she becomes able to see her father differently, namely how her father took her on an adventure. Thus, she rediscovers how, at her core, she is an adventurer.

The influence of guilt and shame

The core question of *who you are* leads to deeper, existential themes such as shame, guilt and loneliness. We call them 'deeper' themes because they are at work further below the surface. They might not come up explicitly in every conversation, yet they help form the foundation of your behavior. These universal and existential themes play an important role because they are largely shaped in the social context. Depending on the culture you grew up in, you are, to some degree, 'directed' by unconscious messages from your family of origin that fit with these themes.

Healthy, sometimes called *anticipatory* shame and guilt function as part of your moral compass. An awareness of potential shame and guilt and a desire to avoid unpleasant feelings or actual consequences can keep you from making social mistakes and from violating commonly accepted boundaries.

Unhealthy guilt can be a major obstacle to growth at the identity level. This feeling, accompanied by physical manifestations such as red cheeks, nausea and/or abdominal pain, occurs when we cross boundaries we have imposed on ourselves as a survival mechanism or to please adults during our childhood. This guilt is experienced consciously but we tend to hide it from the outside world. Often it leads to us retreating from the world when we experience this embarrassment within ourselves. The drivers here are the implicit or explicit messages and rules of the family of origin.

On a less conscious level, shame and guilt are like assassins who kill your joy in life. In particular, the toxic shame that constantly reminds us that we are "not good enough" is like a smoldering fire under the skin. Events in the present can trigger the feeling of "I don't really matter", that I'm "not good enough" and fear of being exposed as an 'imposter' at any time, accompanied by waves of debilitating shame. This type of shame, and avoiding the emotional pain that comes with it, are a key component of many coping behaviors, in depression and aggression, and in forms of addiction.

More than any other type, unhealthy shame, which is based on the belief of being a 'failure', is formed in the early years of life and is related to the emotional availability of attachment figures, your subsequent attachment wounds and how you adjusted to these situations in early childhood. It is hidden so deep in those affected by it, that this form of shame is almost invariably unconscious, yet is the root of most types of expression, behaviors, and beliefs in the here and now.

Unhealthy guilt and shame can negatively affect your self-image and poison all your social interactions. In addition, unhealthy shame is a stressor of sorts that – if left alone – over the years disrupts our system of stress regulation and contributes to a wide range of psychosomatic complaints and autoimmune diseases. So shame also "sits in the body"[14]

Learning beyond discomfort

Change at the identity level is about conscious learning. The client comes to you to learn something they can't learn on their own. Something where the client's existing skills in self-reflection were insufficient. Something the client cannot see without someone to be their mirror. There is clear desire and a sense of urgency for a new movement, for new insight, new space. In the client, this might be accompanied by a feeling of *survival anxiety.*

Survival anxiety is about the client's realization that something *must* change if they are to move on (survive). The discomfort of the old, familiar, situation becomes so unbearable that change is imperative. This urgency is – unconsciously – linked to the awareness of survival and provides the driving force, the will, to change. There is a need to allow someone else, who is sufficiently safe and trusted, into that vulnerable part. For the coach to enable in the client the development he or she cannot manage alone. Someone who can be allowed in close enough and provide the reassurance that allows the brain to focus on learning – discussed in Chapter 2.

In that development, that change, the client wants to 'get rid of' something, to leave something behind. So learning involves not only relearning, but also unlearning. When we start the process of learning to learn, and unlearning, this can touch on the client's discomfort and lead to *learning anxiety.*[15] Learning anxiety is feeling apprehensive about showing new behavior, in a habitual environment that might not be ready for, or expecting, that change. This situation carries the risk of the client feeling rejected. And this stands in the way of learning.

Increasing the survival anxiety might seem the simplest route to the desired goal, but this has the negative side effect of increasing general anxiety without reducing learning anxiety. Helping to reduce learning anxiety, by being present as a secure base and allowing the client to practice with other secure bases in the environment, is the way to deal with discomfort around learning.

It's very likely that the client's inability to manage their own development has negatively impacted their self-image. Or the client's self-image is already so low, from previous life experiences, that they cannot imagine how to make the necessary changes. A positive self-image makes a person feel good. This provides a better starting position for experimenting and accepting the risks and challenges inherent in learning. Ideally, self-image is balanced by positive experiences and caring feedback from people the client lives and works with.

Learning can also be impeded if the self-image is unrealistically high. If it is too positive the client could feel there is nothing that needs to change. When it's too negative the client thinks they cannot change. Because the brain works in such a way that it filters input and only lets through signals that confirm the familiar, it can be really tough to break through the existing self-image. Feedback doesn't get home and defense and denial endure. This supports the client by helping avoid *cognitive dissonance* – the unpleasant tension a person might experience when encountering ideas or experiences that conflict with their own beliefs.[16] Although this might seem to help the client avoid the anxiety, it actually prevents the (dissonant) behavior and so prevents change, ensuring the familiar effect on the environment will persist.

Carol Dweck talks about two different mindsets: a fixed mindset and a growth mindset.[17] Someone with a fixed mindset believes their learning ability is limited, there is only so much of it, it is a form of scarcity thinking. And when you reach that limit, that's it for the rest of your life. Someone with a growth mindset sees no limits to learning: what I don't know, I can still learn.

Clients with a fixed mindset will find it more difficult to experiment at the edge their comfort zone. Somewhere, from someone, they learned that risk-taking only increases the likelihood of rejection. They associate security with *doing what they always did*, even when they are no longer satisfied with *getting what they always got*.

Clients with a growth-oriented mindset are more likely to want to learn at the edge of their comfort zone. At some developmental point, from a person or experience, they have internalized a certainty and confidence that the chance of success outweighs the fear of failure. They even take pleasure in experimenting, in the process of learning, regardless of the outcome. Their experience of learning suggests a positive outcome. For them, lack of 'success' is not failure, they experience no threat of possible rejection and exclusion.

> *During the birth of their second daughter, something was clearly not right. Lex's wife had serious undiagnosed symptoms and doctors were fighting to save her and her daughter. For Lex, this was incredibly confusing emotionally. He comes to the coach with this story, saying that he simply is not familiar with being confused.*
>
> *In their conversation, Lex learns he has many old limiting beliefs such as "talking doesn't solve anything", "men don't cry", "you can solve problems by analyzing them" and "look on the bright side, it could be worse". He realizes that these beliefs have been with him for a long time. The coach reminds him that they have served him well, helping to get him to where he*

is in his life. Moving on, by unlearning them and leaving them behind is proving easier said than done. He is attached to them as if by an unbreakable elastic band.

After exploring the origins of these beliefs with the coach, they agree he should start with vulnerability: whenever he feels vulnerable, he should endeavor to stay in that space while showing and expressing emotions, especially around his wife. He experiences this as a very difficult process, as his wife and others just don't believe him. He feels not taken seriously and this is painful for him.

After a conversation with the coach, Lex decides to ask his wife for feedback: "When we're talking with each other, when do you experience me as bonding with you and when do I avoid bonding?" As these conversations become more frequent, Lex learns that when he allows himself to feel vulnerable, he comes across as tense. He raises his voice and has a hard look on his face. This is painful for Lex to hear. Later, talking with his coach, he discusses his discomfort and learns how he can be more relaxed when talking about difficult subjects with his wife. He finds out that this leads to him experiencing more bonding with her.

On the way to your calling

As the layers of your identity build, created by the responses you give to situations you experience, this can cause disappointment in, and loss of, certain parts of what you believe(d) to be 'you'. Elisabeth Kübler-Ross[18] – who, in the 1960s, pioneered research into grief and bereavement counseling – used four aspects to express the totality of the human identity:

- the emotional aspect – feeling
- the cognitive aspect – thinking
- the physical aspect – the body and bodily sensations
- the spiritual aspect – the philosophical: sense and meaning

Hidden deep under the layering of what you have come to imagine is your identity, lies the core of your 'being'. This makes it challenging to get behind the stories you have come to believe about yourself, in response to events on your life-line, and to know yourself consciously – especially if it's your first real attempt.

Unconsciously, however, you are never estranged from yourself. Your 'true' self has always been reminding you of who you really are and are allowed to be. The art is to become sensitive to its signals, learning to recognize and interpret them. And not to confuse your identity with the roles you play in your life.

Your 'being' and what you make in the world from that place, we know as your *calling*. Your roles in life might change, but your calling doesn't. It answers the question of who you are – and what you want to mean – in every situation in your life: it is your lifelong travelling companion. Looking back along your life-line can help you recognize the signs that help you to identify and formulate your calling. Once you know your calling, you can use it, when looking ahead, to make choices congruent with it, and to respond to life events in ways that fit who you are and are allowed to be, much better than before your calling became your compass. What you do is not who you are and the role you fulfill does not coincide with your calling.

Similarly, the roles you fulfill in life do not define your identity. When roles fit you, when you experience flow and enjoyment, this provides information about the direction in which you might seek an answer. An answer that can then further develop with you. In Chapter 12, on the themes of Meaning and Calling on the Transition Cycle, we will delve deeper into this.

> *It's the final session, and Jane stands opposite the coach: "I am an adventurer", she says, "I take the risk to really welcome people and allow to have joy." She stands up straight, looks directly at the coach, her eyes bright and says with amazement in her voice: "I am totally confident that I can do this."*

Earlier, we looked at Kübler-Ross's four aspects of identity. In any encounter, the dialogue or exchange takes place, simultaneously, via each of these aspects (see also Chapter 6). You work with your client as they respond from each and all of these aspects. In Chapter 2, we wrote about the need for secure base coaches to be present with unconditional positive regard for their clients. Here, this means being present with your client and his or her personal ontology, their system of giving meaning to life, without judgment. We could call it the spiritual aspect of being. For the coach, it can be difficult to accept and follow the client's meaning system because your spirituality has been shaped differently. Unconditional positive regard, however, does not mean that you have to agree with or believe what the client believes. If the narrative helps the client, you work with it. It is one of the levels on which you meet the other person and which benefits from honest, open curiosity.

> *One of Tom's clients was a successful Christian businessman deeply affected by a crisis of faith. But it wasn't his crisis that had brought him to Tom. The man's second son was born with a disability and needed a lot of extra care. This was negatively impacting the man's performance at work. Initially he wanted Tom to help him with time management. But, during the following sessions, other issues were revealed. His grief over the situation had an undercurrent of anger at God. He simply did not know what to do about this, especially as he dare not mention it in his church.*
>
> *Tom had let go of the church in his teens, which resulted in a nasty argument with his father. Now and then, Tom wondered if the order of*

events was the opposite: that he had actually stopped going to church because of the argument. Whatever, Tom took his client's anger at God extremely seriously and explored it deeply with him. For the businessman, it was a relief that Tom was not a part of his (or any) church, while Tom was open to his doubts and desires.

The conversations provided much relief to the client. Although his life was permanently changed by the extra care his son needed, his father-role now had a form he had never imagined. He became certain that God had reasons for putting this on his path, that something was being asked of him. At the end of the coaching contract, Tom asked the man to say a prayer to God out loud. While his client was speaking, Tom closed his eyes, folded his hands and felt inspired by the man's trust.

Important points to take away

- The question of *who you are* is always, really, the question *Who have you become so far?* and, especially, *Who might you allow yourself to be/become?*
- Your identity is not fixed: it consists of layers made of responses to events.
- Your identity shapes you and you, in turn, shape your identity.
- When you start responding differently to past, present and future events, your identity evolves and you rewrite your story.
- The authenticity of the coach increases the security experienced by the client. Authenticity is about knowing the deeper layers of yourself and acting from there consistently and congruently.
- We form our identity through life's experiences. To shape transition is to examine who you have become *thanks* to these experiences and not *in spite of* them. In other words: you turn your loss into inspiration.
- Learning can also be uncomfortable, depending on whether your mindset is *fixed* or *growth-oriented.*
- The question of *who you are* combined with *what you want to bring out into the world* forms the foundations of your calling.
- Your wholeness as a human being, is expressed through four aspects:

  - the emotional aspect – feeling
  - the cognitive aspect – thinking
  - the physical aspect – the body and bodily sensations
  - the spiritual aspect – the philosophical, meaning and purpose.

Self-reflection for the coach

- What words do you use to characterize yourself and what do the words you choose say about who you are?
- What generational aspects play in your identity? How does today's society view/judge events from your past? What influence does that have on how you behave?
- How has your perception of your identity changed over time. How has this affected you as a coach?
- What losses have shaped the development of your identity?
- What masks do you wear when wounds on your life-line are triggered? How does wearing these affect you?
- Which stories no longer serve you? Will you/can you say goodbye to them?
- How are you loyal to your family of origin. What do you manifest this loyalty in what you do and what you don't do?
- How might your wounds bear fruit in your living your calling?
- About what do you feel shame and how does it influence your behavior?
- Where/in what do you feel discomfort when you are learning something new?
- How authentic do you think you are as a coach and how do you test this with your clients?

Notes

1 Van Wielink, J., Wilhelm, L., and van Geelen-Merks, D. (2020). *Loss, Grief, and Attachment in Life Transitions. A Clinician's Guide to Secure Base Counseling.* New York: Routledge.
2 Weisfelt, P. (1996). *Nestgeuren. Over de betekenis van de ouder-kindrelatie in een mensenleven (Nest smells. On the meaning of the parent–child relationship in a human life).* Amsterdam: Boom.
3 Poulter, S. (2006). *The Father Factor. How Your Father's Legacy Impacts Your Career.* Amherst, New York: Prometheus Books; Poulter, S. (2008). *The Mother Factor. How Your Mother's Emotional Legacy Impacts Your Life.* Amherst, New York: Prometheus Books.
4 Francis, R. (2012). *Epigenetics. How Environment Shapes Our Genes.* New York: W.W. Norton & Company. Carey, N. (2012). *The Epigenetics Revolution. How Modern Biology Is Rewriting Our Understanding of Genetics, Disease, and Inheritance.* New York: Columbia University Press; Leaf, C. (2018). *Think. Learn. Succeed. Understanding and Using Your Mind to Thrive at School, the Workplace, and Life.* Michigan: Bakerbooks.
5 Kohlrieser, G. (2006). *Hostage At The Table. How Leaders Can Overcome Conflict, Influence Others, and Raise Performance.* San Francisco: Jossey-Bass.
6 Poulter, S. (2006). *The Father Factor. How Your Father's Legacy Impacts Your Career.* Amherst, New York: Prometheus Books; Poulter, S. (2008). *The Mother Factor. How Your Mother's Emotional Legacy Impacts Your Life.* Amherst, New York: Prometheus Books.

7 Poulter, S. (2019). *The Shame Factor. Heal Your Deepest Fears and Set Yourself Free.* Amherst, New York: Prometheus Books.
8 Vaillant, G. (2015). *Triumphs of Experience. The Men of the Harvard Grant Study.* Cambridge: Belknap Press; Kohlrieser, G. (2006). *Hostage At The Table. How Leaders Can Overcome Conflict, Influence Others, and Raise Performance.* San Francisco: Jossey-Bass. Visser, B. (2022). *Pappa's rouwen ook (Daddies grieve too).* Enschede: Rouwkost. Overdiek, T. and van Lent, W (2019). *Als de man verliest. Omgaan met tegenslag, verdriet en rouw (When the man faces loss. Dealing with adversity, grief and mourning).* Amsterdam: Balans.
9 Legato, M. (2009). *Why Men Die First. How to Lengthen Your Lifespan.* London: Palgrave Macmillan; Scaglione, A. and Shore, P. (2006). *Why Men Die Before Women And How To Prevent It.* Bloomington: Xlibris; Poulter, S. (2019). *The Shame Factor. Heal Your Deepest Fears and Set Yourself Free.* Amherst, New York: Prometheus Books.
10 Van Wielink, J., Fiddelaers-Jaspers, R. and Wilhelm, L. (2023). *The Language of Transition in Leadership. Your Calling as a Leader in a World of Change.* New York: Routledge.
11 Van Gasteren, K. and Verbokkem-Oerlemans, A. (2018). Hoe mannen en vrouwen verbinden. In gesprek met George Kohlrieser (How men and women bond. In conversation with George Kohlrieser). *Tijdschrift voor Coaching,* (4): 65–68.
12 Vaillant, G. (2015). *Triumphs of Experience. The Men of the Harvard Grant Study.* Cambridge: Belknap Press.
13 Veenbaas, W., Verschuren, H., and Goudswaard, J. (2018). *De maskermaker. Systemisch Werk en de Karakterstructuren (The mask maker. Systemic Work and Character Structures).* Utrecht: Phoenix.
14 Poulter, S. (2019). *The Shame Factor. Heal Your Deepest Fears and Set Yourself Free.* Amherst, New York: Prometheus Books; Brown, B. (2013). *The Gifts of Imperfection.* New York: Penguin; Maté, G. (2020). *When The Body Says No Exploring the Exploring the Stress-Disease Connection.* New York: John Wiley & Sons.
15 Coutu, D. (2002). The Anxiety of Learning. *Harvard Business Review,* March: 100–107.
16 Festinger, L. (1957). *A Theory of Cognitive Dissonance.* Palo Alto: Stanford University Press; Aronson, E. (1969). The theory of cognitive dissonance. A current perspective. In L. Berkowitz (Ed.) *Advances in experimental social psychology* (Vol. 4). New York: Academic Press.
17 Dweck, C. (2017). *Mindset: Changing The Way You think To Fulfil Your Potential.* Boston: Little, Brown Book Group.
18 Kübler-Ross, E. (1969). *On Death & Dying. Conversations with the dying.* New York: Macmillan.

Chapter 4

Emotions get you in motion

Emotions are essential to survival in (life) threatening situations and to normal functioning in our relationships with others. Human beings are social animals. That we are able to work together in groups, can develop and cooperate, is down to the role emotions play in influencing our physiological functioning, thinking, motivation, communication, and behavior. Without emotions, we are not full human beings and are socially and morally incomplete.[1]

Or, to speak with Martha Nussbaum: 'Emotions shape the landscape of our spiritual and social lives'.[2] Man is first and foremost an emotional being. He is born an emotional being and only then begins thinking. Not the other way around![3] Emotions do many things: they can be the motor that gets you moving, they can serve as a compass pointing to the right choice and they encourage bonding and communication. In this chapter, we look at emotions and what they mean for learning and development. We see how emotions work in the brain. We describe the function of specific emotions in bonding with others and, in particular, with our secure bases. We illustrate how working with the emotions evoked by loss makes a potential visible in human beings.

> *Kim enters the coach's office and sits down. She cannot keep her hands still and her eyes jump from one thing to another. The coach says: "You seem a bit restless, right?"*
>
> *"Yes," says Kim, "I really am. I was restless all of last week and especially on the way here."*
>
> *"Can you tell me something about your restlessness?" the coach asks.*
>
> *"Yes, I feel that all sorts of things are being touched by our conversations and I don't really know what's going on. I can't stop it or avoid it and it is making me restless."*
>
> *"So you're getting restless from what's being touched by our conversations and you say you're not sure what it's about. Is that correct?" she asks.*
>
> *Kim responds, "Yes, we were talking about the past and I thought things were fine growing up at home." The coach is silent for a moment before*

DOI: 10.4324/9781003424178-7

continuing, *"When I look at you, you seem a bit reticent. How is that familiar for you, holding back?"* *This question seems to open a story for Kim about how she experienced two long periods of illness as a child, where she spent the time mostly alone in a room. She explains that this caused her to hold back. As she talks, she becomes even more restless and very emotional.*

After a while, the coach asks her to stand up and imagine her father is opposite her: the coach stands in the father's place, settles herself, and asks Kim to put words to what she feels when she looks at her father. Kim begins to cry and bows her head. When the coach asks her to keep looking, she suddenly blurts out: "Where were you? You let me down so much!"

Her hands move back and forth. When the coach asks her to allow the movement to do what it wants, it gets bigger and seems to be directed at the father. She keeps reaching out and tapping her father's arm. The coach gives her some sentences to repeat and asks her to be led by the movements her hands are making. "I hate you" and "You let me down. It was too much for me on my own" accompany the firmer punches landing on the arm of the coach, still representing Kim's father. Slowly Kim calms down, tears flow again and she begins breathing more evenly. They look into each other's eyes for a few moments more. "What does it feel like, doing this?" the coach asks.

"It makes me calmer," says Kim. "And I also feel a kind of inner strength. That's a surprise to me."

Emotions are signals

Events around you might trigger emotional reactions, but events in themselves do not cause emotions. Stephen Covey based his famous first habit of effective people – being proactive – on the work of Viktor Frankl: "between stimulus and response there is a space. In that space is our power to choose our response."[4] Events outside yourself can be a stimulus, an incentive, and thereby a trigger. You have the freedom though, as a human being, to choose what your response will be. You are not forced or fated to respond in the same way every time, to repeat the same pattern.

Emotions are signals whether needs in yourself are or are not – or not appropriately – fulfilled.[5] Actually, there are no positive or negative emotions. All emotions are signals you can listen to, that try and encourage you to behave in certain ways: behavior that might help you get your needs fulfilled – to the right degree.

Emotions are meant to get you moving. Etymologically, the word emotion refers to the Latin word *emovere* which means *to set in motion*. Emotions trigger our behavior, and events trigger our emotions. However, there is no fixed link between which events trigger which emotions; this can vary from person to person. However, there is a fixed link between (basic) emotions and needs (see below), even though the perception of when a need is or is not fulfilled varies from person to person:[6]

- scared – need for security
- angry – need for boundaries
- sad – need for support
- happy – need to celebrate life with others.

These four (basic) emotions are a simplification of a complex set of emotions. This classification can be helpful in beginning to get a grip on your inner world. Often, another two emotions are added to give us six (basic) emotions:

- surprise – need for predictability
- disgust – need for wellbeing.

Which emotion is evoked by which event is decided by the underlying need being satisfied – or not – in that situation. Your brain and nervous system are constantly trying to keep you safe, rapidly assessing events in the environment for how threatening – according to your brain and nervous system – they are.[7]

However, your unconscious brain interprets events based on previous experiences, and often does not take into account your development since that 'old' experience. Your unconscious brain has hyper-fast reactions, yet is extremely lazy when it comes to learning. Your unconscious brain is like a computer programmed to always give the same reaction to a situation, or to what it 'sees' in a situation. Unconsciously, you react before your slower conscious brain realizes something is happening. Your brain tries to predict what will happen so it can guide you in how you can best respond, but bases this prediction on old experiences. But you are no longer the young, dependent child, helpless in the face of survival-threatening situations. The programming established at those times, often is not helpful in the here and now. Your brain is still reacting based on what was survival-appropriate then and there though.

Emotions are not universal

A widespread misconception is that people from different cultural backgrounds can universally recognize emotions based on facial expressions. Researchers have tried to substantiate the theory that there are fixed, predefined neural pathways in the human brain along which emotions arise. Each emotion would then have its own fixed neural path according to this theory. However, those neural pathways have never been demonstrated in any (brain) research. And the studies with photos of 'standardized' emotional facial expressions have some faults. Emotions turn out to be much more individual and much more complex in origin: emotions in response to a situation are a creation of what our brain – based on old experiences – thinks would be a good prediction, an appropriate response to the event. With that, however, the fast – lazy – unconscious brain is just as often wrong, owing to the filtering that it applies.[8]

If we compare the brain to a computer, it's not just about the software program – our limiting beliefs for example – but also the hardware, the wiring of the computer. Within your brain are neural connections, hard-wired circuits that form pathways along which your brain directs information. These are personal digital highways that allow your brain to rapidly put your body into a state of readiness by releasing hormones that increase alertness, muscle tension and heart rate. We have all felt these changes in our own bodies. Cognitively, in the moment, you cannot know what these feelings actually mean though. Your feelings, insofar as you are able to experience and perceive your bodily sensations, thus form your inner reality, but might not accurately reflect the reality outside of you.[9] To speak with Anais Nin: "*We see things not as they are, but as we are.*"[10]

When a need that was not satisfied in an old situation arises in the present, your emotional alarm bells go off automatically. This means that if you base your behavior purely on your feelings, you miss a step. That of examining to what extent your thought or belief about the current situation is actually correct. Then, more often than you might like to admit, you find yourself *judging* the situation rather than perceiving it purely. Your fast, unconscious brain then gets in your way, because it is filtering incoming data. You don't perceive what is really happening. This makes it easy to find yourself in transference or countertransference.

Missing out the "thinking step" is also called the "primary response." From the perspective of survival this primary response process is fundamental. For example, when you brush against a hot pan, your hand is jerked away. You do it, but you don't have to think before you act. The time it would take thinking about doing it would only guarantee that you got burned. In relationships, especially when things get emotionally tense or when conflict is imminent, it is more effective though to think first and react *second*. In Chapter 6, about dialogue, we will examine how you can check whether you have properly understood the (intentions of) another person. Then you can, at least, take some time before reacting out of your primary emotion.

What we are learning about emotions

Needs arise out of a mix of genes (*nature*) and upbringing (*nurture*). Many needs and emotions are universal, but this does not mean that everyone has learned to allow and display emotions in the same way or to the same degree. In your family of origin, you learned what was socially acceptable and what was not. You learned to adapt so that you would continue to belong, to stay safe and survive. Because needs cannot be switched off, however, if you were forbidden to show a certain emotion, anger perhaps, you might have learned that you could get that need met in another way. For example, to gain support by holding down your anger and displaying sadness instead, when your need for boundaries was not met.

Stereotypically, it is generally accepted that boys are told "tough guys don't cry" and grow up to be men who mask their sadness with anger. Girls get the message that "nice girls don't get angry." So women learn the opposite: to mask anger with sadness.

Because children – unconsciously – learn at a very young age what is and is not appropriate in the showing of emotions, they soon believe that what they have learned is normal. Only later, at school, in friendships, socially, and at work, do they come into contact with people who, in turn, have learned to get their needs met by handling emotions very differently. As they become aware of this themselves – preferably in relationship with a trusted other, a secure base – people can begin to experiment with expressing emotions in a way that better reflects their underlying need.

After all, just as an emotion is a signal to yourself – necessary for understanding yourself contextually – so is its expression a signal for the other person that your needs should be taken into account. So when you give the 'wrong' signal, you not only make it difficult for yourself to understand what is happening to you, you also make it difficult for the other person to know what you need.

In the workplace we repeat the patterns of our family of origin. Often there seems to be no space for expressing personal emotions, because "It's work, okay?" Yet at work you are still a human being, with all your needs, and your – learned –adaptations and survival strategies. And you want to feel safe at work. Most office or work environments do not always invite us to express how we feel. Sadness and fear, in particular, are tricky emotions to feel, let alone to show in the workplace. Anger is only accepted when it functions as a part of your work. Primarily joy does seem to be allowed. But you're human: you feel what you feel, and sometimes you may not show it. Holding back your emotions, however, makes you very tired.

Emotional vocabulary

Working with emotions means learning to name them, as this helps to interpret and understand them. The more 'emotion words' a person knows, the more accurate the interpretation is. A richer and finer emotional vocabulary helps.[11]

It's just like learning to cook, finding your way around different foods. At first, you probably know what you like and what you don't like. Gradually, perhaps via a workshop or a cook book and practicing, a world of flavors, aromas and colors opens up that, when you started out, you couldn't name or perhaps even distinguish.

As we mentioned earlier, we do not distinguish between positive and negative emotions, since all emotions have a signaling function. Of course: some people see certain emotions as more/less pleasant, more/less acceptable. However, labelling emotions as positive or negative is a barrier to exploring them and, more importantly, to seeing them for what they are: signals of needs that are or are not being met and, more importantly, a means of getting you moving. By movement, we don't just mean physical movement (although that will often be important too) but, above all, exploring what they are really telling us about ourselves. Emotions that accompany 'met' needs are usually more pleasant than those that arise when our needs are not, or not fully, met.

Avoiding emotions

When you experience your emotions as not welcome, there are several possible movements. You might look for a safe space where you *can* express these emotions; you withdraw, or you might try to push your emotions aside through either *acting-out* or *acting-in* behavior. Acting-out behavior stems from unprocessed feelings and emotions and is directed outwards. This creates a psychological state that initiates the behavior of venting unprocessed feelings and emotions onto innocent others. Examples of acting-out behaviour are:

- Sarcasm
- Complaining
- Egocentricity in contact with others
- Bullying
- Tantrums
- Physical or verbal aggression
- Criminal behavior

Acting-in behavior is like acting-out behavior, but inward looking. Examples of acting-in behaviour are:

- Letting your inner critic lead you
- Perfectionism
- Compulsions
- Addictions

There is a direct link between the latter, substance addiction, and insecure attachment.[12] The way in how we attach, we also learn how to cope with

life's challenges. If you have not felt safe enough with an available meaningful other, this directly affects your resilience as a human being. You do not
learn to deal with life's ups and downs; life can then be experienced as a
chore, and addiction can lurk in the shadows. In an attempt to compensate
for the lack of attachment strategies,[13] substance abuse, for example, can be
seen as a form of self-medication (*self-soothing*).[14] People who become
dependent on substances cannot regulate their emotions, their self-care, self-
esteem, and relationships.[15] But also, in a broader sense, addiction can be
seen as the expression of an attachment wound. Unprocessed emotions and
feelings fuel the addiction that is an attempt to make something 'whole' from
what is broken. In this sense, addictions are examples of unresolved loss; of
solidified grief.[16]

Perfectionism and burnout

Avoiding one's emotions gets in the way of learning and meaning–making
and is a major cause of burnout. This avoidance manifests as forms of perfectionism. The perfectionist never experiences lasting joy or lives to their full
potential because "never enough" and "never good enough" get in the way.
So perfectionism leads to exhaustion or, as we now know it, burnout. And
we see that burnout is not the result of working too hard, but working too
hard for the 'wrong' reason. The work has become disconnected from who
the client is at the level of their identity. The inner source from which work is
done has become contaminated. The perfectionist – even if they are not
aware of it – keeps looking for approval. They are repeating old attachment
patterns where approval was not received from those with whom a meaningful relationship existed, or from those with whom a meaningful relationship was longed for. Perfectionism is, as it were, an ongoing inner dialogue of
the client where self-criticism always has the last word. It is also called the
perfectly hidden depression and burnout. So being aware of possible perfectionism is important because perfectionist-clients cannot be a secure base for
themselves. This is because they have not yet learned, when vulnerable, to
bond with external secure bases sufficiently.[17]

Emotions as source of healing

Beside their signaling function – 'telling' you if your immediate needs are
being satisfied or not – emotions play a crucial and far-reaching role in how
and what you learn. Your brain stores experiences from your first neural
connection as an embryo. These experiences are based purely on physical
sensations without any conscious interpretation. However, your brain is
already distinguishing between what is perceived as threatening and therefore
unpleasant, and what is perceived as fulfilling and therefore pleasant. Emotions, in the form of bodily sensations, form the basis of this. Long before

you have language as a child, your brain is building an enormous frame of reference for what you – without knowing and without choosing – find pleasant and unpleasant. From this framework, your brain then seeks confirmation and, increasingly, links certain types of event to certain emotions. This creates your behavioral repertoire, where your brain works more predictively from emotional triggers rather than giving you space to make a conscious decision yourself. Much of your behavior is therefore emotionally learned, with no conscious memory of how, what, or why.

On the path to healing your brain needs a new emotional state, that allows for a different learning experience. Working with emotions is a gateway to new experiences that will be stored in the brain. It can even go so far as to change attachment patterns, as positive experiences build up, over a longer period of time and through repetition, in contact with a reliable, present secure base (partner, coach, trainer, manager). This is known as *acquired secure attachment*.[18]

Emotions thus provide a portal into the brain to overwrite old experiences and rewrite emotional links between events and beliefs. This process is called *memory reconsolidation*:[19] the emotional opening and consolidation of a new neural connection based on a new (learning) experience. In this way, clients can actually learn to react differently on a neural level, because the trigger between an event and the thought or belief associated with it can be redefined. The brain can actually learn that the event no longer has to be recognized as threatening; a different emotional response is evoked which allows the client to behave more appropriately in the current context. The blockage, that prevented the client seeing the reality of the situation, has been removed.

To apply memory reconsolidation, when a trigger refers to the past, the emotion in the present forms the entry point. Moving towards the emotion with your client can thus provide the key to a new learning experience.

As you can imagine, inviting your client – to descend into old memories, with their associated emotions – requires you to be able to 'contain' your client's emotions – and your own. By this we mean not only welcoming the emotions, but also being able to bear the emotional burden. Forming a safe space within which the emotions can be present and can flow. By containment, we also mean that if your client is overwhelmed by emotions, you know how to bring the client back to the here-and-now. That way, you offer a transitional space in which working with emotions teaches your client something new.[20]

Emotions as a way into movement

Emotions are meant to get you moving, as we wrote earlier in this chapter. There we talked about the movement required to get your needs met. A movement of finding companionship when there is joy, reaching out for comfort when there is sadness, asking for support when there is fear or, on the contrary, stating your boundaries when there is anger. However, when you struggle with yourself to get or allow certain emotions to become conscious, it also works the other way round: by starting a movement, the emotion can also start to flow.

When you have trouble sensing emotions in yourself, sitting still and trying hard does not help. This is because you are giving your body the same message as always: emotions are to be ignored or denied. Sit still and it'll pass. So, what does help? Motion, movement, mobility. Literally. Moving freely, keeping your brain out of the process and letting your body 'do the talking' through whatever movement arises from within. Walk around the room, turn a little, shake your arms. And then stand still. Possibly, your standing still is not the same as before. Perhaps you become aware of something inside that wants to come out. Allow it, follow your movement. This really does work as a way to get in touch with your own emotions and help your client get in touch with his inner world.

You can also use your voice to allow or bring forth emotions. When a person is sharing a (life) story, and emotions surface, the person often falls silent. They might swallow the emotions or choke up, unable to speak. Giving words to emotions helps not only to make sense of them but also to allow them. And if, at first, the client's throat or voice doesn't want to cooperate, as coach you can encourage the client to continue and to trust that words will come. The reward will be huge: emotions want to be felt. Otherwise, their signaling function is lost and you learn nothing new.

Emotional hostage-taking

When a situation puts too great a strain on your emotional coping skills or resilience, it can create a condition in your brain where your amygdala is taken hostage – the *amygdala hijack*. The amygdala – actually *amygdalae* as there are two of them – is the part of your brain that makes an emotional connection to events. When this brain area is 'overloaded', because an event is too big to be allowed emotionally, your brain falls back, immediately, on instinctive fight or flight behavior. Although your unconscious brain always reacts faster than your conscious slower brain, the comparison with hostage-taking is true in the sense that you no longer experience any freedom of choice at all.

What triggers an amygdala hijack is personal and dependent on the person's history. Precisely the same situation might seem trivial to you, while another person finds it life-threatening. An amygdala hijack is a response to 'danger'. An event in the present triggers the experience of a situation from the past, often an internal reliving. With respect to the situation in the past, the event itself is not necessarily threatening. For the person it happens to, it constitutes an overload of their resilience. A seemingly minor incident in the present can then be enough for a re-experiencing and an amygdala hijack.

A participant in a group might get 'hijacked' into reacting aggressively to the tone of something you say. As a coach, you can start a helping movement by exploring what is triggering his behavior. What is happening in his body, right now, and with which past situations or people does he associate this behavior? Such an inquiry begins with a paraphrase from an *embodied state*. You bring into the dialogue what you, as a coach, become aware of in the dialogue and what you see happening in the other person. "I see your body tensing up. Is it true that you are surprised by what I am saying?" or "I see your body becoming tense. Is that true?" You'll find more about this kind of intervention in Chapter 6 where we discuss dialogue.

Moving towards the emotion

The task of the secure base coach is to have the courage and willingness to move towards an emotion when it is touched and surfaces. You do this because you know the emotion is a signal, and a doorway to learning. Ways of moving towards the emotion include:

- By paraphrasing you invite the client to stay in the emotion and explore it.

  "I see a tear in your eyes when you talk about this. Is it true that it touches you?"
  "Listening to you like this, I get a heavy feeling in my stomach. Do you recognize this?"

- You ask the client to identify and explore the emotions that arise.

  "You talked, in your story, about a period of your life when you often locked yourself alone in your room. Can you take me with you to those moments, when you locked yourself away?"

- By inviting the client to make a movement that fits the emotion, you allow the client to find a way into a healing movement.

  "When you are talking about that situation, your hands keep stretching forward. To what or where are those hands moving?"
  "You were talking about the period immediately following your mother's death. When you talk about that you always lean forward, ever so slightly. Do you recognize that? Can you follow through on that movement?"

In *moving towards the emotion* something wonderful always happens. It literally gives space to the emotions, welcoming them; they become a source of revelations. It is not uncommon for clients to talk about new insights, or memories resurfacing that they had lost touch with: painful memories, but joyful too. Always sources of discovery, enabling transition. The more you are willing to move with the client towards the emotion and explore what you find there, the closer the client can get to the core, at the level of identity.

Regulating emotions

You learn to regulate your emotions through being in contact with others over the course of your life. We call this *coregulation*. At the beginning of life, it is fundamental to survival. But even as an adult, in situations of insecurity and danger you still need that other, that secure base, to help you come back into (*self*)*regulation*.

Sue Johnson, the globally successful author of books about *Emotionally Focused Therapy*, talks of how she would sometimes be upset after giving a couples' coaching session, either because what she had in mind did not work out or because things actually got worse between the couple. Then she would knock on the door of her 'real English' colleague, who would usually say to her in a soft voice "Oh, Sue, do sit down and have a nice cup of tea." Then she would feel the stress ebb away and, slowly but surely, she would calm down.[21]

Even experienced professionals need a secure base like this when stress levels are climbing. Someone who is available – and calm – so you can re-regulate yourself through the other person's presence.

Learning self-regulation, and the extent of your capacity for it, reflects your childhood experiences with your secure bases. The presence of a reliable, regulating caregiver, brings you into a rhythm of reciprocity where you experience security in being bonded. When parents recognize the needs of their child and respond appropriately, an attuned relationship is formed. This biological synchronicity forms the basis on which the child learns to handle relationships.

Of course, sometimes things go wrong and the child learns to deal with a break in attunement. What happens after the break it is important.[22] Resilience is enhanced when breaks are recognized, acknowledged and repaired. This three-step process of attachment, break, repair is repeated throughout one's life: everyone is always encountering large or small breaks in attunement, including you and your client.

> *Paul arrives at my office for his coaching session. So far, we have been dealing with the losses in his life and the friction between him and his brother. This time, he wants to talk about the burden his business has become for him. The employees aren't working well together, the new manager still has so much to learn, and whenever Paul steps into the gym, he gets a sinking feeling in his stomach. When I ask: "Have you thought*

*about selling your business?," he says immediately "Over my dead body!
Never." Not an option. So we begin looking at what to do next.*

*It remains quiet after this session. Paul doesn't make another appoint-
ment. I don't hear from him for a while so I check in to see how he's doing.
He says he was shocked by my suggestion about selling up. He didn't like
it at all. Still, he agrees to make a new appointment. Instead of treating
this as my 'mistake' (I had not attuned to him properly and sufficiently
understood his body language), I see it as an attunement break that needs
repairing. In the next session, I ask him to tell me what he felt when, in the
previous session, I asked that question. He says he was shocked and felt a
surge of anger and, because of the tone of my voice he did not feel there
was any space for him to say anything about it. And that he experienced
me as moving directly on to "Well then, what now?" without giving him
any chance to respond. He got the feeling he had no choice but to move on.*

*I repeat what I hear him say: "So, because of the tone with which I
made the comment and that I went straight into the next step, you did not
feel there was space for you to share the emotions that arose in you. Is that
right?"*

"Yes!, and you did it in such a loud voice, that especially!"

*"So, especially my loud voice," I repeat. Paul nods and seems to relax
slightly. I apologize for what happened earlier.*

*It is silent for a while and Paul sits with his head bowed. I ask him what
is going on for him. He says he got a picture in his mind of his father who
would preach fire and brimstone in the house in a very loud voice. Safety
meant 'swallowing' his emotions. My loudness triggered that old response
in Paul. We discuss this together and then look at if this is what happens in
interactions with his employees. He discovers how much he suppresses his
emotions, only to explode at another moment, leaving his staff bewildered.
He also notices, to his shame, resembles his father in those moments.*

*What emerged in this session was new and made the coaching relationship
stronger than before. It led to a breakthrough for him and acceleration in
his development.*

In their childhood, some of your clients will have missed the experience of
repairing breaks in attunement, leading them to experiencing much insecurity
and, from an early age, they would have had to self-regulate. For them, you
can be a trusted co-regulator. To be such an anchor for your client, team, or
organization, it is important you are properly self-regulating yourself.

*In a team coaching session, tension arises between the coach and a parti-
cipant. The situation is very tense. While they engage in dialogue, the co-
trainer skillfully maintains eye contact with the remaining participants.
When it all has cooled down enough, everyone takes a break. Several participants come up to the co-trainer and let her know that they felt*

continued bonding with her, through her calmness, which came through in her eye contact. That this made the tension bearable for them. They bonded through her calmness.

The process has left one participant withdrawn. By sitting with her and engaging with her in dialogue, the co-trainer slowly shepherds the participant back into the group.

Important points to take away

- Man is first and foremost an emotional being.
- Events in themselves do not cause emotions; they can however trigger emotional reactions.
- Emotions are signals that needs have, or not, or have excessively been met. There are no positive or negative emotions, they are meant to set you in motion.
- Depending on the messages you received while you were growing up about which emotions were and were not allowed, you likely learned to suppress or mask certain emotions, and/or to overlay them with an 'acceptable' substitute emotion. As a result, their function, of signaling underlying needs, was disrupted.
- Your unconscious brain reacts predictively in the present. It signals potential threat when a need might not be met, by comparing situations in the present with situations in the past. So your fast unconscious brain does not give your slow conscious brain time to weigh things up.
- When emotions are not allowed, you might look for another place to express them, withdraw or try to avoid them through *acting-out* or *acting-in* behavior.
- Because the brain stores experiences even before the child develops words and language, you don't always have conscious memories of why you react to certain situations the way you do.
- The emotional charge accompanying a memory, whether conscious or not, can be changed. An emotional state in the present, where a new experience is offered in a safe environment, is the way in to this change.
- A broad emotional vocabulary helps in interpreting emotions and reflecting on and learning from new experiences.
- When too great a demand is made on your emotional coping skills, an amygdala hijack can occur: the brain is taken hostage.
- To enable learning, the secure base coach has the courage and willingness to move towards the emotion. This literally gives space to the emotion, making it a source of learning and discovery.
- Regulating your emotions is something you learn over the course of your whole life, in interaction with others, and is necessary for survival.

Self-reflection for the coach

- Which emotions were allowed and which were not allowed in your family of origin? How did that shape you?
- Which of your emotions can you easily allow and accept and which not?
- Which emotions in another person can you allow easily and which less easily?
- In which situations have you learned a different emotional reaction than before and/or for which situations do you still want to learn to respond differently?
- What emotions come to the surface easily?
- Which is your habitual way to ignore emotions?
- How and how much can you regulate your emotions?
- What discoveries did you make by moving towards an emotion openly with curiosity and awareness?
- How well, or not, are you able to express your emotions?
- Who can you turn to when you are overcome by emotions? What does that person do that enables you to (re)regulate your emotions?

Notes

1 Vingerhoets, A. (2021). *De Emotionele mens. Waarom onze emoties bepalen wie we zijn (The Emotional Man. Why our emotions determine who we are)*. Amsterdam: Ambo|Anthos.
2 Nussbaum, M. (2001). *Upheavals of Thought: The Intelligence of Emotions*. Cambridge: Cambridge University Press.
3 Cf. Damasio, A. (2006). *Descartes Error. Emotion, Reason and the Human Brain*. New York: Vintage Books.
4 Covey, S. (2020). *The Seven Habits Of Highly Effective People*. New York: Simon & Schuster; Frankl, V. (2008). *Man's Search For Meaning. The classic tribute to hope from the Holocaust*. London: Ebury Publishing.
5 Rosenberg, M. (2015). *Nonviolent communication. A Language of Life*. Encinitas: Puddle Dancer Press; van Wielink, J. and Wilhelm, L. (2015). Will you tell me exactly what you feel? Tribute to Marshall B. Rosenberg. *Tijdschrift voor Coaching*, (2): 18–23.
6 Koopmans, L. (2014). *Dit ben ik! Worden wie je bent met transactionele analyse (This is me! Becoming who you are with transactional analysis)*. Zaltbommel: Thema.
7 Feldman Barrett, L. (2018). *How Emotions Are Made. The Secret Life of the Brain*. Basingstoke: Pan Macmillan.
8 Ibid.
9 Ibid.
10 Nin, A. (2014). *Seduction of the Minotaur*. Athens: Ohio University Press.
11 Also called: granularity of emotions.
12 Maté, G. (2018). *In the Realm of Hungry Ghosts. Close Encounters with Addiction*. London: Vermilion.
13 Schindler, A. (2019). Attachment and Substance Use Disorders. Theoretical Models, Empirical Evidence, and Implications for Treatment. *Frontiers in Psychiatry*, 10.

14 Maté, G. (2012). Childhood Trauma, Stress and the Biology of Addiction. *Journal of Restorative Medicine*, 1(1): 56–63.

15 Flores, P. (2011). *Addiction as an Attachment Disorder.* Plymouth, UK: Jasson Aronson.

16 Van Wielink, J., Fiddelaers-Jaspers, R., and Wilhelm, L. (2023). *The Language of Transition in Leadership. Your Calling as a Leader in a World of Change.* New York: Routledge.

17 Antony, M. and Swinson, R. (2019). *When Perfect Isn't Good Enough. Strategies for Coping with Perfectionism.* Oakland: New Harbinger Publications; Brown, B. (2020). *The Gifts of Imperfection.* New York: Penguin; Ferguson, M. (2019). *Perfectly Hidden Depression. How to Break Free from the Perfectionism That Masks Your Depression.* Oakland: New Harbinger Publications; Coerts, J. (2022). *Van burn-out naar levenszin. De natuurlijke ordening als helend principe (From burnout to a sense of life. The natural order as a healing principle).* Amsterdam: Boom.

18 The concept of acquired secure attachment was introduced by Mary Main: Main, M. (1996). Introduction to the special section on attachment and psychopathology: 2. Overview of the field of attachment. *Journal of Consulting and Clinical Psychology*, 64(2): 237–243. See also Lencioni, P. (2004). *Death by Meeting. A Leadership Fable... About Solving the Most Painful Problem in Business.* New York: John Wiley & Sons.

19 Van Wielink, J., Wilhelm, L., and van Geelen-Merks, D. (2022). Memory Reconsolidation. In: Neimeyer, R. (Ed.) *New Techniques of Grief Therapy. Bereavement and Beyond.* New York: Routledge; Ecker, B., Ticic, R., and Hulley, L. (2012). *Unlocking the Emotional Brain. Eliminating Symptoms at Their Roots Using Memory Reconsolidation.* New York: Routledge.

20 Van Wielink, J., Wilhelm, L., and van Geelen-Merks, D. (2020). *Loss, Grief, and Attachment in Life Transitions. A Clinician's Guide to Secure Base Counseling.* New York: Routledge; van Wielink, J. (2014). Kwetsbaar leven. Over desoriëntatie en heroriëntatie. Interview met prof. Christa Anbeek (Vulnerable living. On disorientation and reorientation. Interview with Prof Christa Anbeek). *Tijdschrift voor Coaching*, (4): 6–11.

21 Johnson, S. (2008). *Hold Me Tight. Seven Conversations for a Lifetime of Love.* Boston: Little, Brown Spark.

22 Dana, D. (2020). *Polyvagal Exercises for Safety and Connection: 50 Client-Centered Practices.* New York: W.W. Norton & Company.

Chapter 5

Your body holds the source for change

Your body is a source of wisdom. It is sometimes also called the temple of the mind. In surprising ways, our bodies contain a lot of untapped potential. However, that potential is also linked to the way our bodies store painful and traumatic experiences. *The Body Keeps the Score* is the revealing title of the bestseller by Bessel van der Kolk, the psychiatrist renowned for his research into the impact of loss and trauma experiences on our body-brain connection.[1] In this chapter, we look at how your body can tell you what your head doesn't yet know. What can your body teach you about bonding? How and where are loss, goodbye, and grief hidden in your body and what healing movement lies there awaiting discovery?

Working with the Transition Cycle themes is like a journey to and through your emotional, cognitive, spiritual and physical domains. We hope to inspire you not only to invite your client to take this step, but also to use these themes as stepping stones to the wisdom of your own body.

Your brain and your body are set up to survive. Your nervous system and brain are fundamentally designed to scan for danger.[2] Many of these processes are unconscious and handed down throughout human existence. Experiences during your lifetime can reinforce this state of unconscious alertness. Your body, because it initially sees everything as a threat, does not always help you stay in a state of curiosity, a prerequisite for learning. Being able to learn, develop, enable transition – requires that you work on recognizing your personal cues of safety.[3] If you interpret a frown from another person as potential rejection, you might see it as a signal that you are failing as a coach. But might you be able to see that frown as indicating deep reflection? Does a raised voice intimidate you, or do you appreciate the other person speaking up? How does your body react and how can you use your body to put your mind into a state of curiosity? How can you acquire the basic sense of safety crucial to being a secure base for the other? Learning to recognize and use signals of insecurity and security requires embodied awareness. And body awareness requires training.

Working with the body can evoke feelings of fear and shame. To become a secure base, you will also have to explore your own body and learn what its

DOI: 10.4324/9781003424178-8

movements mean. It is a process of discovering what freedom awaits you there. To what degree, and in what ways, are you in touch with your body and how do you invite others get to know theirs? This asks for making friends with your body, as this friendship is the basis for your exploring. The body is an area full of concealed experiences. It stores positive and negative experiences.

Two important capabilities, present in your body, are those of regulation and coregulation. Regulation is being able to adequately handle emotions and express them. If you are able to allow yourself to be affected by another person's regulation, this can have a positive effect on your physiological state (bodily sensations and emotions). This we call coregulation.

All positive relationships revolve around coregulation. We learn this as children in the way our caregivers are present and available for this interaction. If the environment where a child grows up is less safe, they learn to rely predominantly on self-regulation and are less able to recognize their body's signals. You start to regulate 'on your own', as it were.

Being able to regulate one's physical and emotional reactions and knowing how to attune to the other for coregulation is a source, for coach and coachee, of learning and development. Getting into a state of good regulation brings relaxation and creates space in the brain, enabling a broader view of reality and an increased ability to learn.

How you move, stand, walk, look, breathe and speak is connected to how present you are in your body and how friendly you are with your body. This affects your ability to be present, physically available in order to attune to the physicality of the other. This asks that you are able to perceive stimuli. Trusting your own body has a strong, helpful influence on your *person effect*, your unique way of bonding with others in positive and negative ways, and therefore on the trust your client feels to let you see them.

We are embodied beings

From the moment Descartes put pen to paper and wrote *I think, therefore I am,* [4] people in the West – at least in terms of their understanding of knowledge and wisdom – have become increasingly alienated from their bodies. Yet we are more than just 'talking heads'. Our body isn't there just to carry our head from a to b. Our conscious brain, the part we notice through self-awareness and the thoughts it processes, determines only two to five percent of our comings and goings. The vast majority, 95 percent, is handled by our unconscious brain and our autonomic nervous system. Our unconscious brain's processing capacity is 200,000 times greater than the one we think with. Thus, our unconscious controls our behavior, feelings, and, funnily enough, even what we think. [5]

Our unconscious brain contains much of what we have learned through past experience. The fact that we can walk, ride a bike or drive a car is because we learned to. The movements of the required muscles are controlled by signals through our nervous system. In turn, our muscles send information back. In this continuous physical feedback cycle, we combine all the information about the state of our body and its effect on what we want to achieve. For example, we learn to walk by first balancing on two legs, then we start taking steps and, soon, we are able to choose direction and, finally, to modulate speed. Our brain is constantly building new neural connections to retain what proved successful. So later, you learn to ride a bike: you balance on two wheels, get up some speed and steer in one direction or another.

In making behavior our own, it becomes automated. We do it without thinking about it. Indeed, when we do start thinking about it, things can suddenly become more difficult. This applies not only to practical actions such as walking and driving, but also to how we react to stimuli and situations and how we regulate our emotions.

As a human being, you inhabit your body. You are an embodied being.[6] Even when you don't realize it, your body is trying to tell you a lot. Through your senses you pick up signals from the environment. However, you don't 'see' with your eyes, you don't 'hear' with your ears and you don't 'smell' with your nose. You see, hear and smell with your brain. Any optical (visual) illusion makes that clear. And if you've ever taken part in those radio phone-ins like "Name That Sound"[7] you'll be familiar with how restless your brain gets when you can't identify it. Also, we all have a taste or smell that instantly triggers a memory and often a physical reaction; pleasant or not so pleasant.

It goes without saying that we experience the world around us with our senses. It becomes special when we realize that our brain, through which we experience our environment, is safely locked inside our skull, totally sealed off from the outside world. And, it is completely blind and deaf. Our brain tries to imagine the outside world via electrical signals from our senses. Our brain filters, selects, ignores and edits all incoming signals to make them fit our brain's ultimate purpose: to keep us safe in a threatening environment. Everything that comes in from our senses (input), is used by our brain to predict what behavior will best fit the situation. And that's the behavior our unconscious brain manifests in the world via our body.

Our brain, however, regularly ignores 'reality'. This is because it predicts appropriate present-context behavior based on old experiences. For our brain, this error is acceptable given how it sees the bigger picture, the ultimate goal: survival of our species.

Your client also enters your consulting room, or training room, embodied. The body of the client or group member 'speaks out for them', so to speak. A body with tight muscles is saying something about residual tension that cannot be let go. Eyes that appear to be 'deep' in their sockets might be saying something about being seen or a feeling being held back. Take time to really 'see' the other person, when you meet in the consulting room or training room. And trust the physical reaction that the other person has to you and evokes in you. Perhaps you feel restlessness, restraint, pressure on the chest, a shiver in your back. In the dialogue with the client, it is valuable to talk about the awareness of these sensations and explore together what is being triggered in each person.

How your brain and nervous system work together

While your brain is scanning the environment to work out how you are doing, it is also 'scanning' signals from your body. Your brain interprets signals from your circulatory system, organs, muscles, nerves, and so on to gather information about your state of being in the world. Conversely, the brain sends signals back through your nervous system to prepare your body for its next movement, particularly when it detects a potential threat: fight, flight, or freeze?

Your autonomic nervous system (ANS) has a critical role here. Along with regulating vital functions such as organs, breathing, digestion, circulation and heart rate, it also regulates your inner state of mind. Your ANS can become 'overstressed' from dealing with too many experiences and then initiate a 'disaster response' to only a minor incident. Those previous experiences can be terrible events such as accidents, disasters, robberies or abuse. However, your ANS can also become overstressed, owing to long-term emotional neglect or exclusion.

Importantly, it is not the events in themselves but your reaction(s) to them that influence how your ANS stress-response develops. With a too high sensitivity setting, it perceives situations as much more threatening than they really are. This can make it difficult for others in your environment to understand what is going on for you, when you react to a situation out of an overly sensitive ANS setting.

> Ellie explains, during her intake with the coach, that she has already been to the GP several times with cardiac arrhythmia. The cardiologist's examinations found nothing at all wrong with her heart or her general physical condition. And yet, increasingly often and mostly during the night, she wakes up with her heart racing.
>
> Exploring her life-line, the coach and Ellie find that she had a brother with a severe intellectual disability that manifested itself in aggressive outbursts. The life-line reveals several occasions when her brother's aggression was very difficult to deal with. When Ellie recounts these moments, it's clear that, as she tells the stories, her body reacts immediately to what she is saying. Her muscles tighten, she stares ahead in a kind of hyperfocus. Ellie discovers with her coach that this is actually her default physical state a she is so easily and so often triggered. Ellie is a youth-care worker and family violence is a recurring theme in her cases. Over a number of sessions, the coach guides Ellie through specific physical exercises aimed at helping her 'stay alert'.

Your body is trying to tell you something and your ANS is responding to these messages before you are aware of them. It takes practice to be able to listen differently to your body, and consciously reassure your ANS that the danger is not real, even if you seem to feel that in your body.

You can also start understanding how this dynamic works in your own body. You start to recognize your own signals of safety or danger and learn to notice them in others you meet. In the second part of this chapter, we will go further into how you can influence, reassure and activate your ANS in order to work with people on a deeper level.

Connecting with the body

In your work, you will meet people who have little contact with their bodies. They experience physical complaints but do not connect this with their bodies. They do not communicate with their body in such a way that they can 'hear' what it has to say and, thus, do not learn to follow their body, to allow it to decide the movement it needs. Most of us have seen this, for example, in clients showing early signs of stress or burnout, or clients that have suffered from complete burnout.

There are five ways into the body, five 'channels' through which you can make contact with it and make transition, big and small, possible:

- Perception
- Respiration
- Movement
- Sound and language
- Touch

Perception

Perception is the first channel: we become aware of our environment and in particular the other(s). What do I feel, what do I hear, what do I smell, what do I see? When we meet a person, our bodies are meeting them too, using all our senses to capture all the available stimuli. Take a moment and sit down on a chair, in silence, and feel into what you can see, hear, smell and taste. Be curious, widen your senses. What would it be like to meet your client in such an 'open' state? Using the wholeness of your body; making this complete you, so to speak, available to the other person? The other person who gets to 'use you up' completely, as it were.

Respiration

The breath is the first contact with life. Thus, as a baby entering the world, your first breath was a welcoming of life into your body. And, so in adulthood, your breath can be a gateway to parts of your body that lie dormant, that are hidden and invisible to you. Perhaps these parts are too painful or shameful: whatever the reason, at some time in the past you split these parts off from yourself. The Hebrew word for breath is *ruach*. It also means spirit, the force that moves, brings creative vitality. Being in contact with your breath is being in contact with (your) life energy.

In the practice of conscious breathing, you try to have control over your body. It is precisely in the deepening, lengthening and slowing of your breathing that the possibility of letting go of control can be found and of giving breath back to that which has been hidden, dormant for so long.

If you really look at your client, whose tears are welling up, you'll see the body reacting too. Usually there is stiffening, swallowing, looking away, holding back or holding on. Sometimes this manifests in the breath, or in the posture, a look in the eyes, or in the tensing of muscles. When tears appear in your client, try exploring the effect of inviting them to continue breathing through those emerging emotions. Perhaps even breathing towards them, consciously directing attention towards the emotion while breathing. Every small change in the bodily response is already a movement. What does the client discover when making contact with the emotion(s)?

Movement

Movement is the third gateway to change and healing. Many of the patterns you are familiar with, as described earlier in this chapter, are not within your conscious awareness. Many bodily reactions are based on past impactful experiences and geared towards survival, which may not always be effective or helpful in the present, let alone in facilitating transition. Actually doing things differently, because it serves you better, requires venturing into the danger area, where you step out of your comfort zone and are willing to learn. Your body will react immediately, with increased heart rate, sweating perhaps, dizziness, tension in the muscles. And with every stored bodily reaction that once served some purpose for you.

> When she looks into the eyes of the man opposite her during a training, her body stiffens and she puts her hands up to her throat. She once learned that men are unreliable and unpredictable. She bows her head, her breath becomes heavy, almost suffocating, and she cries out, "I don't want this, I don't want this!" The coach asks her to keep looking into the eyes of this man and to breathe. Her hands start to tremble. The coach asks her what is happening with her hands. "I don't know," says the client. The coach asks her to make the movement of her hands bigger. Then her hands form fists. "I want it to stop," she says. The coach asks her to make the movement, her hands want to make, even bigger. Then her hands move towards the man in front of her. She makes movements as if pushing him away. "Go

ahead. Do it," the coach encourages her. She stands up and pushes the man away with increasingly stronger movements. She cries while doing this and gradually becomes calmer, her hands dropping.

Sound and language

Expressing what wants to be heard. Not just words, but also sounds, a scream, a cry. This can be a challenge for many clients. Where a person, in response to what was encountered in their family of origin or another formative environment, has 'decided' to hold back, not be heard, become frozen, closed off, allowing the sound that wants to be heard can be healing.

Especially in the West, we are not used to making ourselves heard in situations of loss, distress or emotional events. Funerals are often held in silence, generally there is no dancing or shouting. This is how we keep inside us the sounds that want to and can be heard. Children who are angry are told not to scream, not to be heard. You can add examples yourself. Sounds that belong to emotions are held in, unexpressed. But emotions that are not heard eventually lead to organs making themselves heard through illnesses.

> *'Give it sound, the coach encourages her. She has just told about a period in her life when she experienced lack of safety in contact with her brother. He was dominant, crossed boundaries, spoke in a loud voice. Still, a harsh male voice can take her back to her childhood and make her body stiffen. She points to her throat, 'it cramps here', she says softly. 'What are you saying, I can't hear you', the coach challenges her as she continues to look at her, encouraging her with her eyes and presence to explore this unknown terrain. She gives a firm exhale, as if to push out what is stuck with her diaphragm.*
> *'Give it sound, make yourself heard.'*
> *'I can't' and she grabs at her throat.*
> *'Go on, you can do it.'*
> *She visibly turns on and lets out a deep primal cry that lasts for a few seconds. Tears stream down her face and she sinks through her knees. The coach invites her to come back upright and continue breathing.*

Language spoken by you as a secure base coach from an embodied state enables your client to experience and explore their own body. As you give words in your paraphrase to what you see happening in your client's body, there might be an initial awareness of the body on the part of the client. So your language can invite to explore pain, your language can also encourage to experience joy. In this way, as a coach, you can also make visible where a healing movement is possible.

Giving voice to what is hidden or frozen in the body can feel liberating. As if it – literally – is given breath. Sometimes a sound is enough, sometimes a word or a sentence that has meaning in the client's story. Teaching your client to give words to what the body has to say makes a fundamental contribution to the possibility of meaning-making.

James Lynch did pioneering research on the effects of language spoken from presence. For instance, he discovered how in dialogue from an embodied state, the heart rates of both speakers eventually go down. He also showed how the words "I love you" spoken from presence have a stress-reducing effect, while the opposite is true if they are spoken without that presence.[8]

> *A woman who shares, very emotionally, how unsafe she felt in her family of origin is asked by her coach to tell him what song she listened to most as a child. She mentions a song from her home country. Her coach finds the song online, plays the song and invites her to close her eyes and let the music move her body. "Just follow your body," says the coach. After a few minutes, the woman raises her head and starts spinning around her axis. She dances around the room like this for the rest of the song with the coach as her witness.*

Touch

Besides our senses, the breath, movement, sound and language, there is the wonderfully beautiful and, at the same time, vulnerable physical *touch*. When we are touched as human beings, bonding is created – if the context is positive. Every positive physical contact stimulates the powerful hormone oxytocin; associated with a feeling of warmth and security it is known to reduce stress and anxiety. Oxytocin has the ability to regulate our emotional response and social behaviors, such as trust, empathy, positive memories, processing of signals of bonding, and positive communication.[9]

Besides physical touch, eye 'touch', or eye contact, also triggers oxytocin production. Explore with your clients how much, and in what ways, touch is a signal of welcome and bonding for them, and an invitation to feel physically welcome and to relax. To cite Belgian psychiatrist Dirk de Wachter: "*Man is a being who needs to feel wholly embraced, who needs loving physical attachment, to be touched and held tightly. Especially after the loss of someone very close. Expressing or showing in some way our need for skin contact seems taboo. This is not good. We should dare to ask for skin to skin contact*".[10]

You need to bear in mind that someone else might not, immediately, respond positively to being touched. Although it is true that touch stimulates oxytocin release, this doesn't always create positive, warm feelings. Oxytocin can also amplify negative feelings. Touch, and eye contact, can trigger recall of negative experiences. Any attempt at safe, physical contact requires attunement, care, and consent.

A negative response, such as contraction, not moving or silence, can also be hidden so deeply in the body that we cannot easily reach it with our senses, breath, movement, sound or touch. Then we might be dealing with a *freeze* response, where the old trauma makes the body 'forget' the possibility of movement. We will look at this later in this chapter.

The body and resilience

As we'll see in Chapter 8, it is in our attachments that we develop our resilience. Attachment is how we learn about disappointments, setbacks and transitions. Secure attachment enables you to roll with the punches when life has unpleasant things in store for you. As a child, if you have sensitive caregivers who recognize and respond appropriately to your needs, allowing secure attachment to develop, you learn how to regulate your emotions and are able to contain them. You also learn that you are not alone and can ask for help when you are struggling.

With insecure attachment, you either learn to suppress your emotions, internalizing the message that you have to cope on your own, or the opposite, you don't learn containment or how to calm yourself down. You come to the conclusion that you can't do it alone and always need another person.

Even though you might have had an insecure start, you can also acquire secure attachment in later life, in the company of secure bases. If you learn in life that painful experiences are part of life and that you can ask for support from your secure bases, you can develop a resilient nervous system. This will enable you to deal with difficult situations and impactful changes.

A person's resilience can be weakened over the course of life by profound losses, especially when experiencing many losses in a short period of time. What happens in the body then? Feelings of insecurity and danger release stress hormones such as adrenaline, which make the body ready to flee or fight: muscles tighten, breathing speeds up and blood pressure rises.

> *Hannah came to the coaching appointment by bike, but on the way, her bag got caught in the spokes and she fell over. She got up, took a quick look around to see if anyone had seen her 'stupid' fall, dusted herself off and arrived at my door with a slight dent in a wheel. I can see from the wild look in her eyes that something is wrong, but she waves it away with "It wasn't a big deal."*

Hanna ignores the 'trauma' in her body. It is trauma, in the sense that something has been left behind in the body. Stress hormones, that entered her bloodstream as a natural reaction to the fall, have not been discharged. So the body keeps pumping adrenaline around while Hanna pushes down the signals her body is sending. And this takes a lot of energy. Although this is trauma with a small 't', the same thing happens with capital 'T' traumas.

Trauma

We call it trauma when there is an overwhelming experience we are not able to cope with. It is the body's reaction to an often unexpected, drastic event. Here, it is not so much the event itself that is the cause, as an event in itself is never traumatic.[11]

People can react very differently to the same event. What is important is whether the nervous system can process the event and return to equilibrium. This is more difficult if, for example, you are very young, the event is totally unexpected, occurs repeatedly, lasts too long, is too terrifying and, especially, if you are experiencing it alone. A potentially traumatic event can become traumatic in the absence of a secure base, or, more accurately, in the unavailability of a secure base.[12] It might be that the secure base is there but unavailable to you at the time, or that you fail to accept the other person's offer of help, or – for whatever reason – you could not reach out yourself.

Experiences such as emotional neglect in childhood, parents not sensitive to their child's needs, medical trauma, bullying, mentally ill parents, and loneliness as a result of parental absence (boarding school, hospitalization, imprisonment, military service, and so on), are often not seen as trauma. Yet, later in life, when triggered, they can evoke traumatic reactions. Such reactions can also come up in a coaching session.

So how do you work with that? Back to Hanna. First, you stop her, giving her time and space to realize that her body is still in shock and needs to deal with that. Acknowledging the shock and paying attention to it is a good start. It is often accompanied by shallow and rapid breathing, so the next step is to regulating respiration. You might ask Hanna to put her hand on her belly and direct her breathing towards her hand. You can do some breathing exercises with her, until she is calmer. This way she learns to regulate herself, and returns, to some degree, to the present situation. As a coach, you must check if your client has calmed down enough and if he or she is in contact with you. Eye contact is a key indicator here.

Once your client has calmed down and is able to (re)connect with you, together you can reflect on what happened and talk about how to self-regulate. Pushing away emotions, not addressing the shock while finding it difficult to regulate oneself will occur more often in the client's life than when they have a bicycle accident. This reflection transforms an unpleasant experience into an important learning moment. By working with the body (breathing, touch, eye contact) the stressed part of the brain is calmed: the whole brain becomes available again, and learning is now possible.

When you react to shock you first go into alert mode: you hold your breath, sharpen your senses and you stand absolutely motionless. Like a deer in the headlights. Adrenaline is rushing through your body and you are ready to fight or run away. If it turns out that the 'bang' you heard was just a gate closing, the noise on your roof is not a burglar, but a flock of 'stampeding' crows, that fire you smell is actually your neighbor trying to light the barbecue, then the 'danger' has passed, the state of readiness decreases and calm returns. So our bodies cope well with brief moments of stress.[13]

If the danger does not subside, you need more energy and need to maintain it longer. The release of cortisol compensates for the loss of energy. But if stress builds up and persists, and the body is not given a chance to discharge it and unwind, a toxic cycle is created in which the body keeps pumping adrenaline and cortisol into the bloodstream. If this continues for too long, it severely impacts our resilience. The body stiffens, mental and physical flexibility decrease, and concentration and clear thinking become difficult. The energy that is available is consumed by the state of constant alertness. Rigidity sets in and life energy falters.

Because the body does not return to the state of calm and continues to react as if the event is still going on, the experience does not get integrated. This leads to even minor triggers reigniting the stress reaction, irrespective of the situation being completely different. With knowledge of trauma reactions, you can better contextualize 'strange' behaviors. We could call them 'normal' reactions to unexpected or abnormal events.

> *Miriam has just started as a junior associate at a law firm. During a coaching session, she recounts an incident at work where a client comes to visit her boss. Miriam is in conversation with a colleague and out of the corner of her eye sees the client arrive and report to reception. She immediately feels her body freeze and she can't get her words out. Her colleague looks at her in surprise and asks her what is happening. For a moment she does not understand what he is talking about and then she realizes that the customer reminds her of her father. She lost him in an accident when she was quite young. The client's coat is the same as the one her father was wearing at the time of the accident, which pulled her back into her old pain.*

Often we prefer to avoid the pain and so lose connection with its origin, like happened to Miriam. When someone reconnects you with it at the right time and in the right way, realization occurs. And with the realization comes grief and other accompanying emotions. And this is exactly what is needed: to enter the place that you'd really rather avoid, so that you can come out of isolation and regain access to your feelings.[14] There is literally more air and space, the fight-or-flight response dissipates and coming out of your rigid state makes movement more possible. Rigidity is the opposite of resilience.

Moving towards the painful feelings, sometimes literally shaking the tension and fear out of our body, as a startled deer does when it has survived a threat from a predator, causes the body to come out of the traumatic state.[15]

Because a deer can tremble and shake in this way, it does not get trauma-tized; it is different with us humans, we lock the stress into our bodies. If, during a coaching session, your client stiffens and, for a few moments, is no longer present, it helps to get him moving.

Re-traumatization is subject to many incorrect interpretations. It is crucial that we understand it as the re-experiencing of the trauma, carrying with it the risk that it will cause new damage or that the experiencer is unable, alone, to get out of their violent reaction. With major (traumatic) events the healing movement becomes possible when the coach is able to be and stay fully pre-sent to the client's trauma reactions, as he guides the client to explore an event together. Harmful re-traumatization occurs when, at any point in this process, the client realizes that the coach is no longer present, just like having no or insufficient access to secure bases in the original experience. This can happen because the coach, for example, panics, cannot contain his own emotional reaction and/or has insufficient access to his own experience, knowledge and secure bases. Thus, he cannot provide sufficient safety to guide the client out of the trauma reaction. "See!", declares the client's nervous system, "We're back to square one."

The body and stress

The brain is part of the central nervous system. Another part, the autonomic nervous system, is responsible for action, energy, and lust for life: it's your foot on the accelerator. You use fuel and, like a car, your tank has to be filled regularly. You do this recharging by slowing down and refueling so that you can relax, rest, digest and restore. We are going to look at this process through a framework called the Window of Stress Tolerance.[16] This frame-work is a further development of the Window of Tolerance by Riet Fidde-laers-Jaspers and Sabine Noten, which is based on the work of Daniel Siegel, and later Kekuki Minton and Pat Ogden.

Healthy tension

Figure 5.1 represents a resilient nervous system. A continuous, smooth undulation of charge and discharge, within the upper and lower limits of the window, creates a healthy level of tension, in which you can function opti-mally: thinking, feeling, reflecting, and responding all happen freely and appropriately. From activity to rest and back again like a spring stretching and springing back. In the bigger picture, this is the difference between activity during the day and rest at night. This alternation is also necessary during the day: being active and relaxing, working hard and taking a coffee break or a walk, and then back to work. You reside in your comfort zone, but regularly explore your boundaries. That makes for a lively, interesting life and keeps boredom at bay. It is healthy variation that keeps you resilient.

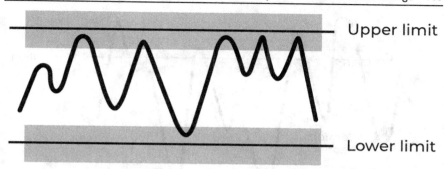

Figure 5.1 Window of stress tolerance: optimal stress level

With your client, you can explore how he deals with his transitions from activity to rest and vice versa.

> *Mark Tuitert (Dutch Olympic gold 1,500-meter speed-skating winner) writes, in his book Drive, about preparing to deliver his absolute best performance. "Together with my teammates, I would skate endless kilometers in training sessions at speeds I would never sustain on my own. Everyone contributes as a part of the 'train' and the bar is raised every month, every week, every day. I enjoy this the most: working with a team that brings out the best in each other.* [17]

This is a perfect description of an optimal level of tension in which the boundaries are constantly being pushed a little, so the window – and thus the resilience – increases.

High tension

It's at the edges that things get daring; where you are challenged to take just a step more, take a little more risk or be less in control. You step a little bit out of your comfort zone. Pushing your boundaries forces you to get more from yourself and to be challenged. The stress experienced is moderate, reasonably predictable and manageable. While it might feel stressful, at the same time it can feel positive. Activities that cross into this growth zone can lead to widening of the window and thus increased resilience. Here, secure bases are indispensable, as Mark Tuitert confirmed when he wrote "Working with a team that brings out the best in each other." Or, as coach, you are a secure base who enables growth in resilience by "leading from one step behind."[18] You lead from behind by being present in such a way that your client leads the way into his own revelations, while his 100 percent caring and 100 percent daring coach has his back.

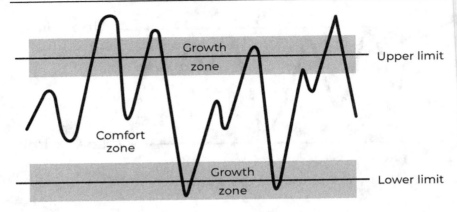

Figure 5.2 Window of stress tolerance: challenging stress level

Back to Mark Tuitert: "To win, you have to stretch the envelope, balancing on the edge of what your body can handle. There is no safe route to gold."

> *One day, however, he wakes up with a slight sore throat and a sluggish feeling. He tries to ignore it because he has scheduled a tough training session that day, which is crucial for his preparation for the coming World Championships Allround. "I refuse to listen to what my body is telling me and I train full on. That only makes things worse: the cold develops into flu, leaving me worse than ever. In those days, I saw sick days as lost training days. His skating coach, Wim den Elsen, gave him a priceless tip. "sick days as natural rest days." Mark again: "'Apparently, it is difficult to admit to yourself that you need rest, and even more difficult to then take that rest and lie around without feeling guilty about the training you're not doing or the appointment you have to cancel.* [19]

This is exactly what *rest, digest and restore* is all about. Recognizing your body's signals for rest and obeying them. You can seamlessly apply Tuitert's speed-skating example to your coaching practice. You probably get clients who have difficulties with observing boundaries, with saying no, always doing just a bit too much. It does not mean that challenges should be avoided, but that the balance between effort and rest is restored and respected: *work hard, play hard, rest hard.*

Earlier, you read that as a secure base coach you offer security and trust (caring), making clients feel secure. At the same time, you challenge them to step just far enough out of their comfort zone, to stretch the boundaries and take risks (daring). Learning from these experiences takes place when they are back in the comfort zone and bonded with you. You learn to know when you can ask for just a little more and when it is right to ask the client to step back. You recognize when there is enough daring and offer the client space to step back into the comfort zone for recovery and reflection. This is where learning takes place.

Unhealthy stress levels

When clients come to you because of a crisis situation, they are likely to be anxious and even in panic. They career through the window, above or below, ignoring the boundaries. This happens especially when there is high, unpredictable negative stress. Going through the upper boundary in the window kicks the stress hormones into action. Under the influence of mounting stress and the anxiety it induces, the body produces *adrenaline*, flooring the accelerator and shifting into top gear. Breathing and heart rate increase and you see behavior like prolonged overwork, hyperactivity, fight-or-flight reactions with hormones racing through the body. Also intense, excessive exercise and obsessive pursuit of hobbies are possible indicators. *Cortisol* makes sure you can keep this up for some time. You are 'on' and can't find the 'off' switch. At some point, the nervous system can no longer cope and you bottom out, crashing out the bottom of the window. You collapse physically and emotionally, exhausted, numb, and uncommunicative.

On the way down, the body's own anesthetics (opioids) do their work. They make you feel numb and lifeless, which is exactly what the body wants. As these opioids replace the 'speed' hormones in your bloodstream, you no longer feel the fear and pain that much. In extreme cases, you faint, or enter a kind of comatose state. This is similar to a phenomenon in the animal world known as 'apparent death' (playing possum), a form of animal deception employed as an anti-predator strategy. It can be life-saving because a cadaver is not such attractive prey.

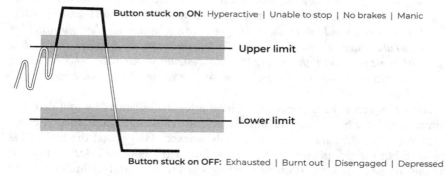

Unhealthy stress

Button stuck on ON: Hyperactive | Unable to stop | No brakes | Manic

Upper limit

Lower limit

Button stuck on OFF: Exhausted | Burnt out | Disengaged | Depressed

Figure 5.3 Window of stress tolerance: unhealthy stress level

When stress levels remain stuck either 'on' or 'off' and the healthy alternation of tension and relaxation is no longer there, this has major health consequences. Constantly having your foot on the accelerator without refueling inevitably leads to exhaustion. Reserves are depleted and then depression or burnout are just around the corner.[20]

> *Mark Tuitert: "Expectations are very high, so I delete all the 'rest' days from my training schedule. During training sessions, I always do more than is required: if the plan is to skate ten laps, I do eleven. If we go on a three-week training camp, I stay three more days. If I have to be on the bike for two hours, it always becomes three.*
>
> *[…] Later, at a training camp in Inzell, I'm walking to the ice rink and I start to feel really rough. It's freezing cold, dark and I'm tired before I even get to the rink. It's just three months till the Olympics start in Salt Lake City and something is very wrong with me. I am sick and severely overtrained, comparable to a burnout in normal life."* [21]

Not listening to your body, stumbling blindly on as Mark calls it, leads to the body giving you a harsh message, it stiffens up and all your energy drains away. Your tank is empty.

> *Paul is the proud owner of a thriving gym business. He has put his heart and soul into it. One day, he receives news that his elder brother, who lives in the Antilles, suffered a cardiac arrest during his regular work-out and died. His brother's family tell Paul that he is not wanted at the funeral; there is still too much old pain.*
>
> *Following his brother's death, Paul is no longer able to do his work as before. On entering the gym, he experiences a huge aversion to being there and goes home as soon as possible. Paul stops giving sports training and delegates that role to his staff. He stays at home and limits himself to handling the organizational and financial aspects of the business. Contact with his staff deteriorates, as Paul is now highly critical of their work and regularly loses it when speaking to them. He prefers hanging out on the sofa watching YouTube videos or Netflix series. To tell the truth, he'd rather stay in bed with his head under the covers. On the demand of his wife, who no longer 'recognizes' him as her husband, he makes an appointment with a coach.*

Until this event, Paul appeared to have a lot of resilience: he founded and ran a successful business, overcame significant challenges and enjoyed every minute of the 60 hours a week he usually worked. He grieved the loss of his brother, but there was more to this story. For years, Paul had pushed himself to the limit in his gym, both in running the business and in his own daily work-outs. He imperceptibly eroded his resilience because, although he pushed himself to the limit, he did not allow any time for relaxation. This also allowed him to deny his feelings about what was going on in the undercurrent of his life that had never been addressed. The sudden death of his brother, the fact that he was not allowed to be at the funeral and the *unfinished business* that still existed between the two brothers led him to collapse. He continued 'on adrenaline' for a while by quarrelling with his staff (fight) and working from home instead of from the gym (flight). But eventually he flew right through the bottom of the window until he spent most of his days watching television on the sofa or hiding in bed under the covers. He pushed himself into a *shutdown*.

This shows how grief can go hand in hand with traumatic responses. Once someone has checked out, is *shutdown*, it is much more difficult to reactivate them and get them back into the window of their comfort zone. Whereas fight and flight are stress or survival reactions, freezing, checking out, and depression are trauma reactions.

Getting started with the body

Through simple, specific exercises, we can remove stress-related blockages that have become stuck in the body and encourage a proper flow of energy. Working with breathing, shaking, and vocal expression the body and mind are brought back into balance, promoting vitality and life force. In this work, we owe a debt to – and draw inspiration from – the approach of Alexander Lowen, which has its origins in bioenergetics.

Here we describe some exercises to get you started. Working with the body takes diligence and practice, but anyone can do it. Try these exercises yourself and use them for your client.

Connecting with your body

Ask your client to stand with their feet parallel about 20 cm apart, knees slightly bent, weight forward, pelvis loose and back straight. Let the arms hang relaxed along the sides. This is the *basic stance*. Now start bending and straightening the knees quickly, creating a jumping motion without your feet leaving the ground. After a short time, your whole body will start *shaking* and your breathing might sound like a dog panting. Do this for about a minute, then stop and rest with the knees still bent – it is important not to lock your knees – and take some deep, relaxed breaths.

Now that we've got some energy moving, we move on to *grounding*. From the basic stance, start stamping: continue stamping while bending the knees deeper, as deep as you can. Continue stamping while returning to the basic posture, tap with the heels, continue breathing with the mouth open, letting out whatever sounds arise. Kick-out your legs, one at a time, kicking harder and harder, then return to the basic stance, turn the hips some more. Feel and touch your legs, feel your feet in the ground.

You do this exercise without shoes, optionally barefoot.

Depending on the type of tension, you can follow up with one of the next two focused exercises.

Get off me – Bend your elbows and then bring them up to shoulder height. This stretches the upper arms. Powerfully throw both your elbows backwards and shout "Get off me." Repeat this, using your voice to express feelings of anger.

Give it to me – You'll need a partner for this exercise: each takes one end of a towel or rope. With both hands, you both pull as hard as possible while saying, "Give it to me." Experiment with pulling softly or forcefully and with how and what you say.

Regulating breathing

This is a three-step exercise and you should participate yourself as much as possible. Step one: you ask your client to breathe in for four seconds and then out for four seconds. Once this is going well, move to five seconds in and five seconds out. Participate as much as possible yourself. Step two: we put more focus on the exhalation. Four seconds in, then six seconds out. If this also goes well, ask the client to pause inhalation for four seconds after breathing out for six seconds before breathing in again.

A longer exhale better supports the body to release stress. You are giving your clients tools to regulate themselves through the breath.

Shaking trauma out of the body

If your client has gone in a state of rigidity and seems at risk of becoming disconnected and shut down, it helps to get them moving. Standing up and shaking the body, trembling, dancing or jumping or some other movement that suits this client. It is necessary for you to join in, as many clients will feel uncomfortable doing these movements. Making sounds while moving adds power and makes it even more effective. Release the 'unshouted scream' or dance or sing the Gloria Gaynor hit song *I will survive*, for example.

Give it breath

Ask your client to lie down on a mat, with a pillow under their head, feet on the floor, knees bent. Imagine yourself as a sort of buddha, or call in the energy of the Holy Spirit – whatever feels right for you and helps you be the secure base your client will need as you guide them into the exercise.

Ask your client to close their eyes and become aware of their body. Then invite your client to give his body breath and to allow whatever is happening in the body. "Follow your natural movement of in and out, contraction followed by expansion. Now make the breath longer, connecting inhalation and exhalation into a continuous circular process and let whatever is there to come up. Just give sound to what is there." Circular breathing allows us to let go of some of our tendency to control.

As coach, you are present and, by speaking softly and calmly, you let the client know you are there. You offer encouragement, possibly by breathing along to the client's rhythm. "Now raise your hips from the floor a little and extend the out-breath, give sound to what is there." Perhaps a *yes* comes up, or a *no*, or *here I am*.

As a coach, you support by being present with encouragement in your voice, looking at your client if needed. First you build this up, then you make the movement smaller and let your client look you in the eye. This can be emotional.

Variation

Ask your client if there is someone they would like to bring along to the next session. Do this exercise with the client, so their companion is both a secure base and witness to what happens during the exercise.

Heart exercise

The client lies on his back with his arms extended at 90 degrees to the body. You ask him to very slowly bring his hands to his heart area. First, during exhale, bring the right hand to the heart, then back, then again the right hand to the heart and back again. Repeat also twice for the left hand. Ask the client to follow the motion of the hand with attention, allowing whatever emotions arise when bringing a hand closer to the heart, to simply be there. Both hands twice equals one round: finish off by simultaneously bringing both hands, on exhalation, to the heart area. When he or she is ready, let them lie on one side while you explore, together, what they are feeling.

Important points to take away

- Your body has its own wisdom, its own memory. Your body stores experiences, which also makes it an entry point for guidance and coaching.
- It is in secure attachment, that you learn how to regulate and contain emotions. As a coach, you can be a coregulator of your clients' emotions.
- A traumatic reaction occurs because your body – when no secure bases are available – is overloaded by an unexpectedly drastic, *potentially* traumatic, event.
- When able to respond resiliently, you stay within the limits of your window of stress tolerance. This means you can access your thinking, feeling, and reflecting and act accordingly. It is a constant undulation between charge and discharge.

- With too much or too little stress, you can exceed the lower and upper limits of your window of stress tolerance. This has major consequences for your health, as there is no longer a balance between charge and discharge.
- The brain tries to gather information from your body's signals about how you are in the world.
- The body responds first. It takes awareness of the body to make a conscious response rather than an unconscious-driven response.
- Connecting with the body can be done through five channels: perception, respiration, movement, sound and language, touch.

Self-reflection for the coach

- What are some of your first memories of being touched? How have these experiences formed the sensibility to touch in your body?
- How did you learn to love your body, and how does this affect how you recognize and respond to the signals from your body that you use in your craft?
- What is your relationship with your body? What parts of your body are you comfortable with, and what parts are you less comfortable with?
- How aware are you of your body? What have you still to learn about 'listening to the body', and how might that affect your craft?
- What is your relationship with stress, and how is this a source of learning and development for you?
- How do you calm yourself during a challenging period?
- What helps you stay within the Window of Stress Tolerance?
- What situations make you go outside the Window of Stress Tolerance?
- How are you able to discharge tension in your body? What might you still learn here and how might this change you?
- How do you guide your clients into feeling into the body and tapping into the wisdom hidden within?

Notes

1 Van der Kolk. B. (2015). *The Body Keeps the Score: Brain, Mind, and Body in the Healing of Trauma*. London: Penguin Books.

2 Carter, E. and Pelphrey, K. (2008). Friend or foe? Brain systems involved in the perception of dynamic signals of menacing and friendly social approaches. *Social Neuroscience*, 3(2): 151–163.

3 Dana, D. (2018). *The Polyvagal Theory in Therapy: Engaging the Rhythm of Regulation*. New York: W.W. Norton & Company.

4 Descartes, R. (1596–1650): cogito ergo sum (Latin for: 'I think, therefore I am'). With this philosophical proposition from his work *Principia Philosophiae* (1644), Descartes tried to lay a foundation of something certain and from which he could build his philosophy further.

5 Dijksterhuis, A. (2015). *Het slimme onbewuste. Denken met gevoel (The clever unconscious. Thinking with feeling)*. Amsterdam: Prometheus/Bert Bakker.

6 Kolthoff, P. (2021). *Stevig staan in intense situaties. Balans in je leiderschap met Embodied Learning (Standing firm in intense situations. Balancing your leadership with Embodied Learning)*. Amsterdam: Boom.

7 Radio game with a mundane sound that, without any context, proves surprisingly difficult to guess.

8 Lynch, J. (1977). *Broken Heart. The Medical Consequences of Loneliness*. New York: Basic Books; Lynch, J. (2000). *A Cry Unheard. New Insights into the Medical Consequences of Loneliness*. Baltimore: Bancroft Press.

9 Wang, S., Lin, C., Tzeng, N., et al. (2019). Effects of oxytocin on prosocial behavior and the associated profiles of oxytocinergic and corticotropin-releasing hormone receptors in a rodent model of posttraumatic stress disorder. *Journal of Biomemedical Sciences*, 26(1): 26.

10 Boormans, G. and Cohen, E. (2020). *Huidhonger. Als je alleen bent na scheiding of verlies van je partner. (Skin hunger. When you're alone after divorce or the loss of your partner)*. Amsterdam: De Arbeiderspers.

11 Bonanno, G.A. (2010). *The Other Side of Sadness*. New York: Basic Books. Bonanno, G.A., Westphal, M. & Mancini, A.D. (2011). Resilience to Loss and Potential Trauma. *Annual Review of Clinical Psychology*, 7: 1.1–1.25.

12 Aten, J. (2020). Who Do You Go to When You Hurt? An Interview with Jakob van Wielink on resilience, trauma, and community. *Psychology Today*.

13 Swinnen, L. (2021). *Activeer je nervus vagus. Een revolutionair antwoord op stress- en angstklachten, trauma en een verminderde immuniteit (Activate your vagus nerve. A revolutionary response to stress and anxiety symptoms, trauma and impaired immunity)*. Tielt: Lannoo.

14 Geenen, M. and Ponjee, T. (2020). Coming out of rigidity gives space. In conversation with Margriet Wentink. *Tijdschrift voor begeleidingskunde*, 9(1): 30–35.

15 Levine, P. (2008). *Healing Trauma: A Pioneering Program for Restoring the Wisdom of Your Body*. Louisville: Sounds True. Levine did pioneering research on how trauma remains trapped in our bodies. In doing so, he shows, among other things, what we can learn in this from animals.

16 Fiddelaers-Jaspers, R. and Noten, S. (2021). *Herbergen van verlies. Thuiskomen in het Land van Rouw (Harboring loss. Coming home to the Land of Grief)*. Heeze: In de Wolken.

17 Tuitert, M. (2021). *Drive. Train je stoïcijnse mindset (Drive. Train your stoic mindset)*. Amsterdam: Maven Publishing.

18 Excerpt from Robert Neimeyer.

19 Tuitert, M. (2021). *Drive. Train je stoïcijnse mindset (Drive. Train your stoic mindset)*. Amsterdam: Maven Publishing.

20 Cordes, C. and Dougherty, T. (1993). A Review and an Integration of Research on Job Burnout. *Academy of Management Review*, (18)4: 621–656.

21 Tuitert, M. (2021). *Drive. Train je stoïcijnse mindset (Drive. Train your stoic mindset)*. Amsterdam: Maven Publishing.

Chapter 6

In dialogue, change is made real

In this Chapter, we look at how dialogue becomes a building block of bonding. Every person has the need to belong – and to *feel* that they belong –, the need to express themselves and to be bonded. Through dialogue you shape the bond in which both belonging and expression are supported, creating a togetherness with the other person in which you can perceive them with all your senses. By giving them your total focus, the other person feels a sense of welcome and belonging. Dialogue is more than a (vital) tool, it is an identity and an attitude to life.

We want this attitude to be characterized by love and autonomy. Every person is unique and brings value, regardless of their gender, role, belief, origin, health or orientations. Every person has the freedom to make their own choices and shape their future regardless of circumstances, but also the responsibility to take into account their freedom and that of others.[1]

Living and working from love and autonomy originates, and takes shape, in dialogue. Forming the foundation for working with the themes of the Transition Cycle, dialogue provides an entrance for real transition. In this Chapter we put the spotlight on powerful elements of dialogue such as caring and daring, listening and tuning in, and paraphrasing.

In dialogue, a truly new perspective can emerge for and between the client and you. We reflect on how self-disclosure – sharing your own vulnerability as a coach – invites the client into the dialogue. You will see how dialogue is a meeting space in which you discover the positive as well as negative impact you have on the other person.

Dialogue

Yazid remembered previous performance review meetings, at former employers, as him sitting quietly during a monologue where his manager lists every aspect of his job that isn't up to scratch. It was always a completely one-sided view. Although, wherever he had worked, his managers had always been satisfied, he also noticed they always found something to complain about. As if 'balance' meant matching every compliment with a

DOI: 10.4324/9781003424178-9

criticism. School had been pretty much the same: although his grades were regularly above average in most of his Economics and Society profile subjects, the dean couldn't stop harping on about his fives in Math.

At his new job, his manager opened the performance review by asking how his experience had been so far. Yazid, feeling confused, looked askance at his manager. She just repeated her question, patiently stirred her coffee and looked calmly back at him. When Yazid started talking about how he was really enjoying his job, his manager nodded encouragingly, inviting him to continue. Sometimes she would ask a probing question, but mostly she would briefly summarize what she heard him say, before inviting him to continue. When Yazid had finished speaking, she gave him feedback on how she had seen him working in the organization. She connected her feedback and examples to what Yazid had just said and emphasized how happy she was that their experiences matched.

They then talked about what Yazid felt he needed, and wanted, to learn in the coming year and how she could help. She described situations where she felt she had seen Yazid struggle and asked him what he felt about them. Together, they agreed a number of development goals. Finally, she asked if Yazid had any feedback for her as a manager and where she could improve in the coming year. Yazid felt seen and taken seriously in the whole process and, in particular, at being invited to give feedback to his boss.

Definition: Dialogue is the search of two or more people for a greater truth than the one they each knew before. Dialogue is characterized by mutual curiosity, acceptance and empathy.[2]

Curiosity

The stance essential for successful dialogue is curiosity, the desire to want to discover something new. You allow yourself to learn. Curiosity draws you into learning something you don't yet know. At the same time, it is about your ability to defer your tendency to judge. However, your curiosity is simultaneously in opposition to your 'lazy' unconscious brain, which prefers to keep the world around you predictable.

In Chapter 4, about emotions, you saw that emotions are signals telling you if your needs are being met or not. This applies equally to judgments. A judgment about another person mirrors an unfulfilled need in yourself.[3] Perhaps you recognize the tendency to put the blame for something that goes wrong outside of yourself, to attribute it to another person or to blame it on 'unavoidable' circumstances. In reality, reflected in the mirror is your own need to feel innocent. So that when you feel the other is being arrogant, that feeling you have is you masking your own need for recognition. By taking responsibility for your own needs, you do not have to demand their fulfillment from someone else. This increases your autonomy, your freedom to meet the other and allow yourself to be known by the other. To discover in the encounter with the other – in a dance in which you are taking turns to lead and be led – something you did not yet know.

> It was Sunday evening and a blended family was relaxing on sofas in the living room. They had just finished the evening meal together, but now everyone was looking at their smartphone screens. The two sisters exchanged a knowing look: sitting here wasn't an option, they had studying to do. Both sighed, but there was a barely audible, yet qualitative, difference in the sighs. Whereas one sister's studies were going well, even though classes were online because of the pandemic, the others were not.
>
> The father felt a subtle tap on his leg from his aware girlfriend. He looked up from the screen, put his phone away and moved across the sofa to sit next to his daughter. "How are you doing?", he asked. "How are your studies going, given that you've been working really hard but your results are disappointing?" A moment later – very emotionally – she said what she'd been avoiding for months, and the possibility that she quit her studies was on the table.

Acceptance

Acceptance, as a precondition for dialogue, refers directly back to the concept of *unconditional positive regard* that we discussed in Chapter 2. It is still true that you don't have to agree with another person in order to accept that they might see or experience things different than you. This doesn't herald the end of dialogue – *let's agree to disagree* – but rather the beginning of it. Because what you cannot accept, you cannot change.

Empathy

Empathy is the third characteristic of dialogue and concerns your ability to relate or empathize with others. We saw, in Chapter 2, that people are neurologically equipped to respond empathically. Judging others, by being afraid of hurting the other person, by wanting to do too well, this ability is blocked. It leads you to putting your needs before those of the other person in the dialogue. You want to ask that 'one good question', or you believe you already know what the client actually needs to look at. You're afraid that if you don't speak out immediately, the chance to help the other person will be lost. In dialogue, empathy helps to get the conversation flowing, and to maintain this interactive flow through the acknowledging effect of the empathic response.

However, many conversations between two or more people can't actually be characterized as dialogue. Sometimes this is not necessary. When you ask someone on the street if they happen to know what time it is, the conversation does not have to meet the conditions of dialogue. And admittedly, in the pub, a robust discussion or debate or a long evening of relaxed chatting can be quite enjoyable, without ever straying into the area of true dialogue.

It gets interesting when you miss an opportunity for dialogue, especially when the opportunity not only presents itself but the situation demands it. And this happens far more often than you are might think. We encourage you to make dialogues not just fundamental to your craft of coaching, but to apply it as a *way of being*. Dialogue isn't something that you do, it is something that you are. The richness of mutual understanding arises when you don't miss an opportunity for dialogue – and thus for discovery and learning. This can be with your partner, your children, your colleagues, your friends, your parents, your siblings. Even if you think the other person is not looking forward to it, it is worth trying to deepen your encounters.

> *His wife walks in the door after a day's work. Dropping her bags in the corner of the room, she walks straight out into the garden and stands there, hands at her sides. He feels irritation rising. Why doesn't she say something, he thinks to himself. He goes into the kitchen and starts chopping vegetables for dinner. He notices he's becoming increasingly irritated. He puts down the knife, walks into the garden, hesitates for a moment and then stands beside her. He takes a deep breath. "How was your day? Is there anything you'd like to share about it?" Sighing deeply, she just turns away from him. Something 'tells' him that he should just go back to the kitchen and leave her to speak when she's ready.*
>
> *However, he does something else: he walks around her, stands on her other side and says softly to her "Do you want to tell me what's on your mind? I would like to hear what you have to say, even if it is painful." The silence continues for a moment, then she says she has been told that the company is being taken over and it is very likely she will lose her job. A tear runs down her cheek. "It makes you feel sad, doesn't it?" he says, looking at her. His wife has turned towards him and, looking at him from time to time, she says "I'm furious." They continue talking.*

Dialogue comes about when, wherever you meet others, you are prepared to perceive the other on four different levels (cognitive, emotional, physical and spiritual). Together with the other person, you set off on a path of discovery by being attentively present, opening your brain, heart, body and mind, checking what you experience with the other person and then exploring further. You can sense a 'rhythm' to the dialogue, like in a dance, of being present with your whole body and mind, opening to the other, checking the other's experience: fully welcoming him or her. A continuous back-

and-forth between you. Learning a dance like the tango takes practice, and so does the dance of dialogue.

Contact and dialogue

Contact belongs to the first theme on the Transition Cycle, which we discuss further in Part Two, Chapter 7. Contact derives from the Latin verb *contingere* which means to touch. To have contact with someone means to touch them. The concept of communication, a means of contact, in turn derives from the Latin verb *communicare which* means to participate or bond. Bonding is part of the third theme on the Transition Cycle.

Dialogue is fundamentally an embodied activity – a touching – that establishes bonding. One human being speaks to another human being. One human being bonds with another human being through words, physical touch, emotion, spirit, energy. People meeting each other touch on cognitive, physical, emotional, and spiritual levels. In an encounter, therefore, body meets body, heart meets heart, involving all the senses. Rarer, and so more special in these times when so many conversations take place via smartphones, with or without someone else in the picture. Touching and being touched is also possible through various media, although not literally of course. But how you make contact, how present you are in your own body and how you seek connection with the other through their image on the screen, enables each of you to perceive and experience the presence of the other.

Bonding as the purpose of dialogue

A dialogue has no pre-intended outcome other than bonding between the involved parties. From that open bond, something can then emerge that invites a larger truth. An example are hostage negotiators. It is precisely because they do not focus on anyone's desired outcomes, but only on establishing real bonding with the hostage takers, that they are so effective. From the bond they make in the dialogue with the hostage taker, an outcome may arise that the hostage taker was initially not prepared to achieve. The willingness of the negotiator – at that moment – to invest unconditionally in the relationship raises the success rate of hostage negotiations to a seemingly improbable 94 percent.[4]

In the definition of dialogue, we find the real challenge here: the willingness to leave the outcome of the encounter open. Therefore, not just any discussion can count as dialogue. A discussion is about being right and trying to be right, at the expense of the other person's rightness. Trying to convince or persuade therefore has no place in a dialogue.

The curiosity which serves as the basis for dialogue always carries the question of how close can you get to the other person. Is the other willing to move with your dance of bonding? Dialoguing, consciously choosing not to try to control the outcome, touches on your fear of rejection, your separation anxiety.[5] That is why conducting a dialogue is so connected to your own attachment history and style!

> *In the past, all the family members had input into what they wanted to do for the holidays, but, ultimately, the father always decided where they went. This was the way the family tried to meet the wishes of all the children and both partners. Although the holidays were always in beautiful places, with something there for everyone to do, Karim had learned that if you want to be the one making the decisions, you have to be at the top of the hierarchy. Participation, he'd realized over time, was more about being seen to do the right thing, rather than doing it.*

Looking at the example, Karim will have to learn to conduct dialogue as a practice of discovering the value of everyone's input. That it is not about one person ultimately deciding, and that dialogue can lead to a greater understanding for all participants.

Perceiving with all your senses

Although you can think of dialogue as an exchange of information between two or more people, that exchange does not always take place 'equally' between all dialogue partners. Earlier, we compared a dialogue to a dance, in which although you are both in motion, who leads can change from moment to moment.

For convenience, we will now assume you have begun a dialogue with a client, a two-way conversation, so to speak. Although you both take turns speaking and not speaking, a significant difference is noticeable during the course of the dialogue: your part, certainly in the beginning, consists mainly of wanting to observe, feel, see, 'taste' the other person. Your presence and observation are therefore primarily aimed at creating a safe setting in which your client feels welcome. At the same time, you try to make sure that you *perceive* your client ever better; more accurately, more fully. That you enter into the dance of dialogue. Perceiving means using all your senses, being in touch with your breath, opening your heart, allowing emotions, welcoming, involving your mind and being guided by that which is greater (spiritual level).

Good listening requires attention and presence on an emotional, cognitive, physical, and spiritual level. And a willingness to turn off your own filters and, as much as possible, to listen without judgment. This is difficult, because your brain is constantly trying to second-guess what is going on. Even about what the other person is telling you. It hinders you getting the right picture of what the other person means. The question is not whether you have and use a cognitive filter, but much more to what extent you are aware of (all) your filters. To speak with Stephen Covey: '*Try first to understand, then to be understood. [...] Next to physical survival, the greatest need of a human being is psychological survival — to be understood, to be affirmed, to be validated, to be appreciated*.[6] To what extent are you willing to invest effort into delaying your judgment until you have enough information, rather than blindly following your assumptions?

> *I find it hard to stay calm, because my boss talks all the time during our coffee breaks, and he keeps making stupid jokes.*
>
> *So you are upset by the way your boss talks. And you mentioned his "stupid" jokes. Would you like to tell me a bit more about that?*
>
> *Yes, sometimes he goes too far for me, making jokes at the expense of others, including colleagues.*
>
> *Would it be accurate to say he crosses a line for you?*
>
> *Yes, I find what he says disrespectful and I it makes me very uncomfortable.*
>
> *It makes you feel uncomfortable.*
>
> *Yes, it always puts me on my guard and I really don't like that. And I'm constantly checking what's happening with the others, how they are reacting. Should I say something or just keep my mouth shut? Am I the only one that's bothered?*
>
> *So if I hear you right, you go on alert and feel cautious and insecure?*
>
> *Yes, insecure; I just don't feel okay!*
>
> *I notice that just talking about it with me makes you angry too, you become rather animated and start talking a bit louder.*
>
> *Yes. Actually, I realize now, it makes me very angry. It crosses a line for me and that makes me feel insecure. I notice that I start avoiding the breaks and I actually find that very upsetting.*

Do you remember an occasion when you felt you were truly understood? That someone really paid attention to your story, gave you all the time you needed? What in particular did that person do? It's very likely that that person actually did *not* do very much at all. *Not* interrupting, contradicting or checking their phone at the same time. *Not* advising, offering solutions or perspectives, comparing, soothing, taking over, coming up with their own examples and so on. It probably seemed like the other person didn't *do* much – although it takes hard work to sit on your hands when the person opposite you is struggling. It is very likely that you experienced that person as consciously being there for you.

It is equally likely that the other person – possibly very subtly – did a lot to encourage you and get you deeper into your story. Possibly the other person didn't just listen *silently*, but listened *actively*, constantly feeding back to you what they noticed in your words, but also in your body language. And all without judgment, without conclusions, without consequences, but with effect. The effect being that you experienced having space to tell your whole story, and to talk from deeper levels than usual. To share your emotions, by letting them flow and, in telling your story in this way, to embrace new experiences, perspectives and insights. The dialogue, as it were, invited you to dive deeper and deeper into yourself. Probably a profound experience: *"I learnt that people will forget what you said, people will forget what you did, but people will never forget the feeling you gave them."* [7]

The power of paraphrasing

The most effective way to actively participate in a dialogue, to really be present, is to paraphrase. Indeed, if you do not paraphrase, the other person has no way of knowing if you are really present in the conversation. The consequence is that the other person will feel neither welcome nor invited.

Paraphrasing is restating the essence of what you hear, see, observe, and perceive, as in the previous case study. Preferably you paraphrase about every three or four sentences to ensure you stay connected and no information or experience – and therefore meaning – is lost. Paraphrasing is giving back what you perceive, shaping the exchanges in such a way that both parties experience bonding. Words are the building blocks of dialogue: paraphrase is the cement that bonds them into shared meaning. It is proof that you are actually able to stand in the other person's shoes, be empathically bonded and, at the same time, be in contact with yourself. Looking fully inward (at yourself), looking fully outward at the other.

What can make paraphrasing so nervy is that we are revisiting our attachment joy and our attachment pain. So the more securely attached we are, the easier it is to paraphrase. The opposite is also true: if we grew up with insecure attachment, it can be a struggle to paraphrase. Reading this now, do you feel any resistance? Paraphrasing is always taking the risk of being rejected, being wrong and thus causing pain (to yourself).

We encourage you to examine your own difficulty and resistance to paraphrasing. And if you dialogue partner – perhaps your client, but could be anyone – reacts by saying that your paraphrasing is inaccurate ("No, I didn't say/recognize that" or other ways in which you perceive that the other person does not recognize themselves in your paraphrase), this is a signal that you need to be more present in the dialogue. You manifest this fuller presence by inviting the other person to explore the subject again, or deeper, or differently.

In dialogue, paraphrasing is the most important tool you have. "Is it true that I hear you say, ...", *followed by as accurate a rendering as possible of what the other person has just told you.* It is a circular process: all of what you perceive informs what you paraphrase, and paraphrasing confirms you have perceived well and enough. It strengthens your bond, because the other person feels heard, seen and welcome and feels there is space for them to commit to the dialogue. *That's where the magic starts.* Paraphrasing opens a field of learning and experience, opens space in the brain to create new pathways and only new pathways can take us to places we've never been and experiences we've never had.

Begin paraphrasing by simply summarizing what you hear; if you can, in your own words. At the level of content, this a useful way of ensuring you understand what the other person is saying. Let's not forget, though, that communication is much more than just content. Communication is about connecting needs, sharing emotions, where the form is determined by the level of safety experienced at that moment. Allowing vulnerability in a conversation therefore depends on the degree of safety. More safety leads to more sharing, to more vulnerability. Therefore, focus your paraphrasing on those aspects of the dialogue that contribute to safety: understanding, acknowledgement, affirmation and challenge (risk-taking).

Paraphrasing takes a lot of practice and requires accepting your resistance, then moving beyond it. It is challenging in the beginning to simultaneously listen and summarize – consciously – before confirming what you've heard. At first, it will distract you from listening 'well', as the double-tasking of giving full attention while forming an authentic summary takes some mastering. However, conscious practice, allied to pure intention, will get you there. Your brain adapts and automates at lightning speed: before very long, it will not be second nature, it will be unconscious.

There'll be times in the early days of practice when you might feel it necessary to interrupt the other person when they are in full flood, passionately, emotionally, excitedly telling their story. This asks for careful assertiveness. If the other person has not yet finished speaking, interrupting them will come across as rude. Perhaps you are distracted by your unquestioned belief in your own perception. Remember that in paraphrasing we repeat our learned attachment movement and its joy or pain. Also, in interrupting, we run the risk of being rejected. It can seem absolutely counterintuitive to practice interrupting in order to experience what it brings, which is more bonding.

If you wait until the other person has finished speaking, before you paraphrase, you are might be so far into the story that you can only remember (paraphrase) the big stuff. In doing so, you relegate the small stuff, where jewels are often hidden, into lost meaning. What can help is indicating what you want to do: "Is it OK if I interrupt you for a moment," "I want to be sure I'm hearing and understanding you correctly, so is it OK if I briefly summarize what you just told me?" Basically, by using subtitles, you ask permission. In our experience, everyone likes it when you indicate that you want to ensure you understand the other person correctly.

Finally, paraphrasing also requires that you learn the art of holding back. To postpone your own judgment and reproduce purely what you hear and not what you think you recognize in it. And no longer waiting for *your* turn to tell *your* story and be understood in *your* turn. Paraphrasing is more than a communication or conversation technique. It is an attitude to life aimed at wanting to bond while maintaining individuality.

In the craft of the secure base coach we identify two variations of paraphrasing:

1   Paraphrase 1.0, in which you give back what you perceive in the other person (hearing, seeing, feeling);
2   Paraphrase 2.0, in which you give something back from your own wisdom.

The case study has many examples of Paraphrase 1.0, where you give back something you perceive, such as: "When you are telling me this, you keep looking upwards, with a sense of hopelessness. Is this correct?"

Paraphrase 2.0, might sound like this: "When I hear you saying this, you seem very lonely. Does that sound right?" or, "'While I was listening to you, an image of a scared little girl came to me. Do you recognize this in some way?"

In the latter examples you can see that you are letting more of yourself show in the contact. Your own experience, your own story comes more to the fore in your paraphrase, without this affecting the amount of care you bring to your coaching. Dialogue is also the art of allowing yourself to be known, showing yourself in the contact. And thus taking an emotional risk, which again directly touches on our attachment style: I make myself visible in the contact, I step into the connection by paraphrasing and thus also accept the risk of rejection. However, if we don't do this – take risks – as coaches (and as human beings) we are avoiding bonding.

Conflict as a source of learning

What if you meet someone who says something that hurts you? What if you get into a dialogue where your client accuses you of something or gets angry with you? Are you able to make a bridge to the other person even when you feel yourself under pressure and you are affected?

Conflict is an act of intimacy, "I find you worthy of my full emotion." Conflict brings us very close to each other's boundaries and sometimes it takes us over them. And it challenges our ability and willingness to keep our focus on ourselves *and the other*, and our mind on curiosity *and bonding*. "I see your anger. And you use words that scare me and touch me. I want to hear you, so will you tell me what is making you so angry?" "You called me a fraud, an impostor. That hurts me. Tell me what it is I do that you see as being a fraud."

Conflict asks you to stay present, to constantly bring yourself back into the here-and-now, into what is actually happening, to shape the bond from your vulnerability, to build a bridge to the other. This arises out of your lifelong commitment to learning and development, to love and bond (reward). The ability to enter into conflict and stay bonded, even when you are intensely touched, increases the bond; it is an act of love. When embracing conflict, the way through it is paraphrase. Perhaps the conflict mirrors something lurking in the shadows of your own life? Bond with that other person and see what you might learn there.

Daring questions

Besides your ability to stand still, perceive and paraphrase, the dialogue is deepened by the questions you ask. The art is not to be already thinking about the follow-up question, as that will emerge from the paraphrasing. Through the practice needed to master the art of paraphrasing, you'll come to trust that the right question will come to mind, at the right time.

Good questions open something that is closed, or set something in motion that had come to a standstill. However, what makes a good question also depends on the context. On a content level, you could say that all questions around themes on the Transition Cycle are useful. In formulating your questions, you choose between closed and open questions: *closed* to check and confirm, *open* to invite and explore. What determines the effectiveness of any question, is the rapport you have with the other person at that specific moment. Because paraphrasing deepens the bond and brings you closer and closer to the other person, it helps deepen the rapport that leads you to ask the appropriate question at a specific moment.

Your relationship with the other, the psychological contract and the degree of caring (security and proximity) that underscores it, determines how your questions are received and so how effective they are. Especially when you begin to ask daring questions.

What is the most daring question anyone has ever asked you? What made this question so daring? And what is the most daring question you *didn't* dare to ask? What made that question 'too' daring?

Without being able to guess what makes a question daring for you, we do believe that a question becomes daring when it carries the possibility to materially affect your relationship with the other person. That relationship is determined, in some measure, by its context. Is it a business, a coaching, a personal or, possibly, a romantic relationship. Whatever the context, however, you might ask, or be asked, a question that triggers something about the relationship. A question that immediately raises the underlying question of whether you are willing to take the risk of finding out the answer. Would you then be willing to take a step towards deepening when rejection might be the result? Or, in the words of Socrates: '*Wisdom begins in wonder*'.[8]

Socrates was a Greek philosopher who elevated questioning to an art. By incessantly asking questions he tried to get closer to the truth, and was mostly busy with themes of virtue or ethics. The eponymous Socratic method starts from the idea that the only thing you can be certain of is that you know nothing for certain.

By constantly asking questions, about what something is and testing the answers for consistency, you eliminate all the possibilities that something isn't, get closer to what it is/might be, and so deepen your understanding of whatever is the subject at hand.

However, by doubting everything and questioning all apparent certainties, Socrates made some serious enemies. He was eventually sentenced to death for allegedly not worshipping the gods of the city of Athens and for his supposed bad influence on young people. With his ability to doubt and question everything, he stood at the cradle of the development of Western philosophy and has left us with a daring example of how questions can bring us closer together.

In the introduction to her book on asking Socratic questions, Elke Wiss evocatively recounts her first, quite painful, experience with the Socratic approach.[9] During a coffee break during her philosophy study, the conversation turned to having children. Everyone had a chance to contribute and most talked about their own children. When Elke said that she did not have children of her own, the course leader immediately asked the next person in the group, not giving Elke any chance to add to her opening statement. Out of curiosity, and to address the palpable discomfort in the group that "No, I don't have children." evoked, Elke came back to the issue, a little later, with another woman in the circle who had also said she had no children. Encouraged by Socrates – who she describes as standing behind her wearing trainers and a Batman cape – Elke asked the woman: "Was that your choice?" "No" she indignantly replied – after a tangible silence in which the rest of the group seemed to be holding their breath – and then, through clenched teeth, "I-did-not- choose-for-that-myself. Absolutely not."

The woman's answer makes the group even more uncomfortable than they already were. Walking back to class, Elke tries to reconcile with the woman, but is told: "I find it very strange that people think they can just ask a question like that."

Her book is an account of what Elke subsequently learned about asking questions: the importance of asking permission, of creating bonding and security to avoid drowning in a 'quagmire of emotions', and about equality and mutual responsibility. These help create a context and the conditions in which it is possible to share the truth of what is on your mind. Even when it hurts.

Underneath every contact there is also a contract, a social or psychological agreement that defines – although mostly unspoken and always unwritten – what is safe in the relationship and 'allowed', and what is not. Trust in the relationship grows when both parties abide by the contract. However, this trust cannot grow further without a willingness to test the limits of the contract, and to assess, moment by moment, the depths of each person's will to show and know themselves.

The daring question (from the beginning of this section) touches on vulnerability, personal or professional, and to the perception of safety in the relationship. Such a question might also cause embarrassment: your own, or your assessment that you do not want to embarrass the other person. Daring questions might also touch on shame. Your own, or your assessment that you don't want to make things difficult for the other person. Being a secure base and offering 100 percent caring and 100 percent daring makes it inevitable, however, that you will ask a daring question. Without the question, there is no daring. It is precisely from your awareness that it is daring that you can manifest your caring qualities first. As a secure base, however, avoiding asking the question is not an option. For that would be an attempt to rescue the other, and then you'd be doing them and the relationship a disservice.[10]

Feedback and the person effect

An unusual variation on the daring question, or when beginning a dialogue, is to ask about your own *person effect*.

> **Definition:** The person effect is the unique way, both positive and negative, in which people come across to others and bond with them.[11]

In every contact, the person opposite us has an effect on us. What the other person does/does not, shows/hides evokes something in us. When we can honestly and openly give back to the other person what is happening for us, the positive and/or negative effects, space is created for learning, growth, and a deeper bond.

Elements of the person effect include:

- Status
- Physical appearance
- Authority
- Nationality and culture
- Age
- Clothing
- Energy level
- Perfectionism
- Optimism/pessimism
- Words and language
- Reputation

Ways you can positively influence your person effect include:

- Empathy
- Authenticity
- Respect

- Curiosity
- Self-disclosure
- Warmth
- Honesty and directness
- Being concrete
- Willingness to confront
- Strength
- Dialogue readiness and skills
- Approachability and availability

We can learn a lot about how we really come across from feedback on our person effect. What effect am I having on the other person: through clothing, posture, word choice and delivery, looking them in the eyes – or not, body language? Is this the effect I want and with which I can be successful? How do I bond with the other person and what is it that I do, that interferes with bonding or even fractures it?

Asking someone for feedback on your person effect is a powerful resource to ensure the way you come across matches who you are and want to be. Feedback is given in the here-and-now, in the encounter with the other person and is about this relationship, where something has happened that prevents or obstructs true bonding. The purpose of giving feedback is to clarify for the other the effect that incident is having on you, so that they can adjust their behavior accordingly in the future. And vice-versa, of course. The recovery of the relationship happens in the present moment because careful feedback, like paraphrasing, (re)connects us with the other person. Ewe harvest future gains too, as feedback empowers the other person to make (more-)conscious choices that align their communication and behavior with who they really are.

Feedback and feedforward

Within coaching and leadership, there is a movement that no longer talks about *feedback*, only about *feedforward*.[12] According to this concept, feedback is of limited effectiveness, because it focuses on what went wrong in the past. The feedback recipient finds this unhelpful as he cannot change the past. Which means it doesn't really do much for the feedback giver, as all he's done is make the recipient feel worse. Feedforward is more about what you would like to be different in the future and assumes the other person wants to change and has the potential do so, to develop. Feedback on person effect, if given while bonded with the other person, fully embraces the concept of feedforward.

The daring aspect of giving feedback, in this context, is that you are suggesting a desired change in the relationship without any certainty that the other person will be open to it. Rejection is lurking. You cannot avoid your vulnerability being seen, when you speak out your need and the change you desired in order to meet it. Any change – now or in the future – always requires saying goodbye to something from the past. You can't slip past this potential discomfort. At least not for yourself; the other person must make their own way in this.

Feedback needs security in the relationship as a prerequisite. Without real bonding, feedback is hard to give and harder to hear. Conversely, but more importantly, it's feedback that can overcome a perceived lack of security and deepen the bond. Good feedback builds security.

It is about reducing the other person's blind spot so that they can make different, more- conscious choices. From here on, whenever we use the term *feedback*, we mean it to include and embrace every aspect and technique of *feedforward*.

The person effect is about what is present – possibly in your blind spot – that is or is not helpful in the relationship. By making this explicit and therefore aware, you receive – possible new – information that you can determine what you want to do with it. This always includes the two explicit questions:

- What am I doing that helps you to bond with me?
- What am I doing that interferes with or prevents you bonding with me?

Sometimes, when I tell you something, you give me a really hard look.

So, if I understand you correctly, there is something in the way I look at you that makes me come across as stern? Would you like to tell me more about that?

Yes. You squeeze your eyes together, your lips tighten and you are quiet just a bit too long for my liking.

So I narrow my eyes, my lips tighten and I take just a bit too long to respond. And how does that affect you?

I start doubting whether I am doing 'it' right and then I actually start worrying about you rather than being focused on myself.

So my gaze, my facial expressions and the fact that I stay quiet for a bit longer take your attention away from you. What can I do to help you get your attention back to yourself?

Maybe a softer look on your face, a smile perhaps and letting me know you've heard me when I tell you something.

So smiling a little more and letting you know, more often, that I am hearing you. Like I'm doing now, for example, by checking if I'm understanding you?

Yes. And how is it for you to talk about it like this?

It clears my head and brings me more back to myself. And then I also discover that this is a pattern of mine, that I let myself be easily distracted from myself.

Shall we talk about that further?

Yes, fine.

The coach smiles.

Important points to take away

- Dialogue is a building block for the bond from which transition can be shaped.
- Dialogue is the search of two or more people for a greater truth than one they each knew before. It is characterized by mutual curiosity, acceptance and empathy.
- Good perception requires attention and presence: emotional, cognitive, physical, and spiritual.
- By paraphrasing, you check whether you have understood the other person correctly and help them get to the essence of their story.
- Without daring in dialogue, there is no learning effect.
- Conflict requires staying present in the tension, bringing your vulnerability into the bond and building a bridge to the other.
- The person effect is the unique impact you have on the other person, whether positive or negative. In the coaching relationship, this affects the bond between you and your client.

Self-reflection for the coach

- What have you learned about dialogue practice in your life, and how does that affect your dialogue ability?
- What is the most difficult conversation you've ever had to start in your life and why? What did you learn from it? Looking back, what would you have done differently?
- What do you encounter when you start (practicing) paraphrasing?
- What daring questions have you ever asked? What made them daring?
- What daring questions have you avoided asking? What made them (too) daring?
- What do you encounter when you use silences?
- How good are you at listening? How would someone who knows you answer this? Your partner, children, colleagues, friends?
- With whom or in what situations do you find it difficult to remain curious and postpone judgment?
- From whom do you still have to get feedback on your person effect?
- What is the most painful feedback you have ever had (on your person effect), and what did you learn from it?
- With whom do you possibly find it daring to ask for feedback on your person effect, that you expect will give you *negative* feedback? What makes it daring with this person or in this context?
- Is there someone to whom you want/plan to give *negative* feedback on their person effect? What kind of feedback? And what does that say about you?

Notes

1 Ethics and code of conduct of The School for Transition.
2 Van Wielink, J., Fiddelaers-Jaspers, R., and Wilhelm, L. (2023). *The Language of Transition in Leadership. Your Calling as a Leader in a World of Change*. New York: Routledge.
3 Rosenberg, M. (2015). *Nonviolent communication. A Language of Life*. Encinitas: Puddle Dancer Press.
4 Kohlrieser, G. (2006). *Hostage At The Table. How Leaders Can Overcome Conflict, Influence Others, and Raise Performance*. San Francisco: Jossey-Bass.
5 Bowlby, J. (1988). *Separation, Anxiety and Anger; Attachment and Loss, Volume 2*. London: Random House.
6 Covey, S. (2020). *The Seven Habits Of Highly Effective People*. New York: Simon & Schuster.
7 This quote is frequently attributed – on the internet – to Maya Angelou, but that is probably incorrect. The oldest reference is to a 1971 collection of quotes entitled 'Richard Evans' Quote Book', in which the quote is attributed to Carl W. Buehner. See https://quoteinvestigator.com/2014/04/06/they–feel, accessed June 20, 2021.
8 From Plato (1987). *Theaetetus*. London: Penguin Books.
9 Wiss, E. (2020). *Socrates op sneakers. Filosofische gids voor het stellen van goede vragen (Socrates on trainers. Philosophical guide to asking good questions)*. Amsterdam: Ambo|Anthos.
10 See also the note on the drama triangle in Chapter 2 on professional closeness.
11 Van Wielink, J., Fiddelaers-Jaspers, R., and Wilhelm, L. (2023). *The Language of Transition in Leadership. Your Calling as a Leader in a World of Change*. New York: Routledge.
12 Goldsmith, M. (2012). *Feedforward*. Mundelein: Writers Of The Round Table Press.

Part II

The practice of secure base coaching

Whereas Part I was about the 'being' energy of the secure base coach, Part II looks closely at the 'doing' energy. We take you on a journey along the themes of the Transition Cycle. Each Chapter is devoted to one theme of this perspective on transition.

In each case, we start by examining the theory and framework of the particular theme. Then we look at some of the research that illuminates the background to that theme. We see how the themes are irrevocably linked to shaping real change in people's lives and to collaboration within teams and organizations.

Then we show you how a coach can apply secure base thinking and practice with individuals and groups. Through case histories and concrete methods you can add to your knowledge of how a secure base coach guides transition. As in Part I, at the end of each chapter there are questions that encourage and challenge you to reflect on your own craft.

At the end of Part II you are offered a feedback and reflection tool based on the Transition Cycle. You can use it in both individual and group sessions.

DOI: 10.4324/9781003424178-10

Chapter 7

Contact and welcome

"I was born when my parents were in deep grief. The unexpected death of my grandfather had turned everything upside down. How do you welcome a new child when you are at the edge of a grave, staring at death? All I've ever known is that at every threshold in my life I hear myself asking: 'Does it matter that I'm here?'"

Floor (32)

"It was the first day at my new workplace, after being unexpectedly laid off by my previous employer. I walked in and the receptionist immediately knew who I was. She gave me a friendly welcome and handed me a beautiful bunch of flowers. My new manager came downstairs to pick me up and personally introduced me to the whole team. This day was the start of a lasting, productive collaboration."

Rik (48)

In every new contact the first contact of your life is touched again, in every new welcome your first welcome. How welcome were you at birth? Who were present and absent? Old memories of feeling or not feeling welcome play an important role in how you welcome yourself and others. How do you welcome yourself from these experiences into a new contact? How do you welcome your clients? How do you step into a new group?

In this Chapter, we will explore how contact and welcome are inextricably linked. They form the basis for every relationship and for cooperation and collaboration in teams and organizations. We will reflect, through these themes, on the role of the secure base coach in guiding individuals, teams, and organizations.

In every contact, your first welcome is touched again

Already, in the womb, the foundations of your life are laid. You receive not only their genes, but also their history and that of all the parents in your family line. This history greatly influences your view of the world and the

DOI: 10.4324/9781003424178-11

way you interact with it. How welcome you have felt with your parents and in your upbringing, is carried with you forever, imprinted in your body and brain. In adulthood, you no longer have active memories of these moments; you cannot bring them to mind, but your body can retrieve them. The responses you learned to give will continue to color your first response to new situations and new events. Your response is unique to you. Even when the context is the same, the answer each person gives will be different. The better you know your own answer, the easier it will be to make a choice appropriate to the kind of bond you want.

The physical and emotional presence and availability of secure bases, at first usually the mother and father, determine your initial experience of being welcome. And, to a large extent and throughout your life, your relationship with yourself and how you welcome others. If the initial experience is a positive blend of love and availability, then you will tend to approach new contacts with confidence, fundamentally assuming that new contacts will be pleasant and that people are available and want to be in contact. What was your birth like? Were your caregivers totally 'there'? Or were they also dealing with stressful issues like work, money worries or relationship problems. If so, then you're initial reactions to new encounters might be that of holding back a little and probing, waiting to see what develops. Am I welcome? Is someone there for me? No matter how young you are, you pick up on those cues and respond appropriately to the situation. This might be playing and laughing or withdrawing; asking for more or less attention; acting the clown, or the helper. The presence of stress factors and secure bases in your first phase of life influences the development of your resilience and your eventual life expectancy.[1]

Throughout your life, you constantly gain new experiences through the contacts you make. These experiences often confirm what you already know, but can also be completely new. If you were born into a large family where there wasn't much attention for you, this experience will be confirmed on the first day of your new job, when your manager leaves you at your computer to get on with your work, alone. Alternatively, it might be that on that same first day, you are welcomed by your new manager, who has scheduled a getting-to-know-each-other coffee hour with the whole team. Either of these new experiences of being welcomed becomes part of your unique way of welcoming others and allowing yourself to be welcomed.

The themes of contact and welcome also come into play between coach and client. At the first meeting between the coach and the client or team, everybody's history is there in the room too. Instinctively, everyone probes each other, puts out feelers. Probing is not something that only takes place at first contacts; it continues throughout the coaching relationship, consciously and unconsciously.

It is further fueled by what is experienced within the relationship. The effectiveness of coaching stands or falls on the trust between both, that is constantly growing, deepening, sometimes perhaps lost for a while, and then recovered.[2] When, as a coach, you are able to act sincerely and congruently and be yourself in the coaching, this forms the basis for the necessary security and trust which make real change possible. Here you lay the foundations of unconditional positive regard, as explored in Chapter 2.[3] It is exactly this form of attention that gives the other person space to explore themselves without the risk of being rejected or criticized.[4]

Relationship building is a delicate process. Even a carefully built trusting, coaching relationship can be damaged by a single experience of one of the parties feeling insecure. Research shows that the coach's willingness and ability to explore these moments in the counseling relationship, leads to real change.[5] This kind of exploration activates processes in the right side of the brain that are different from the emotional development of early childhood. Phyllis Kosminsky and Jack Jordan explain that counseling actually develops language that the right brain can understand, and that the client needs to handle their emotions.[6] A prerequisite for enabling this change in the brain is a safe client-coach relationship.

> *When Floor rings the doorbell of her coach, Joep's, it takes a moment before she hears footsteps on the stairs. Hurriedly, Joep pulls open the door and gestures for her to come in. He points to his phone, wedged between his shoulder and ear, to let Floor know that he is busy with someone. Joep turns and walks up the stairs, still on his call. Floor remains standing in the corridor. For a moment, she feels despair and that ever-present question: "Is it okay that I'm here?" When she comes upstairs, Joep puts down his phone and apologizes for finishing the call. Floor feels herself relax, and how this makes her able to focus on their conversation.*

Properly welcoming the other person requires genuine attention. If the absence of this attention at the moment of welcome, like Joep does in the example, is not revisited explicitly soon into the meeting, it carries the potential to negatively affect the welcome and to erode the client's psychological safety in the relationship.

Things that support the experience of (the other) feeling welcome include:

- Eye contact
- Undivided attention
- Being well presented
- Being calm and restful
- Punctuality
- Being well prepared
- Unconditional acceptance of the client and his problem
- Empathy
- Bonding through language, posture, pace, intonation
- Consciously being physically present

Things that are detrimental to the experience of welcome include:

- Being busy with other things at the moment of contact
- Being late
- An untidy environment
- Being focused on yourself
- Too much talking and too few questions

Isolate or withdraw, the flip side of contact and welcome

Engaging in contact requires opening up to the other person. In contact with others, you are 'touched': cognitively, emotionally, spiritually, perhaps physically. Contact is a dance of touching and being touched. This requires a willingness to open up to the other, at the risk of rejection. If negative past experiences make you afraid to open up (again) to this specific possibility of being touched, you withdraw from contact.

When transition stalls, you end up with the survival strategies on the flip side of the Transition Cycle. The main cause of stalling in the Transition Cycle are moments in your history where there's been hurt or trauma that has not been grieved (enough).

The flip side of "contact and welcome" is "isolate or withdraw." By avoiding contact, you probably avoid the risk of being hurt, for example by rejection, but at the same time you deny yourself the opportunity of new, enriching experiences.

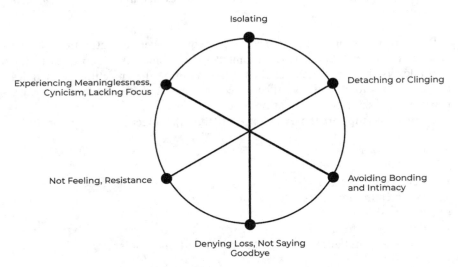

Figure 7.1 Themes on the Cycle of Stalled Transition

Ayse has been working in the investment team of a large insurer for a long time. She has a warm relationship with her team members and manager and, until recently, she derived great satisfaction from her work and work environment. The latter changed with the recent arrival of a new colleague. He does not hide what he thinks of 'foreigners'. Ayse, with her Turkish roots, does not feel welcome with him. Her teammates sense the discomfort and try to break the ensuing tension with a joke or a show of support for her at the coffee machine. The more space the new colleague is given, the more Ayse withdraws.

Isolation and withdrawal are survival movements born of feelings such as anxiety, shame, anger or sadness. The withdrawal movement takes place not only in contact with others but also in contact with yourself. The connection with your own emotional world and needs is broken. This movement has many manifestations. The most visible form is physical absence, but also mental absence, flight behavior in work, sports, or hobbies, putting on armor, withholding your own opinion or not wanting to be (physically) touched are all manifestations of isolation and withdrawal.

As a secure base coach you must be aware of what stalling on the Transition Cycle looks like, and explore with your client(s) how this is affecting your contact.

Contact and contract

In every relationship, there are spoken and unspoken rules. From birth onwards you are receiving messages about these 'rules'. Messages about who you are, what you may and may not do, how people treat each other, what you may and may not talk about. These messages become your unconscious script. Examples of positive, empowering messages (permissions) include "You are allowed to be here. You are allowed to be successful. You are allowed to belong." Negative messages, prohibitions (injunctions) are, for example: "Don't be yourself. Don't be important. Don't be successful." In response to these messages, you develop behaviors that lead to parental approval.[7] The responses you learned growing up, are often so obvious and logical (to you) that you cannot even imagine that these rules do not apply to others or might be different for others.

Bianca comes from a family where you don't talk about feelings. There are often heated discussions at the kitchen table about something that happened, but never about how things felt for the people involved. So when Bianca first meets her coach, she is taken aback when he asks her what she felt in a particular situation. Embarrassed and uncomfortable, she averts her gaze, hoping the coach will let it drop. Instead, he asks her what is happening for her now. She is not used to this and feels even more uncomfortable. The actual cause of her discomfort and her feelings of being disloyal, is her unconscious agreement with the 'contract' from her family of origin: "We do not talk about emotions."

In the initial moments of meeting a client for the first time, they will already have given you many signals about contact and welcome. Signals that often have great significance for their transition and your guidance of it. In each new contact, each person brings their own set of rules: these form the unwritten rules of the relationship.

The way those first moments go determines the content of the contract that is entered into, consciously and unconsciously. Do you meet your client at the door or does he make his own way to your office? Do you get straight to the point or do you start with a cup of coffee? Are all topics welcome, or are there topics you don't discuss? Each of you creates your own psychological contract based on your own rules, needs and expectations. Although it isn't discussed with the other, it decides how each will be when in contact with the other. It often arises unspoken and is based on the experiences of those involved. Both the good and the not-so-good experiences are inevitably written into this contract.

Because you, as a coach, have worked hard to know your own rules and the resulting patterns, you are able to recognize when this is happening to you or to your client, and to bring this into the session.

When Tanja visits Els for the first time, she talks about how her bond with her mother was damaged years ago, when her parents got divorced. And how she chose to cut her father out of her life. Despite the ongoing contact with her mother, she misses the incredible bond they used to have immensely and would like somehow to get it back. In the session, Els feels how she has to navigate between Tanja wanting to improve the bond with her mother and her mother's unspoken wish that she has no contact with her father. When Els mentions this, Tanja flinches, as if she thinks: 'This was not what we were supposed to talk about, was it?'

By explicitly stating the goals of the relationship and each person's role in it, you bring focus to the contact. What is the client's question? What makes this question so important in the client's life that she needs to address it *right now*? This applies just as much to team coaching. In the first meeting you explore the issue and feel into whether or not you are the right person for this client, with this question, at this time, in this place. You might choose to sketch out how you imagine the counseling might go. Should you, perhaps together, come to the conclusion that you are not the right match, this is the time to make that clear.

Anita is asked to coach a team where there is a breakdown in trust between team members. In the introductory interview, the team manager says he does not want to look back, but wants to move forward. That too much time has already been wasted on the past; he wants to move on. Anita tries to explain the importance of connecting the present with the past, but he is absolutely firm. It is not what he wants. Anita decides not to take the assignment.

The secure base coach at work with contact and welcome

Contact and Welcome – Working with Individuals

Entering the room, Bob looks around nervously and asks, "Where should I sit?" "Where would you like to sit?" the coach asks. Bob takes a seat on the chair by the window and looks out. The coach sits down on a bench opposite him. "What is it like for you to be here?" he asks. Bob is still looking outside and seems lost in thought. "I find it a bit tense; I'm embarrassed that I can't sort this out myself and have to ask for your help."

You could take Bob's first question as a polite one from someone who arrives somewhere for the first time. But the shame he later says he feels shines a very different light on this question. As if he is asking himself: "Is there any place for me when I feel ashamed? Am I still welcome with my shame?" Therefore, as a secure base coach, it is it is necessary to be sensitive, and listen with an open heart to all the signals the client sends, consciously and unconsciously. The client has come to you with a life-question and wonders consciously or unconsciously whether he is welcome with you with this question. However, this also applies just as much to you the coach. So in order to make the best of the session for the client, you should be aware of what is going on inside you in terms of contact and welcome.[8]

As you ask your client about how he has learned to welcome and be welcomed, keep in mind how important this question also is for you as a coach. How you shape the contact, together, lays the foundation of the psychological contract between you, which we wrote about earlier in this chapter. That contract is based on previous life experiences of both you and your client. In what ways did you both see your parents, your siblings, your classmates and your friends interacting and bonding with each other? What happened at the times when expectations and desires were met in those contact situations? And what happened when they were not? What beliefs were formed and how do they play a role in the present?

As a coach, it is good to realize that every welcome, every new contact for your client also contains a goodbye. What must the client say goodbye to (leave behind) when he comes to you for help and begins a personal journey with you? People often seek out a coach because they notice that, in some way, their life isn't going the way they want, often voiced as a lack of flow. The causes can be diverse and numerous, but one thing is certain: if a client wants to make a new start, they will have to face the fact that saying good-bye to the old is a prerequisite. *You cannot offer a welcome, if you have not first said goodbye.*

> *"What makes asking for help embarrassing for you, Bob?" the coach asks. "It's simple: I should be able to do it on my own. It's what I've always been told. By my parents, my teachers. It's essential that I can do this stuff myself." Coach looks at him. "And now you find yourself here. So, what makes you unable to do it on your own now?" "I'm just not getting any-where. I go round and round in circles, ruminating, thinking the same thoughts over and over. I need help to unravel those thoughts." "You sound like you're ready to kiss goodbye to the belief that you have to do it alone. Is that right?" Bob smiles. "Yes … maybe. Who knows?"*

To shape real change in your life, you have to welcome yourself. With all the experiences you have had in your life: positive and negative, beautiful and painful, joyful and sad. To attempt this, you need people who can be your secure bases, who welcome you, offering trust and security (caring). People with whom you feel encouraged, strengthened, and challenged (daring) to take risks and let go of old beliefs. Basically, a secure base can be anything and anyone. Usually it is a person, but it can also be a place, or an event, even an experience. Secure bases help you to welcome yourself and all that you hold inside, so that you can bond, in your totality, to the secure base and begin this journey of revelation. When you can lay out all that holds you back and hinders you, with someone who is securely bonding with you, wel-coming you, seeing you, it can be a step into a new beginning and out of the old, restrictive patterns.

When another person truly welcomes you, it changes how you see yourself. It challenges the old, tired, familiar story, offering something new, a different, helpful perspective on the same reality. That is the promise inherent in a conscious, open, caring welcome. As a secure base coach, that's what you strive to be, for all your clients, always.

Contact and welcome – Working with teams

> *Wide-eyed and a little self-conscious, Aleid looks around the room where she and her team receive coaching. The things her colleagues say touch her. This is her first day in this team and her first meeting with her new colleagues. The team manager has decided to start a coaching program for the whole team, because cooperation is in short supply. There are irrita-tions. People have adopted a silo mentality and there are vague references*

to 'old hurts' that nobody will talk about. The team are struggling to meet their personal and business challenges and to shape the changes they need to make.

One of the two team coaches catches Aleid's gaze. "What is happening for you, Aleid?" she asks. "Today is my first meeting with any of these people; I realize I am becoming part of a team in which much has already happened. I wonder how I'm supposed to find my place here."

What Aleid keenly senses is that the team comes with a past. That past is affecting the present and the future. And, naturally, it affects the kind of goodbye given to people leaving the team and how new people are welcomed into it. Perhaps that is Aleid's question: What does my welcome, in and by this team, really look like? And what might that tell me about my place here?

There are two perspectives to starting in any team: that of the joining person and that of the group. The joiner arrives with his history, and the team have theirs, as individuals and as a group.

The first working day largely determines the rest of your career within the team and the organization. This first contact, the attention that is or is not given, helps decide how you entrust yourself to the team and the organization and so begin to develop loyalty to both. Is it a warm welcome? Is there a workplace ready for you? Are you shown around the building? Are a laptop and mobile phone ready for you? Do team members take time to get to know you a bit? Are meetings already scheduled for you with people key to your role? In large organizations, in addition to the immediate workplace welcome, *onboarding* takes place: a welcome to the wider organization, arranged for all newcomers. This way, a network can also be created outside your own team. And, as in Aleid's case, sometimes the creation of a new team or department coincides with a training or coaching program.

Aleid spoke out loud the question that many new team members often wonder but don't ask. That she so clearly responds to the invitation of the team coach, by saying what is on her mind, makes the other team members aware of the history of this group and the impact it has on their behavior and how they work together.

The team coach focuses with the group around two events that have caused conflicts in the team. At the end of the day, a number of team members say that Aleid's question, about how she might feel welcome here and find her place, helped them to face and give meaning to old pain, and to share this with their colleagues. On just her first day, Aleid had made an incredibly positive contribution to the functioning of the team.

Team development requires understanding and recognition from everyone that their personalities and history determine, to a large extent, the dynamics in the group. They must be willing to engage in regular dialogue with each other about that history and its impact on everyone in the team. To develop as a team, the group must be given the opportunity to face and come to terms with the positive and negative impacts of the past. This requires leadership, the willingness to take responsibility for one's own actions and those of others with whom we are bonded. The same applies for the team leader and the coach. This kind of aware, conscious leadership engenders psychological safety, which we'll visit in depth in Chapter 8.

In the context of teams and organizations, change is a constant. Whether large or small change creates growth and development; they are the *raison d'être* of every level: individual, team, organization. Every new change heralds a new beginning which employees have to get used to. Sometimes people adapt casually, almost invisibly, but more often this process will require attention.

The mechanism of first saying goodbye to the old before you can commit to the new applies to every form of change. Even when change is implemented at the organizational level, a transition process usually must take place at the individual level. Not paying enough attention to the transition individuals need to reconnect to the organization is one of the main reasons why change fails so often.

As the team's coach, together with them you constantly reflect on their transitions, what they are going through as individuals and as a group. Everyone handles transition in a different way and at a different pace. Shaping transition requires a personalized approach. As a coach, you must ensure that each employee has the space to reflect on their own transition and connect their process with (that of) the group.

By offering a safe place where everyone's story is welcome, you support the team and each member to let go of the old and embrace the new reality. Because the other employees are witness to this process, the change is endorsed and reinforced. The new beginning is welcomed in together.

Exercises with your client

The life-line

The *Life-line Exercise* comes back in each of the following Chapters. Also known as the *Roots of Leadership Exercise* because it is a deep exploration of how past experiences have shaped your client into who he is today. *The deeper the roots, the higher the growth.* It is the defining exercise in every theme of the Transition Cycle. It is worth devoting a part of every session the looking (again) at the client's life-line – from the perspective of whatever theme of the Transition Cycle you are working through at that time.

Here we explain the basics of the exercise. Using this, you can look at specific themes on the Transition Cycle with your client. You support your client to make adjustments and additions to their life line, allowing deepening to take place.

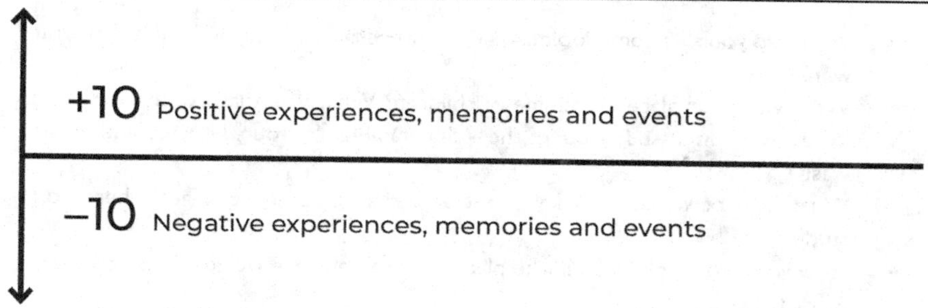

+10 Positive experiences, memories and events

−10 Negative experiences, memories and events

Figure 7.2 The life-line

General
Practical preparation
Give your client a large sheet of paper, A3 works well. It should be robust enough to use again himself, with you or with another person.

Step 1 Prepare
Invite your client to draw a horizontal line representing their life from birth now. At the beginning of the line, draw a vertical line that goes from +10 to −10. This is the scale for the *impact* of events. He should then divide the horizontal line into periods, which you could also call the Chapters of life. Next, your client writes, above and below the line, the impactful experiences and events that have marked his life. If necessary, it might help him to draw a line between the events to get an overview. Allow him to be flexible and creative, to make it his personal life-line. He will do this task in his own time, at his home or office.

Step 2 Explore
Once your client has created their life-line, ask them to bring it with them to your next session to share with you and, in the intervening period, with trusted people they know. It is an impactful way to engage with fathers, mothers, partners, children, and colleagues. You get to know each other in unique and different ways.

Exploring the life-line in the light of contact and welcome
You can look across the whole of the life-line and everything on it. However, it can be more productive and informative to choose an event or focus linked to a specific theme or themes. This Chapter focuses on the themes of *contact and welcome*. Being welcomed, feeling welcome, welcoming another. This forms the basis of every relationship we enter into in our lives and thus also of every professional collaboration. Contact and welcome are inseparable travelling companions.

Reflection questions

• How welcome were you when you were born?

- What did your welcome look like? What were the circumstances in which you were born?
- What was your place in the line of children? What was that like for you?
- What was discussed around the (dinner)table at your house? And what wasn't?
- What kind of welcome did you get at the schools and colleges where you studied?
- How were you welcomed in the places where you have worked and might still work today?
- How does your first welcome color the way you are in the world now?
- How do you welcome people with whom you live and work?
- How do your life experiences, to date, affect how you bond with others?

Welcome to the world

The point of this exercise is to explore your client's welcome into this world:
Use floor anchors (or, if possible, representatives) for:

- your client's birth parents
- the world (family, relatives, circumstances of the birth, such as the place, and so on) into which your client was born.

Have your client stand in front of his parents, with his back to them. Ask him to close his eyes and explore his feelings, what he experiences standing there. (Let him feel into himself – in that place. Prompt him if needed with questions such as: What do you experience in your body? What thoughts come up? Do you feel a movement arising?). Always let him put his words to it.

Tell the client, that when he is ready, he can open his eyes and look at 'the world he was born into'. (Remember, he is looking 'away' from his parents, out into the world.) Ask your client to become aware of what happens when he looks at this world. Wait for his words.

Ask your client to turn around so that he now faces his parents. Ask him to put his awareness on what happens to him when he looks at them, individually and as a couples. Wait for his words.

Continue exploring what you both can learn from these three perspectives.

You conclude the session by looking with your client at how what he has just learned might or does affect his life now.

Guided meditation around welcome

Have your client sit on a straight-backed chair, upright but relaxed with her feet on the floor, knees at 90 degrees and hands resting on her thighs. Her eyes should be closed. Ask her to place her attention on her breath for a minute or two. Then ask her to breath in and out of her belly: four seconds in through the nose, four seconds out through the mouth.

Tell the client that you are going to read a poem – about welcoming everything that is there at this moment.

Choose a relevant poem of your liking, we often use *The Guest House* by Rumi.

Welcome in your body

(This exercise takes about ten minutes: four minutes breathing, four minutes 'jumping' and two minutes sensing and rounding off.)

Stand with your feet hip-width apart for women, shoulder-width for men. Unlock your knees by sinking through them slightly. Relax your hips and allow some space into your pelvic area. Gently straighten your spine by imagining your vertebrae lining up one above the other from bottom to top. You will probably feel your shoulders relaxing and your head aligning itself with your torso. Your jaws might loosen a little; if it feels right to open your mouth slightly, go ahead.

Now close your eyes and take four deep circular breaths: in and out without any pause between them. Breath is an age-old way to get in touch with our body.

Stay in this pose for four minutes, in silence, without changing or trying to 'fix' anything happening your body. Then slowly start moving your legs, by making up-and-down movements with your knees, bending and straightening them without moving your feet. You make a jump, so to speak, without losing contact with the ground. Vary the intensity of your 'jumps', from small movements to bigger movements, deeper down towards your ankles and then more firmly up.

You will notice that the up-and-down movement affects your breathing too, it will probably become heavier. You shouldn't try to change anything that is happening. Continue 'jumping' for about four minutes and then return to the starting pose.

Close your eyes and become aware of what is in your body. Take another four deep breaths.

Round off and write down for yourself what you became aware of in your body.

This is a basic exercise used as preparation for other exercises in the book. We recommend that you repeat this exercise daily, for the coming week, and write something about that you experience each time, what you become aware of, what changes in your body.

Where was your cradle placed?

Lay out drawing paper, pencils and markers.

Ask the client to close his eyes and go inside. Guide him slowly by softly asking him questions (Imagine travelling back in time: from now to ten years ago, and then even further, to twenty years ago ...). In about four steps, you descend through the years of his life to his birth. At each age stage, ask questions about where the client is:

- Where are you now?
- Who is there with you?
- How does it feel to be there?

Go back to the moment of the cradle. Once there, ask the client to take in the environment in which this cradle was located. Then have him open his eyes.
Ask the client to take his time and draw a picture of his cradle and the place it is in. Let him use color and as much detail as he can. Give the client the freedom to do this in a way that suits him.
Then discuss his first welcome. Ask the client to think about the following questions:

- Where was your cradle situated?
- What were the circumstances of your birth?
- Who was there to welcome you into life?
- What stories do you know about your birth?
- How does the place where you were cradled affect how you live(d) your life?
- What have you learned about yourself through this exercise?

You can also give this assignment as homework between sessions. Then, you also ask explicitly about the process of creating the drawing:

- What was it like for you to do this assignment?
- What feelings did it evoke?
- What new insights did it bring you?

Birth announcement card[9]

To visualize the birth of your client and their welcome into the world, you can have them make their own birth announcement card. The aim of this exercise is to experience in what way the stories about and circumstances surrounding their birth influence and color their encounters in the here and now.
Let your client create his birth chart with colored paper, markers, colored pencils, scissors, stickers and other items. This can help him to reconnect with, and perhaps reveal, how he experienced his welcome into the world.
Invite your client, to talk about his announcement card, via the following questions:

- What were the circumstances you were born into?
- In what way did your mother welcome you? And your mother?
- Do you remember any stories about your birth?
- How has the way you came into the world impacted your life?

Variation:

- Stand or sit facing your client.
- Silently, your client takes his self-made birth announcement card and shows it to you. Silently, you look at it.
- After some time, you invite your client to say:

  a   "This is the way in which I am reborn each time I meet someone new."
  b   "This is the feeling I get when others are looking at me."

- Next, you welcome your client in a way consistent with how you are feeling at that moment.
- You explore what this welcome does to your client.

Genogram[10]

To understand the influence of his family history, you can ask the client to draw up a *genogram*. A genogram is a schematic representation of the client's family system and represents much more than a simple *family tree*. It is important that the client draws the genogram of the system he grew up in, known as the *family of origin*. If this is not the family system, due to adoption or foster care, for example, the client can draw a picture of both systems if he is able to.

Give your client a large sheet of paper and have him place the icon for himself bottom center of the paper. He creates his genogram by working upwards from himself, generation by generation. The genogram contains information about:

- Gender
- Nature of the relationship between people: marital or non-marital relationship, divorced, brother, sister, extramarital, and so on
- Year of birth
- Year of death
- Orientation: sexual, religious, political – only if it is relevant

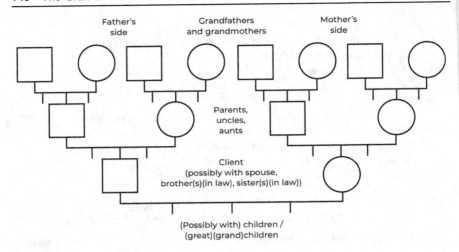

Figure 7.3 Example genogram

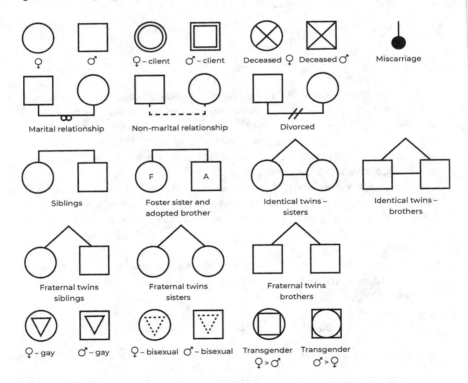

Figure 7.4 Symbols for a genogram

Just drawing up a genogram already brings a lot of insight. What makes it truly valuable is the deepening that comes through the dialogue about what remains unsaid or invisible in the genogram:

- In family history, how did relationships between people develop?
- Were the relationships supported in the system?
- What were the standards like? What was/was not accepted?
- Who were favorites, given preferential treatment?
- Who was left out?
- What was not talked about?
- What family secret is unspoken?
- Who took care of whom? And how?
- What role do the dead play in the system?
- What role does war play in the system?

Exercises with the team

Team Life-line

The Team Life-line makes visible the sequencing in the group: what each team member found when they arrived in the team, how they have got along in the group since then, and what were their highs and lows along that path.

As with the Individual Life-line, we explain the basic details of the exercise below. The difference here is that the individual team members line up in a room/space in the order of their arrival in the team, and each member talks about what they found when they arrived into it, how they have got along in the team since then, and what have been their highs and lows.

Variation

You can also choose to focus on a single theme (of the Transition Cycle). For example, you can reflect with the team on the themes of this Chapter, Contact, and Welcome. Once again, beneath the general description of the exercise, you will find questions to help you support the team in reflecting on the theme explored in the exercise.

General

By sharing these experiences, the group gains insight into the history of the team, and how that is embedded in the history of the organization. Patterns that have developed become visible. This feeds into a mutual understanding of each other's behavior and the what choices were made and why. In addition, sharing the highlights creates a sense of pride, a great, positive energy. By sharing their all-time lows however, the team gains insight into individual pains that often can play a broader role in the group. By reflecting on these together, healing is encouraged. Start with these five basic steps:

- Step 1: Hand out A4 sheets. Have each team member write, in large letters, in landscape orientation, the date (day, month and year) they arrived in the team.
- Step 2: Hand out two post-it stickers to each person: one for a highlight, one for an all-time low.
- Step 3: Now ask everyone to line up in the order of arrival in the team. Notice how they sort this out between each other.
- Step 4: Ask each person to settle in; take a good look around, see who is standing where? What feelings do you get standing in your place?
- Step 5: Ask, from first to join through to last to join, these questions: When did you arrive? What did you find? How have you fared since then? What were your highlights and all-time lows?

Accounting for the size of the team, do your best to spend the same amount of time with each team member. Divide your attention between the individual and the team while in dialogue. Paraphrase what you hear back and what you experience and ask probing questions.

Exploring the Team Life-line in the light of Contact and Welcome
Below are helpful questions for exploring Contact and Welcome with the team you are coaching on these themes. You can then map out and clarify for team members how these themes play a role in this group. How do team members welcome themselves and each other? How do they make contact with each other? Are there situations in which they avoid contact?

Reflection questions

1   What was your welcome into this team like?
2   Which of the current team members were already there? How did they make contact with you? Did they make you feel welcome?
3   How do your experiences with contact and with welcome in other groups play a role in this team?
4   What expectations did you have when you arrived in this team?
5   Which expectations have come true?
6   And which have brought disappointment?
7   How did you welcome those who arrived after you?

New beginning

Changes in team composition herald new beginnings. Although some employees might have been around for a long time, it is important to reflect on and officially usher in this new beginning. Marking a new beginning cannot be done without also paying attention to what is being left behind.

This exercise can be done to mark changes, such as:

- Mergers of teams and/or organizations
- Name changes
- Organizational-structure changes
- New premises/new team-location
- New systems implementation, new ways of working
- New manager/team leader.

In the physical space you are gathered, draw a line down the center. One side represents the old (situation) the other the new. Together with the group, decide which side is which. Could be an old/new management structure, old building/new building, scrum/agile, office working/remote working, etc.

Everyone stands first on the old side and, individually, answers all these questions:

- What are you grateful for on this side?
- What do you have to let go of and leave behind here? (They write this on a post-it which they put on the ground).
- What will you take with you to the new situation? (They write this on a post-it that they carry with them)

You finish by checking if anyone has anything to add. If not, you ask them to move to the other side when ready.

Again ask participants to share one by one:

- What is it like to be on this side?
- What do you find here?
- Is there anything else you need to bond with this new side?

Possibly another movement to the old might be needed to leave something behind. If no more movement is needed, round off the exercise.

Reconnecting

The whole team stands together in a group facing a representative (can also be an object or floor anchor) standing for all the reasons **to go along** with the change in the team/organization.

Invite everyone in the team to take a step forward towards the representative and say in one sentence: "A good reason for me to go with the change is …."

Some members will need to make several moves, but ensure everyone steps forward at least three times. Continue until everyone has said all they have to say.

Then look at the other side. Choose another representative for all the reasons **not to go along** with the change in the team/organization. The group faces the representative again. Everyone is asked to take a step forward towards the representative and say in one sentence: "A reason for me not to go along with the change is …."

Again, ensure everyone does at least three rounds.

Finally, ask the participants if they want to swap sides.

Concluding question for everyone: "Has everything been said that needs to be said?)

The group forms a circle. Everyone is asked to take a step forward and complete the sentence: "What touched me most is …." If this resonates with anyone in the group, they can also take a step forward while the other is speaking. When the speaker is finished, all return to their place in the circle. This continues without discussion. Everyone must take their turn.

Contact in groups

Ask every person to draw a chronological line showing all moments when they first met, in person, a new group/team. Have them also describe how they made contact in those groups.

Have them share, in pairs or threes, any moments, good/not so good, that stand out:

- What was good about that moment?
- What was not so good about that moment?
- What do you look at or pay attention to when you step into a new group?
- Where do you look for support?
- Do you feel drawn to the group or do you – internally, emotionally – move away from the group?
- For each question, talk about how it was different for you entering a new group as a member or as a/the leader.

Round out the conversation with:

- How did you present yourself in your first contact with this group/your current team?
- And what did/do you choose to hide?

Welcoming each other – again
Have team members face each other in pairs.
Ask them to adopt an open attitude and become quiet for a moment.
Ask them to close their eyes and focus on breathing from the belly. Inhale through the nose, exhale through the mouth.
When all are quiet and still, ask them to slowly open their eyes and look at each other.
Ask them to welcome each other with their eyes.
Ask them to put their awareness on what is happening in their bodies.
After a few minutes, have them share with their partner:

- How was this exercise for you?
- What did you feel? Where did you feel it?
- What thoughts came into your mind?
- What did you discover about the way you welcome another person?
- What does this mean for how you work with this colleague?
- What would you like to keep about the way you just welcomed and bonded with each other?
- What would you like to change about how each of you did this?

Repeat this exercise several times if necessary and desired.
Round off the exercise with individual reflection and writing time.

Important points to take away

- Every contact refers back to your first contact; every welcome to your first welcome.
- In contact with others, you are touched by, and touch, the other: cognitively, emotionally, spiritually and, sometimes, physically.
- The flip side of *contact and welcome* is isolate and withdraw. By avoiding contact, we don't risk getting hurt, but we also miss out on beautiful experiences.
- As a secure base coach, you are aware of how you handle contact and welcome and are able to explore these themes with your clients.
  Written and unwritten rules apply to making contact. To ensure psychological safety, these must be made explicit.
- Contact comes before contract.
- At the start of a coaching session, a mutual agreement makes the following things concrete: the client's presenting question, the roles of each person, the process, rules about confidentiality and practical issues such as location, price, and duration of the coaching contract.
- We can only welcome ourselves and others when we are willing to consider what we have to say goodbye to.

Self-reflection for the coach

- What did my own first welcome look like?
- How do I welcome myself into life?
- How do I welcome others into my life?
- How do I welcome (new) clients?
- How have I experienced giving and receiving welcomes in groups, as member and leader?
- How do I make contact with others?
- What do I notice about the way others make contact with me?
- For me, what are inspiring examples of organizations where explicit attention is paid to 'welcome' and 'contact'?
- What rules, written and unwritten, have I been taught about how I make contact and welcome others?
- In what kind of contact do I tend to withdraw or isolate?
- What is challenging for me in making contact?
- When have I felt unwelcome in my life?
- When have I felt welcome in my life?
- What kind of contact did I consciously seek with people?
- What kind of contact did I avoid?

Notes

1 Zik, J. and Berkowitz, S. (2019). Early life stress. Update on neurophysiologic effects and treatment. *Current Opinion in Psychiatry*, 32(6): 528–533.
2 Nocross. J. and Lambert, M. (2011). Psychotherapy relationships that work. *Evidence-Based Responsiveness*. New York: Oxford University Press.
3 Rogers, C. (1957). The necessary and sufficient conditions of therapeutic personality change. *Journal of Consulting Psychology*, 21(2): 95–103.
4 Pos, K., van Wielink, J., and Wilhelm, L. (2014). Het verduren van het gebrek aan maakbaarheid. Maakbaarheid als het grote verhaal (Enduring the lack of malleability in the society. The malleable society as the big story). *Tijdschrift voor Coaching*, 2: 7–11.
5 Flückiger, C., Del Re, A., Wampold, B. and Horvath, A. (2018). The alliance in adult psychotherapy. A meta–analytic synthesis. *Psychotherapy*, 55(4): 316–340.
6 Kosminsky, P. and Jordan, J. (2016). *Attachment-Informed Grief Therapy. The Clinician's Guide to Foundations and Applications*. London: Routledge.
7 Koopmans, L. (2012). *Dit ben ik. Worden wie je bent met Transactionele Analyse (This is me. Becoming who you are with Transactional Analysis)*. Zaltbommel: Thema.
8 Van Wielink, J., Fiddelaers-Jaspers, R., and Wilhelm, L. (2023). *The Language of Transition in Leadership. Your Calling as a Leader in a World of Change*. New York: Routledge.
9 This exercise is based on van Wielink, J., Wilhelm, L., and van Geelen-Merks, D. (2020). *Loss, Grief, and Attachment in Life Transitions. A Clinician's Guide to Secure Base Counseling*. New York: Routledge.
10 Ibid.

Chapter 8

Attachment and resilience

"I was born in Bosnia during the war. I remember being four years old and sitting with my mother in the air raid shelter under our flat. My father had just left when the air-raid alarm went off. The shelter has become a familiar place. A place where we sing songs and play games. A safe place amid these very insecure times we live in."

Mohammed (32)

"For ten years, as a strategy consultant, I have been my boss's right-hand (wo)man. When she is on stage as our COO, I make sure her story is right and everything is in place. When she called last week saying she was sick and asked me to take over her presentation, I freaked out. Panic consumed me, I just couldn't dare. All I could hear was my mother's voice: 'Don't try to grab that, it's too high for you.'"

Anne (48)

All humans have an innate need to experience close proximity to other people. Indeed, it is a biological necessity for survival. How you form new relationships and bond with others is largely determined by how you learned to do so in your first phase of life, in the contact with your parents or caregivers. When we talk about the first stage of life, we mean the first 18 years or so. Do you feel welcome? Is someone there for you when you reach out or do you have to do it all alone? Is it okay to show emotions? Or better to hold them in? In every new relationship you enter into, your first attachment experiences are revisited, becoming a filter through which you view these new experiences. Your early attachment history acts as a predictor for the new experiences. It makes it difficult – but, fortunately, not impossible – to experience secure attachment if you are acting – in the present – from an old insecure attachment style. If new secure bases are sufficiently and reliably present, acquired secure attachment can develop later on.[1]

How resilient you are is partly determined by the availability of secure bases and your attachment style: secure attachment ensures more resilience.[2]

DOI: 10.4324/9781003424178-12

The examples your secure bases showed you, for handling adversity, strengthen your resilience. It is then tested again and further developed through challenging life-experiences. The way you bond with others during these experiences affects your resilience and its development.[3] Resilience thus refers to your ability to continually relate to the changes that come your way.[4]

In this Chapter, we explore the different attachment styles and their influence on how we shape relationships and behave in groups and organizations. As a secure base coach, you need to know and understand these dynamics and be sensitive and insightful in using them with your clients.

Our attachment style forms the basis of every relationship

John Bowlby is the originator of modern attachment theory: "*By attachment we mean any behavior that results in a person achieving or sustaining proximity to a very specifically defined other, who is considered better able to cope with the world.*"[5] In the 1950s, along with his colleague Mary Ainsworth, he conducted important research on the attachment between mother and child. He showed that attachment in humans and animals is a naturally occurring process. It is *unconscious* behavior aimed at experiencing proximity with an available other: '*The awareness that an attachment figure is near and available gives someone a powerful and pervasive sense of security and encourages them to value and continue the relationship*'.[6] It facilitates the primary care and security provided by parents to children in the first phase of life when the child is totally dependent on the parents. The presence of this care and security forms the basis from which children can explore and discover the world. The foundations of our attachment style are thus already laid in the first phase of life, the phase when a child depends on others for care and security.

If a child experiences that someone, a secure base, is available to meet his emotional and physical needs of security, care and challenge, the child will have a secure attachment experience. However, this is not always the case. Should this secure base not be available – or not sufficiently reliably, appropriate to the child's needs – the child is then likely to have an insecure attachment style experience.

Bowlby examined attachment movements between mother and child, but the attachment process happens with every contact a person experiences throughout a life. Inevitably, we collect and become a blend of attachment experiences.

Modern attachment theory distinguishes between two main concepts: secure attachment, and insecure attachment. Insecure attachment can be further subdivided into insecure attachment with *too little* emotional boundaries, and insecure attachment with *excessive emotional boundaries*.

Secure attachment

'As the youngest in a big family, I always wanted to join in with my older brothers. When I was four, I also wanted to climb the big oak tree in our backyard. My father took me to the tree and helped me stand on the bottom branch. It felt a bit too high and I asked him to lift me down again. Instead of lifting me down, he encouraged me to climb up a little. That started me on a lifetime of climbing. Once in a while in trees, but mostly scaling sheer rock faces in the mountains."

Tim (34)

Secure attachment can occur when a secure base – which creates the security from which a child can explore and expand his world – is *sufficiently* and *reliably available*. By *available* we mean the combination of (physical) presence and (emotional) accessibility, including sufficient dialogue. By *reliable* we mean repeatable and predictable in behavior: responding similarly in similar situations, in such a way that it fits the situation. And by *sufficient* we mean that the secure bases do not have to be perfect. In Tim's example, his father is willing to let him discover what it is like to climb the tree. He is available and provides enough security for him to take the next step even though he is afraid. Tim thus learns how, in contact with secure bases, he can allow his desire to climb the tree to overcome his fear of falling. This experience makes Tim not only climb more trees, but also to take on bigger challenges, like mountains. In the words of Bowlby: "*Life is best organized as a series of daring ventures from a secure base.*"[7]

A child with secure attachment has secure bases that provide care, support and security, and are a source of inspiration, challenging the child to explore, take risks, and experiment in order to learn and grow. The child learns that showing and exploring emotions leads to a deepening of the relationship and to development and growth. With secure attachment, caring and daring are both optimally – i.e. 100 percent – present.

Insecure attachment

However, not everyone grows up in a situation where secure bases are sufficiently available to create a secure environment where learning and development are possible. When secure bases are absent or insufficiently reliably available for the child's needs, insecure attachment can set in. Insecure attachment takes two forms: with too little emotional boundaries – between the emotions of the parent(s) and the child – and with excessive emotional boundaries.[8]

Too little emotional boundaries

> *"I was five years old when I fell out of the climbing frame in the play-ground in our street. My mother had warned me not to climb it. She said it was too dangerous. When I came home with my head split open, she was inconsolable. That was the last time I was allowed to go to the playground."*
>
> Masja (42)

Insecure attachment with too little emotional boundaries, occurs when there is a high degree of care and security, but not enough room for experimentation, risk and challenge. People with this attachment style have learned to avoid risk as much as possible and to avoid the path less travelled. However, when they do try something a bit risky, and it goes 'wrong', as it does for Masja, and come home bearing the consequences, they get confirmation of the original (warning) message. In Masja's case she learns from the pain and fear of her mother that it really is best not to take risks, because when you do it hurts or saddens others.

The child learns that while there is room to share experiences and show emotions, the other person allows and expects their emotions to dominate. This child is confused and, out of loyalty for the other person, will limit or even completely stop reaching out to others and expressing emotions. In insecure attachment with too little emotional boundaries, there is a lot of caring but far too little daring.

Excessive emotional boundaries

> *"I'm standing with my son in the changing room at swimming class. Opposite me is a father with a little boy who is almost in tears. His father takes an embarrassed look around the changing room and hisses at him to stop. When he doesn't, the father gets angry. He grabs the little boy by the shoulders, looks him in the eyes and snarls, "Boys don't cry. Stop this minute!""*

Insecure attachment with excessive emotional boundaries occurs when there isn't enough care, support and security to give a child the confidence to explore his world. The crying boy seeks proximity to his father. However, his crying makes his father push him away and deny his behavior and emotions. A child with an insecure attachment style with excessive emotional boundaries experiences a lack of support and comfort, or even disapproval, when he lets his emotions show. The child learns to hide emotions, sort things out himself, and not to ask for help.

In insecure attachment with excessive emotional boundaries, a child lacks the secure bases that provide, when needed, a safe place, offering them comfort and care, where they are welcome with all their thoughts, behaviors, and emotions. In contrast, they do experience a high level of challenge, so they mostly set out on their own. Conversely and unhealthily, they learn that, as the other person cannot or will not deal with their emotions, they must not dare to share them. This can lead to the perception that others are not needed to grow and develop. In insecure attachment with excessive emotional boundaries, there is little caring and a lot of daring.

It is also possible that a child learns a combination of the two forms of insecure attachment. We then say that a child is *ambivalently* attached. Children who are ambivalently attached emotionally challenge potential caregivers to test their availability. They have a great need to bond with others but, owing to their fear of abandonment, they test the bond continually.

Acquired secure attachment

As you now know, the foundations of your attachment style are laid in the first phase of your life, in contact with primary caregivers. However, although key, this phase is not decisive. Every life has a mix of secure and insecure experiences. Your attachment style, at any point in your life, is the aggregate of these experiences: for most of us this will be secure or insecure. Every new relationship begun is approached through the lens of your basic attachment style. Your old attachment experiences predict how you internalize new experiences, making it difficult for a person with an insecure basic attachment to experience safe attachment even when it is being provided. Difficult but not impossible. In the sufficiently reliable presence of new secure bases, *acquired* secure attachment can still occur.

Secure bases

Bowlby's attachment theory is primarily about attachment between people. In addition to people, things can also be a secure base. Some examples include:

- People: any and all immediate and extended family members, teams, societies, etc.
- Places: country, town, village, house, river, tree, pub, etc.
- Events: wedding, funeral, (sports) match, disaster, accident, etc.
- Experiences: the experience of a friendship, being rewarded for a special achievement, being unexpectedly complimented by someone, getting a chance to do something special, becoming a father or mother, a good marriage/partner relationship, etc.

- Goals: achieving targets, getting promoted, becoming a parent, running a marathon, organizing a charity, etc.
- Other: pets, faiths/beliefs/religions, values, ideology, symbols, genders, etc.

Actually, *anything* can be a secure base for you, if it offers a balance of caring and daring. Put another way, secure bases are your sources of inspiration. After all, what inspires you gets you moving. Even a negative and even traumatic experience can become a secure base if, in the learning recollection of the experience the positive prevails. For example, Edith Eva Eger says, for example, about her experiences in Auschwitz: "Not only did I survive it, it gave me the gift of being able to guide others. I turned Auschwitz into a classroom."[9]

Everyone is resilient

Resilience can be described as the capacity to recover or bounce back. It is the ability to adapt successfully despite difficult or threatening circumstances, and the skill to maintain a stable equilibrium.[10] Resilience enables you to keep your *mind's eye* focused on the positive in challenging circumstances. It is something you develop in connection with your environment. The example you were given on how to deal with adversity is instrumental in developing your own resilience. Did your parents react from victimhood to setbacks in life? Did they sit by and do nothing? Or did they seize opportunities when times were challenging? Did they challenge themselves and others to explore what was possible?

> *After my little brother died in a car accident, my mother withdrew. She did not know how to deal with this grief. History repeated itself. Her mother too had lost a son at a young age and had never smiled again after that. My mother followed her mother's example.*

To focus your mind's eye, you need secure bases. First and foremost, people who support you in difficult times, offer security, and encourage you to get up and try again. They are able to listen, empathize with you and be curious about what it is like for you. They endure your and their own discomfort with the emotions that arise in this contact.

> *When my boyfriend suddenly broke off our relationship, I collapsed. I locked myself in my room and spent a week just lying in bed. During the week, my best friend came by every day. At first, she just comforted me. After a few days, she reminded me that I had been here before, that I knew what to do. By trial and error, I picked up where I left off. I started exercising, cleaned up the pictures and after three weeks I went out with*

my friends again. Yes, I had been here before. And, it was still painful, but this time I had faith that I would recover, and that helped me pick up my life again.

So resilience is built in connection with your environment and in your bond with your secure bases. They help you trust that, after moments of adversity, better times will come again. This confidence – in your own abilities and qualities – helps you to show perseverance when it serves yourself and others. By sharing peaks and troughs in your life with others, you can experience – if you choose to – that your life path is unique and that your life in and of itself is meaningful.

Detaching or clinging, the flip side of attachment and resilience

In every new encounter, your attachment style is fundamental. The attachment style you developed, in contact with your caregivers and other important secure bases will form the basis for how you attach in new encounters. If you are predominantly securely attached, you will enter new relationships with confidence and be curious about what each relationship can bring. It is different if you are insecurely attached. Children who are predominantly insecurely attached will have difficulty building relationships from a basis of self-confidence and self-esteem. Expressions of healthy self-confidence and self-esteem include:

- a joyful attitude to life and being generally happy with life
- balance of giving and taking
- focusing on opportunities
- ability to give and receive compliments
- spontaneity and flexibility
- playfulness
- creative response to problems
- satisfaction with acquired experiences
- able to share intimacy
- finding others important
- openness to life and to others

The flip side of 'attachment and resilience' is 'detachment or clinging'. Detachment is a survival strategy involving the constant moving in and out of contact. Doing it alone feels safer than doing it together. Doing it together has the risk that the other person won't play ball with you. The opposite is that you cling desperately to the other person, that you cannot and will not let them go.

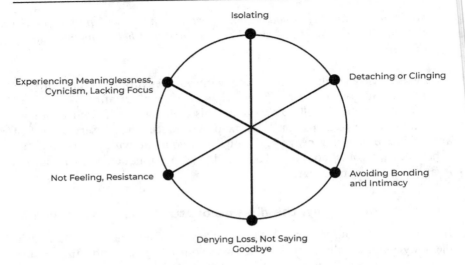

Figure 8.1 Themes on the Cycle of Stalled Transition

> *Pete hired Sandra nine months ago. Sandra has a lot of purchasing experience and began enthusiastically. After only a few days, Pete notices that Sandra asks a lot of questions. As time goes on, she asks for his opinion more and more. After six weeks, he decides to discuss this with her and tells her she needs to improve. His message hits hard. Sandra panics and, instead of trying to solve things herself, asks him for even more affirmation. Pete decides to have another conversation with her; bit this time not about her results, but about her behavior. He discovers that she used to be rejected by her father when she made mistakes and that this has made her anxious and made her seek reassurance by asking for help. Together, they agree on how to move forward. Six months later both can look back on how well things have gone since they spoke.*

The movement of detaching and clinging takes many forms. Sometimes it conspicuous, other times subtly present. Signs of detachment include people withdrawing, no longer having an opinion about anything, indicating they do not consider anything important, that nothing bothers them, frequent job changes, having few friendships, being unable to accept compliments, being distrustful. Expressions of clinging include being overly loyal, asking for a lot of help even when it is not really needed, having difficulty letting go or endlessly seeking affirmation.

Psychological safety as a basis for excellence

In Chapter 2, we described the importance of psychological safety in the coaching relationship. Psychological safety is a term widely used in modern coaching literature, but it has ancient roots. In the 1960s Edgar Schein and Warren Bennis wrote about this phenomenon in their research on anxiety in people during (organizational) change.[11] In the 1990s Amy Edmondson built on their work with a study on medical errors in hospitals. Her key discovery was that successful (read: effective) teams reported more errors than teams that performed less well, were less effective, and less likely to achieve set goals.[12]

Psychological safety is the shared belief and experience that the relationship and/or team (or group) is a safe place, where you can be yourself without the risk of being rejected. No single person decides that the relationship or team is safe. Psychological safety occurs when people experience an optimal balance between caring and daring. As a result, people experience that they are welcome to be completely themselves, without any risk of being judged. As the coach, you play an important role in creating an environment in which a client, individual or team feels safe to experiment and so make excellence possible.

Pursuing excellence is the mindset in which growing, learning and developing lead and guide our actions. We are willing to do today what it takes to be better tomorrow. It is about experimenting, taking risks and making mistakes. It asks that we engage in conflict with each other in order to discover new truths together, learn from this and move onward with this new knowledge and experience. When caring and daring walk hand in hand, the psychological safety can be created in which excellence becomes a reality (Figure 8.2).

Your attachment style affects how you move through the Window of Excellence. As you read in the previous section, everyone has their own attachment style and, to a large extent, this determines the degree of psychological safety you experience in a relationship or group. If you are predominantly securely attached, you will excel more naturally than if you have had predominantly insecure attachment experiences. If you know this about yourself, you can recognize and acknowledge your behavior, making it easier to learn new behavior when desired.

> *Carla grew up in a protective environment. Her mother was afraid of many things and was always urging her not to take (unnecessary) risks. Now Carla is managing the service department at a financial house and has to deal with an under-performing employee. Her coach encourages her to start a conversation to explore what is the real issue. But Carla is afraid of the reaction and avoids the conversation. She lets the situation continue, while putting her focus on getting more out of the other team members in order to achieve targets.*

Avoidance is the mindset in which relationship is more important than results. It sometimes looks and feels like excellence because everybody is having a pleasant time together, but the necessary conversations do not take place, conflict is avoided and there is a strong aversion to taking risks.

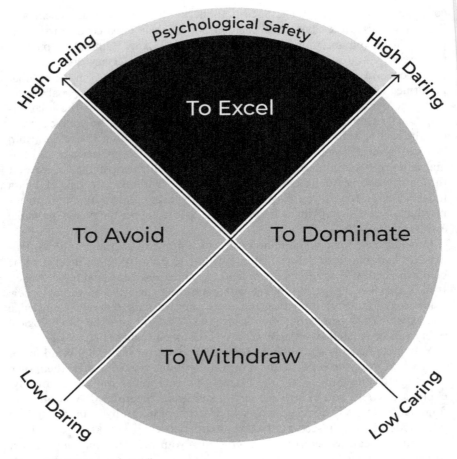

Figure 8.2 Window of excellence
Source: Klaartje van Gasteren, Marnix Reijmerink, Jakob van Wielink, inspired partly by the work of George Kohlrieser, Susan Goldsworthy and Duncan Coombe (2012).

Anxiety and fear of disturbing the relationship keeps Carla from starting a conversation with her coworker about her performance. By no longer involving her employee in the teams results, Carla moves from avoidance to withdrawal. She disconnects from the dysfunctional employee and focuses on the rest of the team. Her coach invites her to excel by encouraging her to have an open conversation with the employee.

> *One day, when Carla comes into the office, she sees the employee sitting at the coffee table, complaining about the pressure she is under. This is the last straw for Carla. She walks up to her and demands that she walk with her to her office. When the door is closed, she gets incredibly angry and*

demands the work in question be completed today. If she does not deliver it
by the end of the working day, she will be fired.

Dominance is the mindset in which the goal is more important than the
relationship. In her anger, Carla moves into dominance, not knowing how
she can stay connected in the conversation. The longer you wait, the harder
it becomes to move back into the mindset of excellence. As much as this
always remains possible, you must consciously choose to move into it and
bond – externally physically and internally mentally – with secure bases that
help you make this happen. It always requires being more caring and/or
more daring when interacting with others. And in the vast majority of cases,
a move towards excellence will require some measure of vulnerability,
genuine curiosity and asking questions.

In every interaction you move through this window and your attachment
style determines how you move. This dynamic is also found in groups, both
between members and in the dynamics of the group as a whole. To a large
extent, the movements of the leader influence how the group as a whole
moves through this window. The leader goes for it, so to speak, inviting the
group to follow.

Johan is consulting with his team and Henriëtte takes the floor. She is
worried about the slow progress of the new project. Johan dismisses her
concerns, saying that the deadline is still a long way off, and moves on to
the next topic. Henriëtte falls silent, followed by the rest of the team.

Crisis tests and increases your resilience

A crisis – for example the corona crisis – triggers old attachment movements
and tests your resilience. At the same time, it is a superb opportunity for
tapping into your developmental and growth potential. Working this way, a
crisis can become a transition. It brings growth in your identity and you (re)
discover or strengthen your calling. A crisis takes you from an old reality to a
new one. What does this new reality look like for you and everyone you lead?
As a coach, how do you adapt your leadership to the new situation?

How do you recognize, in crises in your own life – and that of your clients – the movements of just surviving and those of living through? How do
you talk about them? Figure 8.3 shows how the different phases of a crisis
occur and affect you and those you lead.

The window shows how there is a reality, prior to the crisis that floods
over you like a wave. A pre-crisis phase in which 'normal' *life* runs its course.
Once the crisis starts it gathers momentum, sweeping all before it. Nothing is
fixed or certain any more. And the need to be in contact with your secure
bases becomes palpably greater. It is a phase where you notice that some
deep-seated attachment movements and patterns occur automatically, as old,

ineffective behavior rears its head. In the face of (impending) loss your resilience is tested. You try to fall back on what once offered security and safety. You are deep in the phase of *surviving*.

At some point, a kind of stabilization arises in the current situation. A phase where you can, more or less, reflect on what has happened to you. What was painful when the crisis was in full flood? Looking back, which past experiences helped you deal with this crisis? And which secure bases were supportive? Perhaps the crisis has had some positive effect on your personal leadership qualities or approach. A treasure unearthed in the ruins of yesterday's reality. This is the period when you reap the rewards of the resilience you have built up throughout your life. This is the phase when you are *living through* the crisis.

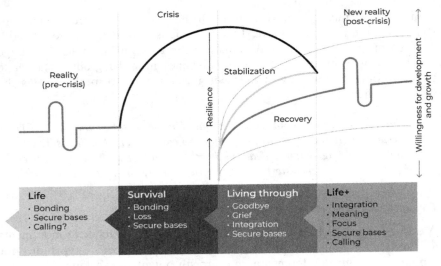

Figure 8.3 Window of crisis and transition
Source: The School for Transition and partners

This third phase is the precursor to a new episode: when you move into post-crisis. The phase of *Life+*. The phase in which you, alone and with others, give meaning to what happened and celebrate what you learned. This allows new focus and a (new) vision of your calling to emerge. Who are you now? And what does the 'new' you want to bring out into the world?

Life+. Why the '+'? This final phase is an incredible opportunity, bonded with others, to focus your mind's eye on learning, development and growth. It is the phase that helps you find a (new) balance between caring and daring. Crisis is one of the ways Life invites you to excel. A phoenix rising from the ashes.

The secure base coach working with attachment and resilience

Attachment and resilience – Working with individuals

Rose, a coach, gets a call from Janneke looking for help: she finds it difficult to form relationships or to let anyone get close. This limits her in several areas of her life. While on the phone, she tells Rose how she has spoken to several coaches but rejected them all: not the right profile; no click; too well known in her network and so on.

Here, in the first contact, there are signs about what Janneke has learned about putting her trust in others and thus the attachment style she has developed based on those experiences. These signals allow Rose, with caring and daring, to connect with Janneke's needs. For instance, Janneke's way of responding shows she has lacked a safe foundation in her life, one in which her emotions were welcome and she felt heard and seen. Although Janneke is hesitant, she decides to start the process anyway and Rose takes her on as a client.

After a number of sessions, Janneke calls Rose. She wants to stop the coaching. It doesn't feel safe enough after all. Rose listens, paraphrases and asks her what she is doing that makes Janneke feel insecure. Janneke is upset for a moment. It's just a feeling.

Janneke very emphatically probes how safe it is this close to Rose. As if she is testing the thickness of the ice by putting one foot on it, ever so lightly, and then pulling back. When Rose asks what she does that makes Janneke feel insecure, Janneke is momentarily confused. As if she had not expected this: a reaction out of open curiosity, willing to listen, regularly and carefully checking how she's doing, and willing to ask vulnerable questions about her own behavior. Someone who gives the impression that she'll stay with Janneke whatever happens.

What Janneke isn't able to realize is that Rose **is** willing to stay, and to observe and endure her own discomfort and emotions alongside Janneke's. Bowlby saw this often: *Being a secure base is largely a waiting game.*[13] In her life so far, Janneke has rarely if ever experienced being with another person who, when Janneke becomes emotional, is willing and able to accept them wholly; to listen to them without becoming distracted, put off, or pushing them away:

Rose and Janneke decide to resume the coaching. Rose keeps inviting Janneke to tell her what she is thinking, feeling, experiencing. Together, they explore what's behind Janneke's feelings. Janneke talks about the loneliness she experienced in her childhood. How she remembers that every time she was angry or sad, these emotions were not accepted by those around her. Both her father and mother made it clear to her that being angry or sad was not nice for them. "Now you are making me sad too," her mother often said. And her father would literally say that he wasn't going to spend his life sitting around waiting for her to get angry. He already had enough stuff of his own to deal with. And so she increasingly withdrew whenever she felt painful or confusing emotions arising.

An important aspect of coaching individual clients is exploring together how the client learned to attach to others. And, in that context, to reflect on what a person learned in their life about caring and daring. What events on the life-line had the most impact on the unique blend of these two attachment movements? What meaning did the client unconsciously attach to certain experiences? At what moments did the client consciously reflect on the impact and also the loss that possibly accompanied certain experiences? And when not – and why not?

Because of the coach's own journey in exploring his attachment history and its influence on his life – and coaching – he is able to guide the client on her path. What attachment joy and what attachment pain does she experience in her life? And how much, to a greater or lesser extent, has her attachment history contributed to the resilience she has developed? To examine, in depth, experiences where resilience was tested is important.

In the conversations with Rose, her coach, Janneke discovers that her tendency to withdraw when she gets emotional brings on a sense of loneliness and despondency. As Rose shows her that contact and bonding is always possible, even when emotions overwhelm you, she learns that she has a choice: lapse into her old pattern or choose to step forward, by speaking out about her feelings. When she does, she notices that the other person is more likely to stay in touch because Janneke takes the first step herself. She no longer has to be a victim of her own emotional hostage-taking, but she can very consciously break that 'habit' by taking a risk. Rose makes her realize that the more (emotional) risks she takes, the safer it can be for Janneke with any other person.

The extent to which the client develops resilience is predictive of how they will react when things get stressful. By looking back along the life-line to influential events, it is possible to explore what resources, in the form of secure bases, the client has at his disposal to cope with the stress and shift their focus to the positive.

Attachment and resilience – Working with teams

Mariët was put in as the team's new manager. After one-to-ones with everyone individually and the entire team had met a few times, it was clear to her that this was a group of professionals who were all very good at what they did with their customers. But together they didn't function as a team. Each was on their own island. They really were not involved with each other. Whenever they did meet, the atmosphere was generally friendly. However, there was no collaborative working and thus no learning from each other.

The previous manager's approach was to give everyone maximum space. For him, everything was fine as long as the customers were happy. He had paid no attention to the underlying bond within the team. In the past, when this bond had become necessary, and there were team members who wanted to engage with him and each other, he would say, "I don't want any fuss." Before long, team members had given up on strengthening the mutual bond and focused only on their work with their clients. Slowly but surely, personal development stalled and customer dissatisfaction crept in.

In the dynamics of any team, there are always triggers arising that confront people with their own behavior and that of each other. These triggers originate in the way you learned to entrust yourself to others over the course of your life. At the start of your life, this was an unconscious process in which you discovered, through trial and error as it were, whether your thoughts, behavior, and emotions were welcome or not in contact with others: "If I let everything I feel and experience show, will the other person stay? And will I also be able to remain present in the contact? Or is it insecure, with the consequence that I learn to swallow my emotions, keeping them to myself or just let them out in vehemence and anger."[14]

In the underlying dynamics and the cooperation within a team, everyone's early and later attachment experiences are palpable and visible. As a team coach, you can make team members aware of their own attachment style. What did they learn in their lives about caring and daring? What are their ways of bonding with others? How do or don't they contribute to overall psychological safety within the team? In relationships and collaboration with others, are they more focused on maintaining the relationship or on achieving the goal?

The unique mix that each individual team member brings to the team dynamic determines the overall mix of attachment styles. When team members gain insight into their own unique mix of caring and daring, they are better able to understand their own behavior and that of their colleagues. This understanding enables the team to improve team performance.

If team members can truly entrust themselves to others, this will positively influence the dynamics in the group: their actions emotions, vulnerability, and beliefs connect rather than obstruct. When bonding with others, they will be more inclined to increase risk-taking, facilitating personal and team growth. In a team, the basic attachment style of each individual will always be triggered. The total composition of styles in the team determines how the members of the team trust each other.[15]

At the same time, individual attachment style is not all-important in team dynamics. Research shows that people express their own attachment style differently in different situations. Four facets appear to play a role: self-image, previous experiences, expectations, strategies.[16]

How do I see myself and others?

A person's self-image is based on the direct and indirect messages they have received about themselves and the interpretation and meaning they have given to these messages. This self-image determines how they see themselves in a team or other kind of group.

What are my experiences in groups?

Over the course of your life, you move in, with and through many different (types of) groups. You begin, of course, in your family of origin. At the dinner table you learn to relate to others for the first time, so to speak. But the class at school, the sports team, school societies, and work teams are also examples of groups in which you learn, to a greater or lesser extent, to trust people and to set goals.

Table 8.1 Overview of behaviors related to attachment and self-esteem

Predominantly secure attachment	Predominantly insecure attachment with excessive emotional boundaries	Predominantly insecure attachment with too little emotional boundaries
• Has a predominantly positive image of both self and other. • Will easily seek collaboration and give, and expect to receive, trust in that. • Allows vulnerability to show in collaboration. • Is both relationship- and goal-oriented. • Has a mindset of excelling.	• Often has a negative image of others. • Will not trust or give permission to the other person easily or quickly. • Will tend to keep others at a distance emotionally. • Will focus on goals in collaboration and only make functional bonds that are necessary for achieving those goals.	• Often has a negative self-image. • Does not trust himself to have control over how relationships (individual and group) unfold. • Will try to keep in touch with everyone. • Will not enter into conflict easily. • Will not take actions that might jeopardize collaboration.

Table 8.2 Summary of behaviors related to attachment and previous experiences

Predominantly secure attachment	Predominantly insecure attachment with excessive emotional boundaries	Predominantly insecure attachment with too little emotional boundaries
• Accepts both positive and negative experiences.	• Will mostly suppress negative and painful experiences.	• Remembers mainly negative and painful experiences.
• Learns from positive as well as negative experiences.	• Focuses mostly on achieving goals.	• Lets negative experiences guide his actions.
• Is willing to take risks.	• Little or no focus on social interaction with others.	• Is especially concerned with keeping relationships 'whole'.
• Uses learning experiences to excel.	• In collaboration, is more daring than caring.	• Does everything possible to avoid new negative or painful experiences.
• When working with others, is both relationship- and goal-oriented.	• Does not contribute to a mindset of excelling, tends to be rather dominant.[17]	• In collaboration, is more caring than daring.
• Is caring and daring at the same time.		• Does not contribute to a mindset of excelling, tends to be rather avoidant.

In these different groups you gain experiences concerning being welcome, feeling safe or insecure and around vulnerability. Do you feel welcome in this group? Can you be yourself here? Can you express yourself and the emotions you feel here? Are you allowed to make mistakes here?

What are my expectations of social interaction?

As Table 8.2 shows, your interaction with others serves a purpose, although you are not always aware of this. Depending on your basic attachment style, you either seek affirmation, support, security, appreciation and love in contact and collaboration with others (in insecure attachment with too little emotional boundaries), or you are actually looking to use interaction with others to strengthen your own position and keep others (emotionally) at a distance (in insecure attachment with excessive emotional boundaries). Sometimes your interaction is strongly focused on strengthening and maintaining the relationship and sometimes on achieving conscious or unconscious goals.

In teams, people can appear to be acting quite pragmatically when working with others. The attachment movement that each individual learned to make in the course of his life remains their basic guiding principle, but the goal that someone has in mind when entering into a social interaction ultimately determines their attachment movement. Ultimately, not only do you want ensure your physical safety, you are also completely emotionally attached to survival.

What strategies do I follow?

In a team, people seem to be, consciously or unconsciously, more calculating than you might believe. Is someone's strategy in the interaction focused only on their relationship with the other(s)? Then that person will do everything possible to maintain contact and not put it under unnecessary pressure or at risk. They will, at all times, avoid conflict. If they make a mistake, they will not talk about it and if they see someone else making a mistake, they will always respond with understanding. However, if someone's strategy is focused only on achieving (team) goals? Then that person makes the relationship with others secondary. Neither of these two strategies – both of which are very understandable from the perspective of attachment and attachment styles – results in sustainable collaboration from a mindset of excelling.

> Back to Mariët's team and manager. The excessive amount of freedom given to team members had not only created a sense of purposelessness among them, but also a lack of cohesion among individual team members. No coherence. "I don't want any hassle," the manager had said. And, by allowing everyone maximum freedom, he didn't avoid hassle, he actually created it.

Freedom without structure creates ambiguity and this leads to people feeling insecure. When people feel insecure, they tend to fall back on the patterns of the attachment style that they 'know' best. A long time ago in their life, these patterns helped, but they are a long way from being effective in every other situation.

Leaders and employees create, through a culture of caring and daring, a context in which hard work, enjoyment, willingness to dialogue and conflict, celebrating success, learning from mistakes, ownership and meaning-making contribute to an overall mindset of excelling. In particular, the importance of being willing to constantly engage in dialogue with each other about what is going on in the organization and in the team should not be underestimated in the pursuit of excellence. When we say 'leaders and employees', however, we cannot ignore the fact that the role of a team's leader is always more important in achieving excellence than that of the team members. This has everything to do with the principles of transference and countertransference, which you read about in Chapter 2. If you are not aware of this people will end up, as the old saying goes, doing what you do and not what you say.

As a coach, you can contribute to the development of bonding, trust and resilience by creating a setting in which dialogue leads to awareness of one's behavior and its impact. You must give the example and lead this yourself.

By mirroring, questioning, paraphrasing, encouraging; by bringing in and challenging your own wisdom and vulnerability. What is happening to each of you, individually? What is happening in the team? What impact does this have in the short and longer term? What is your long-term focus? What are you learning? As a coach, what am I coming up against?

Exercises with your client

Exploring the client's life-line in the light of attachment and resilience

Attachment forms the starting point for discovering the world through trial and error. In that trial and error, you develop your resilience that enables you to cope with setbacks, disappointment and pain.

Questions for reflection

- Which aspects of secure and of insecure attachment are you familiar with? How do these affect the way you take risks in your life?
- How would you describe your (emotional) bond with your father? How safe do/did you feel with him?
- How would you describe your (emotional) bond with your mother? How safe do/did you feel with her?
- What sweet and what sour fruits are you reaping personally and professionally from the way you attach?
- How safe do you think others feel with you?
- Which secure bases inspire you and provide enough bonding and safety for you to take risks?
- What was said around your family (of origin) dinner table? How has that shaped you?
- What was left unsaid at that table? How has that shaped you?

Recognizing attachment styles

Explain to your client the four different attachment styles. For each style, invite him to share what he does and does not recognize in himself, and others within his various systems. Now ask deeper questions of your client to help him embrace this self-examination.

Enquiry[18]

This exercise helps your client to explore his basic attachment movement, by asking the same question over and over again. He gains insight into every facet of attachment.

Ask for silence with you and your client. Make sure you are both comfortable. For a period of three to five minutes, ask him the same question over and over again: "Can you tell me what is good about not attaching?" After each answer from your client, whatever it is, say "Thank you." You are an embodied presence, receiving your client's answers with an open heart; doing nothing with them.

Each time you ask, "What's good about not attaching?", you can adjust how you ask the question. Perhaps a different tone, or emphasis on different words.

Discuss with your client what this process is bringing up in him.

Physically experiencing attachment styles[19]

Your body stores attachment experiences as memories. Memories formed from your earliest moments. So young that you didn't know how to give words to experience. This makes it difficult to mentally access such memories, to get them from your brain. But your body — as a whole — often can make that wisdom accessible. By recreating, for the client, the early attachment situation, such memories can be recalled.

In this exercise, as a coach, you respond in different ways to your client's conscious reaching out. These reactions are similar to reactions the client might have experienced at a young age in contact with attachment figures. The aim of this exercise is to give your client insight by experiencing in the present what might have happened in those situations in the past.

Ask your client to come and stand facing you, about a meter away.

- Invite your client to go back to a moment when, as a child, he reached out to a parent or another attachment figure for support or proximity, and then ask him to reach out his arms to you.
- As coach you always respond as if you are the parent or attachment figure, in a number of different ways:

  a   By not responding at all
  b   By ignoring the movement or beating away the client's outstretched arms
  c   By frenetically grasping the client and not letting go, even if it causes discomfort to the client.
  d   By receiving and welcoming the client.

- After each movement, help the client to come back to the present by moving, briefly changing posture and stating that it is safe here, in the present, that you are there for him.
- Ask the client what he experienced with each of the different reactions from his 'parent/attachment figure'. Use his answers to go as deep as possible.

Finally, discuss with your client how this exercise was for him.

Secure Base Map[20]

Secure bases come and go in the different phases of a life. This exercise helps your client map this out.

Take a large sheet of paper. Have your client make three sections, separating his life (the sheet of paper) into: **Then**/past, **Now**/present and **Later**/future. For each period, have the client recall which secure bases were there Then, which are there Now and which secure bases might remain Later in his life. And which new bases might be needed in the future, in order that your client can do what he has to do and can continue learning.

This inventory can be a simple list, but the more creative and imaginative your client is in representing his secure bases at different stages of his life, the more value and impact this process will have. He can try drawing, painting, cutting, and pasting pictures from magazines, or arranging other symbols: whatever works for him. The image below is just an example of how a simple secure base map might look.

Together with your client, explore this map. What stands out, what is it like for your client to make this map? What does the client discover about themselves?

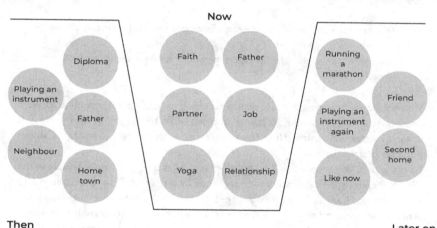

Figure 8.4 Secure Base Map
Source: The School for Transition and partners

Bodily experiencing your own attachment movement[21]

With this exercise, you help your client to experience his attachment movement bodily. In this way, he gets insight into how his body responds in various situations when a certain mental, physical or emotional need is – or is not – met.

Over time, many people lose awareness of their body's physical response because their own behavior in many situations is mostly automatic and unconscious. A result is that they don't know if or how their reaction relates to their need. When it appears that the need might not be met, sometimes they are already making a movement without noticing it.

For example, when someone counts on having to solve something in a certain situation on his own and thus assumes that no help or support will be available, he already begins an inner withdrawal. This closes him off to his environment, reducing even further the chance that his needs will be met. A vicious circle. In this exercise, if this movement manifests, it will be demonstrated by the client taking a step backward.

But when the opposite applies, and someone is able to reach out to another person, because they really believe that help, support and proximity are available in a given situation, they will make a forward movement. In this exercise, the client will demonstrate this by taking a step forward.

The exercise
Ask your client to stand in the middle of the room. Ask him to close his eyes or, if he is uncomfortable, to focus his eyes on a point on the ground. As the coach, you say specific sentences (provided below) and, immediately after, your client makes a movement:

- He steps forward when the question prompts him to reach out to the other person
- He steps back when the question prompts him to withdraw and distance himself

When your client finds it difficult or has no idea if his movement would be forward or backward, he is 'allowed' to take a step sideways, to the left or to the right, it doesn't matter which side. This allows him to experience that movement is always possible in any situation.

As the coach, you are speaking on behalf of (representing) meaningful people in the client's life, living or dead. Start each sentence by introducing the character you're representing: "I am ..." Invite your client to first make whatever movement the sentence evokes, and second say the sentence. After each (withdrawal) movement, you ask your client what he needs in order to return to the (neutral) starting position.

For this exercise to work, you need to be familiar with some people from your client's life and network. This can come from his stories, examples from his lifeline, through his secure base map and possibly by studying the genogram your client made. The sentences you speak out on behalf of these people must always start by naming the relationship the person you are representing has to your client. This helps you to understand the movement evoked. Here's an example:

I am Henk. I'm your father. You're my son.

As coach, with this exercise, you can alternate between important people from the client's life: mother, daughter, sister, friend, girlfriend, partner, or any important relationship.

In each of these relationships, you can help your client explore the whole spectrum of emotions: from joy to sadness, from fear to anger. In particular, when a sentence evokes resistance in your client, his attachment movement will be meaningful. Example sentences include:

- I love you.
- I'm happy with you.
- I miss you.
- I want to spend more time with you.
- You need to try harder.
- You have to adapt.
- You have to behave.
- You have to think of others.
- I'm mad at you.
- I'm sorry.
- I don't want you to be angry with me.
- I don't want you to be afraid of me.
- Will you forgive me?

You can invite your client to intensify certain attachment movements by asking them to cross their arms in front of their chest when stepping back. This is a defensive gesture which also protects the heart. With a forward movement, he can open his arms wide.

Exercises with the team

Exploring the team's life-line in the light of attachment and resilience

Below are questions that can help you explore the themes of attachment and resilience with the team you are coaching. You can clarify for team members the roles these themes play in the group. What did individual team members learn about caring and daring in their lives? And how does that influence their behavior in the team? How does their personal attachment movement strengthen team collaboration, and how does it (potentially) hinder it?

Reflection questions

- For you, who in this team is a secure base and why?
- What were the times when you felt safe in this team?

- What were the times when you felt insecure in this team?
- What is the balance between caring and daring in the team? How does this affect the team, and you personally?
- For you, what was an incident or event that tested the team's resilience? What do you think the team learned from that? And what did you learn?

What were the times when the team got into the mindsets of excel/avoid/dominate/retreat? What caused that to happen each time/mindset?

Team under the magnifier
This exercise helps you explore with the team what the team is attached to and bonded with.

- Give each person a large sheet of paper.
- Every person draws circles to represent each team member including themselves.
- In their own circle, they name everything they are attached to.
- In the other circles, they name anything they think the other team members are/might be attached to.

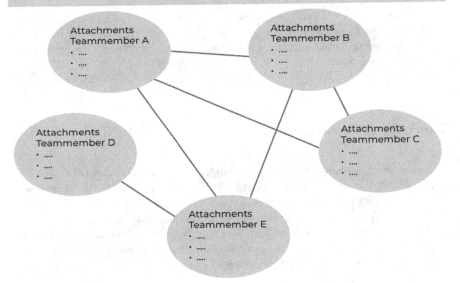

Figure 8.5 Team under the magnifier

- Team members discuss the different sheets and circles with each other to explore each other's attachments. Together, they arrive at one collective new sheet of circles and personal attachments that team members recognize for themselves. Use colors and lines to indicate relation between similar attachments.
- Reflection questions that might be helpful in the discussion:
    - What is the significance of these attachments for this team member(s)?
    - What are everyone's opinions about these attachments?
    - Which attachments does each person value and which not?
    - What does this appreciation and/or negative judgment mean for mutual bonding and collaboration?

Failure-experiences and resilience

This exercise helps you reflect with the team around triggers existing in individual team members (and thus in the dynamics of the team). This is a systemic exercise that you can do using members of the team as representatives. You can also choose to put down floor anchors or work with figures on a table; just remember to define the space (the Field).

- Invite one of the team members to briefly share with the team a (failure) experience that was challenging for him.
- Have the team member create a representative/floor anchor/figure for themselves.
- Have the team member set up the triggers that made the failure experience challenging:

    a   What is the trigger?
    b   What is the worst thing anyone could say/do to him?
    c   What tendency arise in him then?
    d   What does the trigger do to him internally?
    e   When he falls, what makes him able to get up again?
    f   What thoughts, feelings and physical movements help him spring back and enable him to make a conscious choice?

- Explore with the team member what is happening to him now, in this field.
- What movement arises? What (different) choice can the team member make now?
- What has the team member discovered? What lessons can he learn from this?

What intention arises in the team member about his role in team collaboration?

Exploring the Window of Excellence

In this exercise, the team members, in threesomes or foursomes, explore how different team members moved through the Window of Excellence in various situations. The aim of the exercise is to gain insight into one's own actions in such situations and to determine in dialogue what, looking back, would have been needed to embrace the mindset of excelling together. What behaviors and choices would have contributed positively? In each situation, what would a mindset of excelling have meant for mutual cooperation and for achieving the goal?

- Each group receives a printed version of the Window of Excellence.
- Each group is given figures with which to do table-top exploration.
- During exploration, encourage everyone to watch each other closely, paraphrase each other and always try to take the dialogue deeper.
- Have team members take turns describing a situation that was challenging for them.
- Have team members use the figures to explore and understand how they and other stakeholders moved through the window in this situation.

  a   What did they want to achieve in this situation and what was the outcome?
  b   What happened in the dynamics between those involved and/or with the dynamics of the team as a whole?
  c   Looking back, what would it have taken to return to the quadrant of excellence?
  d   What has each individual team member learned, from this process, about their own actions/behavior in the team?
  e   What lessons can the team learn from this exploration?
  f   What do the different learnings mean for future collaboration in this team?

Based on this exploration, what new (working) agreements do the different team members want to make with each other?

Crisis and Transition

Every (significant) change, every crisis, is an opportunity to learn, develop and grow. The four phases of the Window of Crisis and Transition show this very clearly.
In this exercise, you engage in a conversation about the four phases. You facilitate the dialogue and bring the outcomes together. You then discuss what agreements should be made and how these agreements will enable growth and development.

Phase 1: Life

- How would you describe your life/team/organization before the crisis? What was the direction and focus then?

- What was in the mind's eye?
- How were you bonded to others?
- What themes were at play in this phase?
- What role did loss and restoration play in this phase?
- How did you live your calling?

Phase 2: Surviving

- What happened to you/your team/your organization during the crisis?
- What was the first inclination you felt in yourself?
- What characterized the first days/weeks? Do you remember this from earlier in your life?
- What dynamics became apparent in your team/organization?
- What did this phase ask of your (personal) leadership?
- What helped you? What were your sources of inspiration/important secure bases?
- What did you lose in this phase? And what, perhaps, have you gained?
- How was your calling helpful during and immediately after this crisis?

Phase 3: Living Through

- What was most painful for you in this crisis?
- What, for you, marked the tipping point from crisis to restoration?
- What experiences and secure bases (from the past) were helpful in your recovery?
- What did you have to say goodbye to? What did you want to leave behind?
- What was the positive impact of the crisis on your (personal) leadership? What did you choose to keep?
- What did you discover about yourself in this crisis? What has this brought you?
- What new perspective has this crisis given you on your calling?

Phase 4: Life+

- How would you describe life post-crisis?
- How is it different now from before?
- What did you learn?
- What do you have at your disposal now that wasn't there before this crisis? What is the '+h' of LIFE now?
- What does this mean for your calling and how you are living it now?
- In which of your roles could you live your calling (personal, professional, organizational, social) more fully?

What are you willing to do, and leave behind, to shape your calling in the new reality?

Important points to take away

- Everyone has an innate need to experience proximity to other people.
- Everyone's attachment style forms the basis of every relationship.
- Secure attachment can occur when secure bases are available.
- Unavailability of secure bases can lead to insecure attachment.
- Resilience builds in accordance with secure attachment;
- The flip side of attachment and resilience is detachment or clinging.
- Psychological safety is the shared belief and perception that the relationship and/or team is a safe place to be yourself without risk of being rejected.
- One person does not determine whether the relationship and/or the team is safe.
- It takes psychological safety to excel.
- Every change and also every crisis triggers our old attachment movements and tests our resilience. At the same time, it is the ultimate opportunity for tapping into developmental and growth potential.

Self-reflection for the coach

- How have I experienced caring and daring in my life?
- Was I challenged, earlier in my life, to take risks?
- How do I handle risk-taking now?
- How do I deal with calls for help? When to help? When not to?
- Who do I feel safe with?
- With whom or what do I experience support?
- Who encourages and challenges me?
- Do I presume trust or do people have to earn it from me?
- When did I feel that I had excelled?
- Am I – when it matters, when things get stressful – more focused on the relationship (caring) or on the outcome (daring)?
- What is my dominant attachment style? And how do I notice it as I move through the Window of Excellence?
- How have I developed resilience in my life?
- When was my resilience really tested? What did I learn from those moments?

Notes

1 Main, M. (1996). Introduction to the special section on attachment and psycho-pathology: 2. Overview of the field of attachment. *Journal of Consulting and Clinical Psychology*, 64(2): 237–243.
2 Werner, E. (2005). Resilience and Recovery. Findings from the Kauai Long-itudinal Study. *Research, Policy, and Practice in Children's Mental Health*, 19(1): 11–14.
3 Cross, R., Dillon, K., and Greenberg, D. (2021). The Secret to Building Resilience. *Harvard Business Review*, January 29.
4 Portzky, M. (2015). *Veerkracht. Onze natuurlijke weerstand tegen een leven vol stress (Resilience. Our natural resistance to a life of stress)*. Antwerp: Witsand.
5 Bowlby, J. (1988). *Attachment and Loss, Volume 1–3*. London: Random House.
6 Bowby, J. (1988). *A Secure Base. Parent–Child Attachment and Healthy Human Development*. London: Routledge.
7 Bowby, J. (1988). *A Secure Base. Parent–Child Attachment and Healthy Human Development*. London: Routledge.
8 Fiddelaers-Jaspers, R. (2014). *Jong verlies. Rouwende kinderen serieus nemen (Loss at a young age. Taking grieving children seriously)*. Utrecht: Ten Have.
9 Reijmerink, M., van Gasteren, K., and van Wielink, J. (2019). Ik heb Auschwitz veranderd in een klaslokaal. In gesprek met dr. Edith Eva Eger (I turned Ausch-witz into a classroom. In conversation with Dr Edith Eva Eger). *Tijdschrift voor Coaching*. March.
10 Van Wielink, J., Fiddelaers-Jaspers, R., and Wilhelm, L. (2023). *The Language of Transition in Leadership. Your Calling as a Leader in a World of Change*. New York: Routledge.
11 Schein, E. and Bennis, W. (1965). *Personal and organizational change through group methods. The laboratory approach*. New York: John Wiley & Sons.
12 Edmondson, A. (2018). *The Fearless Organization. Creating Psychological Safety in the Workplace for Learning, Innovation, and Growth*. New York: John Wiley & Sons.
13 Bowlby, J. (1988). *A Secure Base. Parent–Child Attachment and Healthy Human Development*. London: Routledge.
14 Reijmerink, M. (2021). Helping teams excel – Influence of attachment and psy-chological safety on team performance. *Library of Professional Coaching*, on http s://libraryofprofessionalcoaching.com/concepts/strategy/coaching-with-groups-and -teams/helping-teams-excel-influence-of-attachment-and-psychological-safety-on-t eam-performance, accessed on October 28, 2023.
15 Mikulincer, M. and Shaver, P. (2017). *Attachment in Adulthood. Structure, Dynamics, and Change*. New York/London: Guilford Press.
16 Rom, E. and Mikulincer, M. (2003). Attachment Theory and Group Processes. The Association Between Attachment Style and Group–Related Representations, Goals, Memories, and Functioning. *Journal of Personality and Social Psychology*, 84: 1220–1235.
17 Van Wielink, J. and Wilhelm, L. (2019). Cultuurverandering door coaching (Cul-ture change through coaching). *Tijdschrift voor Ontwikkeling in Organisaties*, 1: 46–51.
18 This exercise is based on van Wielink, J., Wilhelm, L., and van Geelen-Merks, D. (2020). *Loss, Grief, and Attachment in Life Transitions. A Clinician's Guide to Secure Base Counseling*. New York: Routledge.
19 Ibid.
20 Ibid.
21 Ibid.

Chapter 9

Bonding and intimacy

"Three reorganizations in four years. The last one is still ongoing and the next is already announced. Thinking about it still makes me angry. It's been five years since I left, I could no longer go with it; there was no other option. At that tempo, I couldn't keep on throwing myself into a new role, a new team, a new manager. Now, five years later, I notice how I haven't really settled into my new job. I'm wary, waiting for someone here to decide my future for me."

Bea (41)

"We've been together for five years now, Sandra and me. It was love at first sight and, in the beginning of our relationship, there was a lot of intimacy between us. Last year, this started to happen less and less. I had a heart attack and lost confidence in my body, which affected our sex life. I notice that this frustrates and disappoints Sandra. I wish I could change this."

Mitch (30)

The degree of vulnerability you share co-determines the degree of bonding you experience in a relationship. The greater the bond you feel with each other, the more intimacy is possible in the relationship. Attachment is the unconscious process by which you are drawn closer to another person. Bonding is a conscious process and thus differs from attachment. Bonding is a choice to deepen the existing attachment relationship through vulnerability. People can be married and firmly attached for decades, but hardly bond: the same can happen with employees and the organizations they work for.

The degree of vulnerability you are willing to share is largely determined by previous experiences. In the past were you welcome with all your thoughts and emotions? Do you trust the other person to be careful with your vulnerability? Has your trust ever been betrayed? What has letting your vulnerability show given to the relationship? How deep do you want this relationship to go? What level of bonding is necessary for you?

DOI: 10.4324/9781003424178-13

In this Chapter, we explore how bonding deepens when you give form to your intimacy. We will show that conflict is a special – and along with sexuality perhaps the most special – form of intimacy. We will see how, as a secure base coach, you can work with these themes with different clients.

Bonding is a choice

Bonding is how – by choosing to share your vulnerability – you deepen your attachment relationship. In the previous Chapter, we described how attachment is an unconscious process. Bonding is a conscious process in which you, moment by moment, choose how much of yourself you let the other person see, how much you are willing to show of yourself. The more willing you are to let your vulnerability show, the more the relationship deepens. In every relationship, you make this choice, based partly on the purpose of that particular relationship. The degree of bonding you pursue with a colleague might be different from the degree you pursue in a friendship or with an intimate partner.

> Pete has been working as an interim manager in the financial sector for 15 years. A role that gives him freedom, and the inside track on many companies. It was a conscious decision to start working his own business, At the time, it was a conscious decision to start for himself after two disappointing jobs where his contract was terminated after only a year or so. Both times he was given a similar reason: that he was difficult to gauge; hard to tell if he was really committed. Now, after 15 years of self-employment, he wonders whether he wants to continue working as an interim manager or whether he might be better off returning to salaried employment.
>
> He starts a coaching engagement with Kurt, to investigate what has actually happened. Before long they're talking about his father, who also disappointed his employer at a young age. He always told Pete that an employer is loyal only to his salary and not to his employees, so you should work hard but not show too much of yourself. Pete realized that he had never put effort into establishing relationships at the places he worked, had been focused only on getting results. As an interim manager, this came in handy when taking on difficult contracts and then leaving again, but he now realizes that this didn't help him when he was an employee.

Focusing only on results invites no bonding. Focusing only on the relationship doesn't get results. It is important that in a relationship, be it work or personal, there is a balance between focusing on the relationship and focusing on results.

> Anais is a mother of two sons. Her eldest, Kyran, is 12 years old and in Grade 8. This year, he will receive his final recommendation from the

school, which determines what level of secondary education he can follow. The question is whether he will be able to go to HAVO (roughly equivalent to American High School). In recent years though, Anais has tried not to put too much pressure on him, so Kyran has mostly played football instead of studying. Anais decides to have a conversation with Kyran to find out what he wants. He explains that he would like to go to HAVO, but doesn't know if he is able and what he needs to do to get there. Anais asks him what she can do to help. Two things, he says. "First, you can help me plan so I can study and play football and, second, you can help me to stick at it when things aren't going so well."

The way you are attached determines, in part, your ability to bond with others. The more securely attached you are, the more confident you will be in establishing bonding with others. Insecure attachment leads to either a certain degree of detachment or excessive dependence in the bonding. Unconscious experiences from your attachment history have an impact on your conscious choice to bond or avoid bonding. The more experiences you have had in your life of people being available and reliable, the easier it becomes to bond and to shape intimacy. Sexuality is a very special form of intimacy in that you open up both physically and emotionally – and perhaps even spiritually – to the other person. You reveal yourself in all your nakedness, at the edges of self; edges where we are also exposed, susceptible to being hurt.

Through vulnerability and dialogue you build intimacy in a relationship. As a secure base coach, you might consider trying to build a high degree of intimacy in the coaching relationship. You create a proximity that supports you and your client together to find and stay with the tension that enables growth.

Dialogue

Bonding flows from a willingness to engage in dialogue. Face to face in shared curiosity, each allowing the other to discover something they do not yet know. A dialogue is a coming together of emotional, cognitive, physical and spiritual aspects. In every dialogue, these four aspects are present, consciously or unconsciously. Dialogue goes much further and deeper than 'talking'. It is more a fundamental attitude and at the same time the craft of observing in, through and beyond language. Dialogue requires embodied presence; see the dialogue model in Figure 9.1.

Kim has been coming to her coach, Bram, for a long time. She lost her son four years ago and is trying to find meaning in her life again. Today, they talk about how an important part of her life was dedicated to her faith, but with Max's death she lost her faith in God. "How can there be a God, when these kinds of senseless things happen." When she talks about God, her fists clench and her voice hardens. Bram enquires into what God meant to her. What did his presence bring into her life? How was she aware of his presence? And how did her grief close the door to God's love?

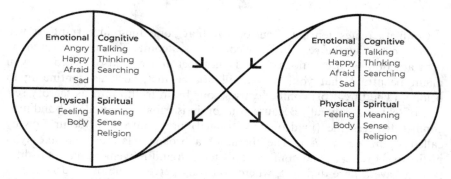

Figure 9.1 Dialogue model by George Kohlrieser, based on the work of Elisabeth Kübler-Ross[1]
Source: From Hostage At The Table. How Leaders Can Overcome Conflict, Influence Others, and Raise Performance (2006, John Wiley & Sons Inc), reproduced with permission of the Licensor through PLSclear

One of the main barriers to dialogue is starting from a place of agreeing or disagreeing with something. The openness and curiosity that are essential to dialogue are interrupted by this primary – and quite normal – reaction; your brain analyses information and tries to place it in a known *frame*. To engage in dialogue, you have to put a lot of effort into distinguishing between accepting something and agreeing with something. Unconditional positive regard lets you accept the other person's reality and experience – no matter how bizarre, abject, unhealthy or at odds it is with your interpretation of reality. You can't change what you don't acknowledge, says Dr Phil.[2]

Dialogue is profoundly linked to transition. Our ability to say goodbye and grieve, hinges on our willingness to face up to what we have lost. Grieving is also letting go of resistance to the way things have gone – the 'disagreement' that we often hold onto to – in order to reopen a path to the future, a future characterized by curiosity about the other, the different, the unknown. Being able to grieve and to dialogue go hand in hand.

Conflict and battle

Next to sexuality, conflict is one of the highest forms of intimacy. In conflict, two or more people find out that they have different thoughts, feelings, experiences and perceptions. Conflict evokes tensions that can weaken the bond. The art, in conflict, is to get to a state where, after exchanging and exploring the views each holds, you allow space to discover a greater truth than you knew before.[3]

Definition: A conflict is a difference – of experiences, perceptions, thoughts, and feelings – between two or more people or groups, characterized by tension and emotions.

Conflict creates tension. Tension, in that something important to you might be lost in the search for a common outcome. Tension is caused by contradictions and emotions. You do not feel understood or heard, or you might be afraid that your needs will not be met, such as continuing to belong. (The threat of) conflict causes your brain to flip into its factory setting of 'eliminate threat'. Because your brain is tribal – focused on bonding – conflict triggers the (inadequately trained) brain into what John Bowlby called *separation anxiety*. The threat of a broken relationship makes you instinctively retreat from conflict. This tension and movement makes it difficult to have a pure dialogue, where you fully perceive the other person and respond accordingly. Often your emotions make you defensive or unable to see your own part clearly.

In fact, your brain is much more focused on reassurance than discovery and learning. Your brain has been 'taken' hostage, so to speak, by an amygdala hijack.[4] In a hostage state you come – as Edith Eger says – with your primary impulses, your reaction, but not your response.[5] When you are able to respond, your connection with yourself, with your breath, and with your vulnerability is restored. The heart remains open, the other is 'allowed' to see you. Conflict is essentially good and often necessary. After all, there are no healthy families or organizations without – sometimes very big – differences.

In a permanent hostage situation, conflict turns into battle. The focus is no longer on wanting to understand or learn from the other in order to reach shared goals, but on winning, beating the other, proving you're right. Whereas in conflict you still want to understand each other and are curious about what there is to discover, in conflict differences harden and you end up opposing each other. Battle is not about here and now. It is a transference pattern in which old pain is reawakened and old patterns are triggered. This is mostly an unconscious process: your heart closes to avoid feeling the pain, and your brain stops receiving so you are no longer hearing the other person.

The moment you get into a battle, stress hormones are released that signal danger. Your defense mechanism is triggered and reacts to the threat. The other person responds similarly to this 'violent' reaction, their survival mechanism clicks into action, making neither of you able to perceive the other. Both of you are trapped by old patterns that make excelling impossible.

Marieke is under pressure to schedule a new demo for a client; she decides to ask her new colleague Alex to join her. She wants to include another of her colleagues, Jan, who is also working with this client, so she decides to message him and ask if he sees any objection to Alex attending. She expects his agreement, but Jan replies that he would like to bring a different colleague. Marieke is taken aback by his (unexpected) response and starts typing an angry reaction. Before pressing send, she decides to vent her feelings and check her thoughts with a friend. She realizes that she does not feel heard and seen and, crucially, that her anger does not resolve this. She decides to send Jan another message with a question in it. This lightens her mood and she feels she can now reconnect with Jan and hear what he wants to say.

Overcoming battle is only possible when you are aware that you are battling. This can happen, for instance, when you discover that you long for more intimacy in your relationship, a better career, deeper friendships, more fun, **and** you start to see that your tendency to battle is getting in the way of this. You might end up being right, but at the cost of being happy. You can't change what you don't recognize and acknowledge. If you are aware of being in battle mode, you can learn to actively reassure your brain. There are many ways to do this: by taking a deep breath, counting to ten, taking a walk, talking with someone else or simply by taking yourself out of the situation for a while. When the brain calms down again, space is created to reconnect. By truly wanting to hear and understand, the path back from battle to conflict to resolution can be found.

Avoiding bonding and intimacy leads to stalling

The degree of secure or insecure attachment you knew in your life has a major influence on whether you are inclined to bond when feeling vulnerable. The more insecure your attachment is or has been, the more wary you might be; you are also less inclined to show that you feel vulnerable. Avoiding bonding and intimacy might stem from fear of being hurt or rejected, or because you never learned this in the past.

Kelly grew up in a family with four brothers. At the dinner table, her father did the talking and would tell her brothers what things were really like in the outside world. Her mother listened in the background. When Kelly asked a question, she invariably got the same answer: "Girls don't need to know that." Now Kelly is working as a secretary at a law firm. When her boss asks her for her opinion, she realizes she falls silent, not knowing if she even has an opinion, let alone how to express it.

Another reason to avoid bonding and intimacy is if they cause you to re-experience the pain of loss. If the loss has not been truly grieved, there is a real chance that the fear of such a loss happening again is greater than the desire to bond. Thus you discover again that grieving and the ability to engage productively in conflict go hand in hand.

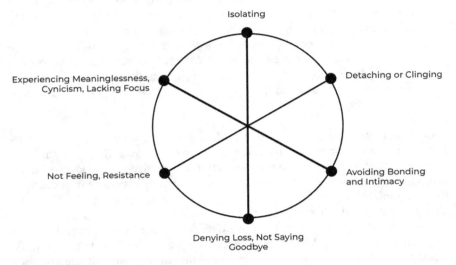

Figure 9.2 The Cycle of Stalled Transition

> In the first year of their marriage Anton's wife died in an accident. After years of (grief) therapy, he meets and bonds with a new partner. However, fate strikes again. She gets lung cancer. After a year-long illness, she dies in his arms. At that point, he decides never to enter into a new relationship: "I'm never going through this again."
>
> Jan is an entrepreneur. He started his first restaurant when he was 21. For the first three years, business was good, but the competition came into the street. He began to lose some customers and, over time, he found himself increasingly in the red. At the end of his fourth year, the business was no longer sustainable and he declared bankruptcy. Although entrepreneurial blood still courses through his veins, he doesn't dare to risk opening another restaurant.

Avoiding bonding and intimacy can manifest in different ways: not letting anyone get close, having difficulty with people being nice to you, not accepting love or support from others, preferring not to affect others or be moved by them, not wanting to make love or to make love without real contact.[6] Basically, these are survival reactions, and many are very similar to the behavior we see in detachment. There is value in examining these movements and exploring their origins; from there you can start looking for a healing movement.

The paradox: the more risks you take, the safer it gets

In the previous Chapter, we talked about the importance of psychological safety as a condition for excellence. Although your first reaction is often to back away from tension, things can actually become safer when you learn to use the support of your secure bases to move towards it. Taking emotional risks pays off. It tests and strengthens the bond when you dare to stay. This is the paradox of the secure base.

> When Yvonne is coaching this team, she notices many minor, seemingly innocuous comments are made about Jan and eating. Jan seems to be preoccupied with food throughout the day. When he is not yet back after lunch, people joke that he must have made one more visit to the buffet table. Yvonne decides to ask a question: "Do you often joke about Jan's appetite." First silence, then defensive comments: "Yes, but he doesn't mind." "It's just a fact that he always eats a lot." "It's just a little bit of fun, that's all." "Nobody minds a joke." Some team members haven't spoken. Yvonne questions them directly. It seems they are not comfortable with the 'jokes', but aren't sure how to handle this. Meanwhile, Jan comes back into the room and is surprised to hear what they're talking about. He says he doesn't like it either and, a long time ago, decided not to make a fuss about it. Yvonne guides a dialogue between the team members in which everyone gets the chance to speak.

Through Yvonne recognizing that this was a form of teasing and her willingness to raise the issue directly in the team, she creates space to work with the tension together. Her guidance creates a safe base for the conversation. The dialogue and the agreements the team members make together, increase the feeling of safety within the team.

Psychological safety increases when you are willing to take risks. This can apply physically, but is absolutely true emotionally. Are you willing to get into and stay in a difficult conversation? How do you learn to speak your mind (and heart) while feeling the fear of rejection? How do you learn to stay so that you can also hear the other person and understand each other?

The person effect – testing the bond

As you read in Chapter 6, the degree to which you bond with others is determined by the person effect. Everyone has their unique way of influencing this person effect. Some elements you can adapt to the context or moment, such as the way you dress, how you bond with others, the language you use. Other aspects you can't simply adapt, like your age, gender, height, nationality.

To gain insight into how you bond with others, you have to test the bond. You do this by asking for feedback on your person effect. What is a positive way in which I bond with you? What is a negative way? And what is their effects on you? This will begin to give you a picture of your person effect in that particular relationship.

It is up to you to judge what you do with the feedback. If you get feedback that suits how you want to come across, then of course that is fine. In that situation, do more of what works. If you get feedback that is unexpected or makes you uncomfortable, then it is worth exploring how you can change this by changing your person effect. Does your person effect bring you closer to deeper goals you are pursuing in your life, or does it take you away from them?

> *Irma is giving a presentation with a male colleague. When the audience enters, he stands by the door while she welcomes the people into the room. When it is her turn (the plan is that she will say something about the person effect), she asks if anyone in the room is willing to share something about the first impression she made. A man stands up and says that as she was not at the door, but in the room, he had got the impression that she is the assistant. This is not what Irma wanted. She decides that, in future, she'll ensure she also welcomes people arriving for the event.*

Asking for and receiving feedback requires a learning mindset. Being open to feedback from others offers new perspectives and allows you to refine your self-image. It shines a light on your blind spots about yourself The more insight you have into how you come across, the more able you are to be authentic. And you can't get closer to authenticity without concrete feedback. When someone tells you that they feel welcome with you, that is positive feedback, but you can only get a repeat such feedback when you know exactly what you are doing that makes the other person feel so welcome.

Feedback is a constant in your life. From an early age, your parents and others give you feedback on how you do things. A toddler taking their first steps will (usually) receive positive feedback, in language, sounds and gestures. This encourages the child to keep trying. The more securely attached you are, the easier it is to give and receive feedback.

The secure base coach at work with bonding and intimacy

Bonding and intimacy – Working with individuals

> *Guido was inconsolable when, at the age of 16, his best friend Cees was killed in a scooter accident. They had known each other since childhood, shared joys and sorrows, been like brothers to each other. Guido had not had such a friendship with anyone since Cees died.*

That was until he met Sarah at a university roommate's graduation party. A remarkable woman who immediately stole his heart with her fearless candor. She asked him questions that no one had ever asked him before. Questions that touched on his vulnerability. Their friendship grew into a love relationship. They married and had two daughters; life could hardly be better. Then fate struck, again. Around her 35th birthday, Sarah was diagnosed with a very aggressive form of breast cancer and died within three months.

Guido's world collapsed. Why was life testing him so cruelly? He had consciously committed himself to Sarah and now he felt disillusioned. He asked himself: "Why should I still choose to bond? With people? With places? Why should I pursue any goal at all? Everything and everyone dear to me is lost." Guido realizes that he can no longer feel any joy. He is on autopilot, not living, just surviving. Love feels far, far away.

He does not want to load this feeling onto his daughters, so he decides to seek help.

You can become incredibly disappointed with life. Disappointed in your bond with people. For so many different reasons. When you lose them unexpectedly, when a friendship ends, when you lose your job and have to say your goodbyes to a job and colleagues you put your heart and soul into. These are just examples of moments when you chose to entrust yourself to someone or something, but life, circumstance or people made a different choice.

As a coach, you no doubt meet people who, for whatever reason, have become disappointed in their bonds in life: with others, with places, with goals. As a result, they have often lost connection with themselves too. When they then come to you for help, you must understand that, for them, they are taking a big risk. It is important to acknowledge this, tell them that you can see this, feel how hard this must be for them. By exploring with the client how it feels for them, you not only create a sense of welcome and safety but you also invite them into (new) vulnerability, new intimacy.

You can only do this when you are willing to dare in bonding with your client and when you can welcome any reaction. Often, in fact, you'll strike a painful chord with people. And when that happens, your particular way of bonding and your own tendency to move forward or backward in the face of unease are triggered.

In every encounter with a client, you step forward and feel what happens – to you and your client – in that stepping forward. This is the moment the moment that, for example, Viktor Frankl refers to in his work. The moment between stimulus, which comes from outside us, and response, our internal outwardly expressed reaction to it. Between these two moments is a space, in which you as a human being can experience freedom of choice, the freedom to consciously choose your response.

Coaches need to be constantly aware of this and make their clients aware of it too. When talking with your client, the purpose of this all-encompassing (mental, emotional, physical and spiritual) enquiry is to test the bond. What is happening to us, right now, and to what extent does this reflect the client's experiences with others?

The coach guides Guido in an exploration of the meaningful relationships in his life. This brings to light how many caveats he, without knowing, brings into every bond. As a result, these prophecies are, inevitably, self-fulfilling: he always ends up disappointed. Whether it is one of the personal relationships with his family, his children, his friends or professional relationships with colleagues and clients, in every bond, he gets exactly what he expects, but not what he desires. He experiences a high degree of superficiality and transience in each contact, which means he does not experience the emotional depth he really longs for, the bond he is unable or afraid to shape himself.

They look at every facet of what, out of pure self-protection, he does in all his encounters. Mentally, it erodes Guido's self-confidence to behave frankly and freely in contact with other people. He is wary and extremely cautious, constantly testing the bond, so it never gets the daring it needs to actually develop. There are also physical consequences. In contact with others (especially if he is speaking to someone for the first time, or has not known them for very long), his breathing and heart rates elevate significantly, making him chronically fatigued. Previous medical research into the causes of this fatigue yielded nothing.

In discussions with his coach, he discovers that his fear of completely entrusting and giving himself to others is building up enormous physical tension. Emotionally, it is precisely this fear that has him in its grip, is keeping him hostage. His fear links directly to the terrible losses of his friend Cees and his wife Sarah. Altogether, this makes Guido regularly wonder how, even if, he can find meaning in his life. Does my life have meaning if I am unable to bond with people? What is the effect on me and what do I pass on to my daughters about bonding and taking emotional risks?

Bonding and intimacy – Working with teams

The manager of a team of engineers at a large energy company enlists the help of Eric, a specialist in team coaching. In the initial exploratory meeting with Eric, the manager explains how the team's work is falling short of expectations. He thinks that the team overall are trying hard, but that results, and their contribution to growth of the organization are poor. There is little collaboration and transparency, so work is frequently duplicated or left unfinished. This gets everybody irritated. In spite of an earlier attempt by the manager and a different coach, poor relationships between team members continue to determine the dynamics in the group. The situation is exacerbated by several team members being on long-term sick leave, apparently suffering from burnout.

In Chapter 8, you read that in a team or group, people tend to repeat their original attachment movement. The way they first, and unconsciously, learned to put their trust in others is always triggered in exchanges in the group: the moment two or more people attempt something together, they trigger each other. However, people not only unconsciously entrust themselves to others to a greater or lesser extent, they also do so consciously. We saw, earlier, that we call this conscious process of entrusting oneself the *bonding* process. Whenever you are in this process with one or more people, you are always concerned with the degree to which you let them see how vulnerable you are feeling moment by moment. What you do or do not show of yourself has an effect on the others in the team and thus on effective collaboration.

Here's an example.

In the team (in the case study above), people avoid each other. It's clear that tensions exist but they are not addressed. Everyone, it seems, avoids real contact. They make sure they get their own work done, but are not, or not sufficiently, concerned about their contribution to the organization's performance as a whole. Everyone immerses themselves individually in the operation and only does that which fits with their idea of necessary.

Eric starts working with the whole team and discovers in the first session that they all find it challenging and uncomfortable to stand in pairs, in silence, opposite each other, looking into each other's eyes. By inviting – and also daring – them to really feel what the eye-contact exercise does to them, he initiates a conversation about what 'bonding' means to the members of the team. He asks each to say something about their discomfort, about what is evoked in them physically, mentally and emotionally.

Eric asks the team to form a line, in order of first to join the team through to last to join, and to exchange with the person next to you how you have been doing in the group since joining, and what was a high and a low point for them. A lot of learning happens, for Eric and the team. A woman, Julia, shares how, on her first day, she was in a meeting in which a colleague was reprimanded about something she had said in the meeting. This has made Julia cautious about voicing her opinion in the team. This is the first time team members have heard from each other about their first moments in the team, and how that continues to affect their performance. Sharing their 'highlights' does create a positive energy and pride that has a strong unifying effect on the team. Crucially, sharing their 'lowlights' makes visible the fault lines that have developed and how they undermine bonding and collaboration.

In coaching this team, the first session proves to be a pivotal moment: standing in their vulnerability, with all the emotions that come with it, team members share where they have lost trust in each other and the team. Eric gives everyone space to tell their story. By observing carefully, paraphrasing accurately and asking deeper questions, Eric gets more and more information out into the open. It is no longer only about what happened, but also about how people experienced it, what emotions it evoked, the resulting choices they made, and how all this affected how they bond with the group. This allows the team to reflect on what has been lost in the bonding process between them and how this has caused people to become disconnected from each other. Eric's choice to use the *Team Life-line* intervention enabled team members to share, recognize and to acknowledge, and so to heal what was broken ... the mutual bond with each other.

As a team coach, the art and challenge is to help heal the bonds. Transition takes place when bonding is in place. Nobody can do it alone. Teams have a right to exist because they have a goal or task to accomplish together. The moment some people in the team lose sight of that goal, because of fear, frustration, pain, sadness, whatever, cracks appear in the bedrock of the team. The team loses traction when not everyone is pulling in the same direction. As soon as the team is under pressure, those small fault lines turn into large cracks.

There is always at least one person in the team who can feel the foundations are getting shaky. And that person has to handle the challenge of speaking this out in the group. If he doesn't, or can't, for whatever reason, the group gets further out of balance. Other team members will be affected and will in turn, be challenged to ring the warning bell.

Team members bear responsibility in the group for their own behavior, but also for that of their teammates. They could ask themselves the question: what am I doing that causes my colleague to do what he is doing? Being part of a group is far from optional. You cannot choose to be in the group sometimes and not in it at other times. You have rights in a group, but also duties. No one is more important than the team.[7] The same applies in a family. There, too, you reap the benefits of the bond with your siblings (your colleagues), and you are jointly responsible for the health of the bond. You cannot outsource that to the other person.

Being properly in a team means managing the balance between autonomy and being part of something bigger than yourself. Finding this balance is impossible alone, because your autonomy and your place in the team are determined by the space you are allowed by others. This applies to every team member, including the leader. We call this *the balance of giving and taking (or exchange)*. When the balance is disturbed, it affects the bonds in the group.[8]

Team coaches are tasked with guiding this process by using all their senses to perceive – in a broad sense – what is happening between team members in exchange and in bonding, and then asking questions about it. Patterns that have developed in a team or group need to be uncovered. This allows the team to build trust, develops willingness to accept and enter into conflict with each other, and increases mutual commitment and individual and joint willingness to take responsibility and joint focus on results.[9] This contributes to the perfect balance between caring and daring which facilitates a team mindset of excelling. This mindset and the interpersonal and working climate it can create ensure that transition, that real change, becomes possible.

Exercises with your client

Exploring the life-line in the light of bonding and intimacy
Bonding (Chapter 8) is about the unconscious underlayer of how you shape relationships. It Bonding applies when you are doing this consciously. How you choose to be close to others and, from there, to shape meaningful relationships. Intimacy in these bonds and relationships comes from being able to surrender to the other when you are feeling vulnerable. And being an invitation to the other to do the same. So we see that vulnerability is a prerequisite for intimacy.

Reflection questions

- How do you bond with others?
- Who would you like stronger bond with and why?
- How close do you let others get?
- How do you keep others at a distance, too, perhaps?
- What have you learned about conflict? How does this affect the way you bond with others?
- What have you learned about when conflict escalates to battle? How does this affect the way you bond with others?
- Are there unresolved conflicts in your life that need resolving?
- Are you a good listener? How do you know that you are?
- To what extent do you let your vulnerability show when bonding with others? How does this affect you? Affect the other?
- How do you shape intimacy in personal relationships and professional contexts?
- What is your understanding of the word 'love' in personal and professional relationships?

Life-line and conflict
Ask your client to create his life-line (see the life-line exercise in Chapter 7). Using this life-line, have your client tell you about an early experience of conflict and ask him the following questions:

- What conflict and with whom?

- What was the conflict?
- What were the circumstances?
- In what way did you not go for it?
- What would be different in your life now if you hadn't held back?

Ask your client:

- "Tell me more about this."
- "Is it true that I hear you say ..."
- "I get the feeling that ..., is that right."

Make notes as your client tells their story.
At the end, ask your client to summarize their story in two to three brief sentences.
This brings focus.
Now tell the story back to the client back to the client.
Ask deeper questions:

- What did you learn?
- Looking back, what would you do differently?
- What would you say now to whoever you were then?
- In what ways would you encourage and challenge the person you were then?

Bodywork on the edge
This is a bodywork exercise in which you let your client feel how he takes his place in the world, how he meets others, applies pressure, experiences counter-pressure, physically counter-pressing, and vocalizing (shouting "No!", shouting "Yes, this is me!").

- Play music that shakes the body. For example, *Watusi Warrior Drums* by Slagerij van Kampen (Kampen Drummers).
- Now have your client take a seat opposite you, toe to toe. Find each other by physically touching. Challenge your client by pushing and pulling. As words surface, let your client speak them. Challenge your client to vocalize what he is feeling. Loud to soft – whatever wants out. Meanwhile, play appropriate music in the background. For example, the song *Castle* by Halsey.
- Let your client seek their own movement, seek their own power and yours.
- Close with music. For example, *Only the Winds* by Olafur Arnalds while looking at each other in silence.

Provocation

In this exercise, you let your client experience how negative triggers bring on physical, emotional and mental reactions. The aim of the exercise is to discover that these negative triggers and their consequences need not lead to a hostage situation. As coach, you support the client to encourage and challenge himself to stay bonded, to be curious and to ask the one provoking to say some more. *In the eye of a storm, there is the sound of peace and silence.*

- Sit facing each other.
- Have your client tell you about a situation in which he felt or still feels insecure.
- Respond to what he says from sharpness, be provocative. Be daring without caring.
- Encourage your client to breathe in and paraphrase what you just said: "I heard you say that …. Tell me more about this."
- Continue for ten minutes.
- Then have a dialogue with your client about what he learned about himself in this exercise.

Letter

Ask your client to write, at home, a letter. Tell your client: "Imagine you have 15 minutes to live, what would you say and to whom? Write it all down."
Have your client bring the letter to the next session and ask him to read it out, aloud, to you. The aim is to get your client more used to expressing what is inside him, what needs to be said.

Variation

Put two chairs facing each other. Your client sits on one chair and imagines the recipient of the letter is sitting on the chair opposite. He reads the letter to him/her. At points while he's reading it out, invite him to take a moment to switch seats and sit on the empty chair to 'hear' what has just been said. Let your client respond from the perspective of the 'occupant' of the empty chair(s). Then let your client take a seat back on his own chair and continue reading aloud. When your client has finished reading the letter, invite him to take a seat on the empty chair again. Ask him to respond from the heart, a second time, from that chair. And then to return to his 'own' chair and, a last time, say what is in his heart.

Person effect
In Chapter 6, we described the person effect and the value of asking for and giving feedback about it. In this exercise, you let your client give and receive feedback.

- Your client sits or stands facing you. You ask him to say two sentences to you that are about the person effect you have on him or her.

  - "The positive effect you have on me is ..."
  - "The negative effect you have on me is ..."

Make sure your client is really giving his full attention to the actual effect you have on him. For example: "The positive effect you have on me is that the way you make contact with me and the way you keep eye contact makes me feel welcome. The effect is that in our conversations I open up easily and dare to be vulnerable." After your client says these sentences, thank him and swap roles with him, with you giving the positive and negative examples. Suggest to your client to ask five people he knows for feedback on his person effect. Discuss this in the next session. What is the client learning about himself?

Rewrite our Book of Rules
Every human being has a 'book of rules' that is part of his or her father and mother factor. In it are the spoken and unspoken rules that determine how you should function with respect to various themes in personal and professional life. This exercise is about recognizing, acknowledging and examining those rules of behavior. And rewriting them where necessary or desirable.

Have the client bring separate photos of his father and mother, to use depending on what is the issue in process.

In addition, make a number of floor anchors that include themes that appear in the *Book of Rules*, such as money, status, love, ethics, relationships, conflict, men, women, sexuality, and any other themes that the client wants to bring in.

Have the client place the picture of his father or mother on the floor and let him place the theme floor anchors around it from his gut feel.

Research with the client:

- What makes him choose this constellation and what makes it feel right? Does it need adjusting?
- Which anchors is he drawn to explore? Which ones instill fear or want to be avoided?
- When he stands on each floor anchor, what comes up about the *Book of Rules*? What emotions arise? What happens in his body? What has he learnt about this theme from father/mother? What is he still carrying that does not belong to him? What can be returned to them?
- What would the *Rules* be like if he were allowed to rewrite them?

Explore your journey as man or woman

Each of us has received implicit and explicit messages from our fathers and mothers about what it is to be male or female. This exercise is about recognizing, acknowledging and exploring those messages and their effect, up till now, on the client's journey as a man or woman.

Have the client bring a picture of his mother **and** one of his father.

First, have the client sit opposite the mother's picture.

Inquire with the client:

NB: depending on the gender of your client work with being female or being male.

What did you learn from your mother about being a man or being a woman? What examples were there? How did that affect your development? What did you get, what did you miss? What did you pick up elsewhere? In which part of you do you bond easily with your mother and in which part do you keep a bit of distance? What do you want or wish for when you face your mother? Where in your body do you feel that and what movement do you want to make? In your relationship with your mother – or in the absence of one – what did you learn about bonding, safety and trust? And what did you learn from her about risk-taking and about exploring the world?

Then have your client take a seat opposite the picture of his father.

Inquire with your client:

What did you learn from your father about being a man or being a woman. What examples did you receive? What did that mean for your development? What did you get, what did you miss? What did you pick up elsewhere? In which part of you do you bond easily with your father and in which part do you keep a bit of distance? What do you want or wish for when you face your father? Where in your body do you feel that and what movement do you want to make? In your relationship with your father – or in the absence of one – what did you learn about bonding, safety and trust? And what did you learn from him about risk-taking and about exploring the world?

Conclude with:

What did you learn about being male/female in this exercise? How do you recognize that in yourself at this moment? What leadership quality did this help develop? What leadership task lies ahead of you?

Exercises with the team

Exploring the team life-line in the light of bonding and intimacy

Below are questions that can help you explore the themes of bonding and intimacy with the team you are coaching. You can map out and clarify for and with the team members how these themes play out in the group. How bonded are the members, to the team as a whole and to each other? Are they willing to share how vulnerable they feel when speaking out in the group about what they think, feel and experience in working with the others? And are they willing to subordinate their own interests to those of the team? Do they also have fun with each other? Do they experience depth when collaborating?

Reflection questions

- With whom on this team do you feel a bond? How did that happen? What do you do and what does the other person do?
- With whom on this team do you feel a lesser bond? Why is that? What do you do and what does the other person do?
- In this team, do you dare to speak out about what you find difficult? If you do, why? If you don't, why?
- Is making mistakes accepted in this team? What contributes to that and what might also detract from that quality?
- Do you have fun in this team? How does that happen?
- Do your encounters in this team have enough depth for you? What makes that possible? What do you do and what does/do the other(s) do?
- Do you accept conflict when necessary? What helps with that? Or what causes it to fail?
- What conversation, topic or theme do you avoid? How does that happen? What does it take to get it discussed?
- Do you take responsibility for your own and also each other's actions in this team? How does that look, and how does it affect collaboration?

Life-line and your experience in groups
On large sheets of paper, have each team member draw their life-line since childhood with their positive and negative experiences.
Members discuss these life-lines in pairs.

- What pattern do you see in how you bond?
- What makes an experience positive or negative?
- What do you see from the perspective of the Window of Excellence?
- What secure bases were there for you? And which ones were not?
- How does your history in groups affect your behavior in groups now? And, specifically, in this team?
- Now for the 'bonding thermometer'. On a scale of 1 to 10, give each experience a rating, where 10 is the best and 1 the worst.

Now put the team in a large circle. Team members have the chance to respond to this question: "To what extent have you bonded with this group?"

When someone wants to say something, he steps forward one meter. If what he says resonates for another team member, that person can step forward with them. Everyone gets a chance to speak out. There's no limit to how often anyone may step forward.

You then explore a second question in the same way: "What specifically could you do to make a deeper bond with this group?"

Now allow a few minutes for each team member, silently, to reflect on what they discovered, in this exercise, about themselves and about the team.

To round off, let each team member express, in one sentence, the core of what he discovered.

Fish on the table

A very useful exercise to flesh out the theme of conflict in a team, is *Fish on the Table*. Given this name by George Kohlrieser, it is a metaphor for something tricky, difficult, perhaps painful that needs to be brought out into the open in order to 'clean it up' together and repair the bonds with each other again.[10] By putting the fish on the table and having a dialogue about it with all the emotions that it brings up, you are discussing what is essential to you.

When team members are empowered to clearly state what is standing in the way of optimal collaboration with one or more people in the team, space is created for reconnection.

Step 1. Have people walk in pairs and explore together what particular fish each wants to put on the team's table. They need to describe precisely what the tricky, difficult, or painful thing is for them, how it affects them and what they hope and desire. What would they like to be different?

Step 2. The team members stand in a semi-circle in the room facing you. One by one, they come and stand next to you in front of the group. Together you discuss their 'fish', working through the questions from Step 1.

Step 3. Then – with you beside them, possibly with your hand on their shoulder or in their back – they tell the team what their fish is and what they desire here.

Step 4. You invite anyone in the team, for whom something about this person's fish or desire resonates with them, to come and stand behind this colleague. There's no obligation: only if the fish/desire evokes something in the other person, however small or large.

Step 5. You invite the (first) person to consciously look behind him and take on board that one or more colleagues are standing there (or not). What realization does he get from this?

Step 6. The semi-circle reforms and you invite the next person to come forward. Start again from Step 2.

Psychological safety

When group and individual enjoy a balance of caring and daring, psychological safety can develop (see Chapter 8). This exercise enables you, literally, to build this feeling of safety in the team. You allow team members, step by step, to experience the degree of safety they feel with individual team members and in the group as a whole.

Step 1. People face each other in pairs, in silence. Have them look each other in the eyes. Tell them to direct their focus inwards to the physical reactions happening in their bodies. What is brought up by gazing into the other person's eyes and he into yours'. Where in your body do you feel that? Do you feel safe? Do you feel unsafe? Tell them to allow whatever comes up to unfold.

Step 2

- Each pair chooses an A and a B.
- B asks A: "What am I doing now that builds safety between us?"
- A answers. In four sentences, brief and precise. No discussion by anyone.
- B thanks A for the answer.
- B asks A: "What am I doing now that erodes safety between us?"
- A answers. In four sentences, brief and precise. No discussion by anyone.
- B thanks A for the answer.

Step 3. Each pair switch roles.
Step 4. Let the 'pairs' say goodbye to each other.
Step 5. People form new pairs and repeat the exercises until everyone has spoken to everyone.
Step 6. Have people reflect individually (silently) and write down what they have learned about themselves and the team.
Step 7. Have each team member say, in one or two sentences, the core of what they learned about psychological safety in themselves and in the team.

Firing Squad exercise

The goal of this exercise is simple: to consciously put team members in a situation where they are under significant pressure. This will trigger their primary attachment movement and behavior. They are, so to speak, put in front of a firing squad, that will try to unbalance the team member through harshness, provocation, and criticism. Because the team member is repeatedly instructed, without respite, to take a deep breath and paraphrase what was just said to him, he might start to experience that he can choose to remain curious about what the other person has to say. This strengthens the ability to engage and remain in dialogue.

Step 1. Place enough chairs for everybody in a semicircle opposite a single chair.

Step 2. Invite one of the team members to sit in the single chair, while the remaining members of the team sit in the semi-circle.

Step 3. Have the team member in the chair tell the group about a situation (inside or outside the team) in which he felt or still feels unsafe.

Step 4. Let the other members of the team in turn 'fire' sharp, provocative remarks at their teammate. Let them be daring without caring.

Step 5. After each 'salvo', encourage the targeted team member to take a deep breath and paraphrase what his colleague just said to him: "I hear you say that .... Is that right? Have you anything else to say about that?" Without giving him a chance to elaborate on that conversation, the next salvo comes.

Step 6. Do this for seven minutes per person (or less if the group is too large).

Step 7. Have the next team member take a seat on the chair. Repeat the process until everyone has been in the firing line.

Step 8. Have people reflect individually and write down what they have learned about themselves and the team.

Step 9. Have each team member tell, in one or two sentences, the core of what they learned about themselves and about the team.

Important points to take away

- The key difference between attachment and bonding is choice. Bonding is the conscious choice to deepen an existing attachment.
- The degree of vulnerability you are willing to show/share determines the degree of bonding you experience.
- The more (emotional) risk we take in contact with others, the more secure the bond can become. This is the paradox of the secure base.
- Dialogue is the most powerful way in which a bond is shaped.
- A dialogue is a coming together of the emotional, the cognitive, the physical and the spiritual.
- Conflict and sexuality are the ultimate act of intimacy.
- Conflict is something you conduct in open-hearted bonding with the aim of discovering something, together, that neither of you knew before. War is something you wage against each other with a closed heart, where everyone loses in the end.
- The extent to which we bond with others is determined, among other things, by the person effect. How we come across is partly under our control (clothing, vocabulary/syntax, degree of interaction), and partly not (gender, age, nationality).
- The secure base coach builds bonds and intimacy in order to shape transition.

Self-reflection for the coach

- How do I bond with others?
- How close do I let others get? How do I keep people at a distance?
- What is the most difficult conversation I ever had? What made it so difficult? What did I learn from it?
- How do I shape intimacy with my clients?
- How did my parents shape my view of vulnerability? What does this mean for how I welcome my own vulnerability and that of my clients?
- What have I learned about conflict?
- How do I deal with conflict? Do I welcome conflict or try to avoid it?
- What battle am I fighting right now? And what pattern am I repeating in this?
- What would my partner, my children, my colleagues, my team members say about my listening skills?
- How pure is my perception, when observing what is happening with the client?
- Am I having enough fun? Why/why not?
- When was the last time I said sorry? And the last time I should have but didn't? How did this affect me and the other?

Notes

1 Kohlrieser, G. (2006). *Hostage At The Table. How Leaders Can Overcome Conflict, Influence Others, and Raise Performance.* San Francisco: Jossey-Bass.
2 McGraw, P. (2000). *Life Strategies. Doing What Works, Doing What Matters.* New York: Hyperion.
3 Van Wielink, J., Fiddelaers-Jaspers, R., and Wilhelm, L. (2023). *The Language of Transition in Leadership. Your Calling as a Leader in a World of Change.* New York: Routledge.
4 Ibid.
5 Eger, E. (2018). *The Choice: Embrace the Possible.* New York: Scribner Book Company; Eger, E. (2020). *The Gift. 12 Lessons to Save Your Life.* Amsterdam: London: Rider & Co.
6 Fiddelaers-Jaspers, R. (2021). *Met mijn ziel onder de arm. Tussen welkom heten en afscheid nemen (Feeling lost. Between welcoming and saying goodbye).* Heeze: In de Wolken.
7 Van Wiggen, O., with van Aggelen, L. (2016). *Niemand is belangrijker dan het team. Een militaire visie op leiderschap (No one is more important than the team. A military vision of leadership).* Arnhem: White Elephant Publishing.
8 Scheffers, A. (2021). *Waarom zelfs de beste teams ontsporen... En hoe ze hier weer gezond uit kunnen komen (Why even the best teams derail... And how to come out of it healthy again).* Culemborg: Van Duuren Management.
9 Lencioni, P. (2002). *The Five Dysfunctions of a Team. A Leadership Fable.* San Francisco: Jossey-Bass.
10 Kohlrieser, G. (2006). *Hostage At The Table. How Leaders Can Overcome Conflict, Influence Others, and Raise Performance.* San Francisco: Jossey-Bass.

Chapter 10

Loss and separation

"It's been four years since I turned into the street and saw the chaos. Smoke, flashing lights, fire trucks, the street full of people. It took only a few minutes to realize that it was not just a house, it was our house. That was the day my husband, our children and I lost our home. Everything we'd built, gone forever. Four years later and we are still in the process of building a new home, filling it with new things. Everything went up in flames and, every time we buy something for the new house, I feel a sense of loss again, of something gone forever."

Ankie (59)

"We didn't see it coming. The director of the family business where I worked always believed he would be successful. He didn't ask anyone for help when business started going badly. On that Friday afternoon, when he called us all into his office, nobody thought he would be telling us he was bankrupt. He couldn't even pay us this month and had filed for bankruptcy earlier that afternoon. In total bewilderment, I stumbled out of the building. When I got home I told my wife the bad news, I no longer had a job. We both cried: for the owner who saw his family business go bust after more than 70 years. And for ourselves, wondering just how we were going to pay the rent next month."

Frank (61)

Separation is a part of life. Every welcome contains its separation. The moment you are born, one thing is absolutely certain, you will die. This is the great arc of life. Between being born and dying, there will be many goodbyes and their separations. Big and small. Planned and surprising. And with every separation, something is lost. A separation is the closure of one thing, but also the prelude to something new. *Separation* is the *preparation* for something new. For what is to follow.

In this chapter, we explore how loss is woven through our lives,[1] how it affects the way you shape your life in the present, and how the healthy weaving of loss into the present life cannot happen without conscious separation.[2]

DOI: 10.4324/9781003424178-14

Loss takes many forms

The question is not *if* there are losses in your life, but *what* the losses are. Regardless of the question a client, team or organization presents when coming for counseling, it will have been created in part by loss. The secure base coach looks at the request for help partly through the lens of loss.

When loss affects you, you must relate to it. Grief is the price you pay for the bonds you make in your life.[3] The extent to which you are affected by a specific loss depends on many factors, including:

- the type of loss
- the bond you have with who or what is lost
- if the loss was expected or unexpected
- if the separation came too soon for you
- your attachment style
- if you have secure bases around you
- your history of loss(es)
- the way you learned to deal with loss
- your culture.

Each of us deals with loss in our own unique way. The knowledge and experience you have accrued is your guide through the landscape of loss. Your past experiences provide essential guidance on how to deal with new losses.

> *Yvonne loses her job for the second time in a matter of months. She revisits the coach, Willem, who helped with her earlier job loss. She tells him she is restless and has noticed that she is withdrawing from contact. Willem starts the session with a guided meditation, to help her get in touch with the restlessness in her body; he invites her to explore what helped her to quieten the restlessness last time. A key element at that time, Yvonne explains, was a conversation with her manager. By understanding exactly why she was dismissed, she was able to come to terms with it and take this learning into her new job. A place where she wanted to take the next step in her professional growth. Fired for a second time, Yvonne needs to return to her last boss and ask for clarification about why she was dismissed again.*

Looking back, you can often see that by 'interweaving' the loss, growth can follow.[4] Interweaving a loss is about working with and living through the themes on the left side of the Transition Cycle. When you interweave a loss, you grieve what has been lost, and you integrate the loss into life. This means you are, as it were, picking up the pieces of the puzzle and putting them back together again, recognizing that the puzzle has changed and some pieces are missing and cannot be found. There is no integration without acceptance. Grieving is a consequence of the choice to accept separation, to face the reality of loss. As we will see in the next chapter, grieving opens the door to the possibility of meaning-making, a necessary step on the path to finding joy (again) in bonding with others.

At the moment of loss, of course, it is almost impossible to grasp that growth can be a consequence. Growth cannot be imposed, or forced. However, exploring previous loss experiences with clients can help them connect with their resilience now, in the present. It helps them anchor previous – even very recent – learning experiences and use them as a source and compass in a landscape where loss has removed all the signposts. You can then feel some measure of control as you rejoin the path, the process. Control that the brain needs to make the puzzle anew. Learning in and with loss makes it possible, again, to experience and grow self-confidence and trust in the world around you.

Forms of loss

When we think of loss, we often initially think of a person or people we have 'lost'. However, loss takes many forms. Each form of loss brings with it different questions.

Table 10.1 Examples of forms of loss

Forms	*Questions at hand*
People	How do I carry on without you?
Attachment	With whom, what or where do I feel safe?
Intimacy	Who or what do I feel a bond with?
Grounding	Where do I belong?
Structure	What is my role?
Health	Who am I if I can no longer do this?
Identity	Who am I?
Future	Where am I going?
Meaning	What is the point of this?
Control	What are my responsibilities?

Billy was four when his mother took him from Curaçao to make a new home in the Netherlands. He had to leave his friends behind and ended up in a country where everything seemed to be different and all he knew and had learned didn't seem to help. He struggled to adapt to his new surroundings and began to withdraw more and more.

When he was 15, his mother decided to return to Curaçao and Billy felt happy as he boarded the plane with her. As an adolescent, back on his native soil, he could feel how much he had missed his country. A few years later, at 19, he is about to return to the Netherlands to study. Before leaving, he takes the time to say goodbye to everything he loves so much there. Back in the Netherlands, he is now able to look back fondly at Curaçao, but he can also fully embrace his new, student, life, one he chose for himself.

Usually, different losses are triggered by similar events. The secure base coach explores the landscape of loss. What losses have there been? What was/ is the most painful of these losses? Was there room for parting? What secure bases were available? How do these losses affect how you manage your life now? Where is there unfinished business?

With the loss of her mother, 58-year-old Agnes became an orphan. She really hadn't expected her mother's death to have such an impact on her. She realizes that she was a daughter, but no longer is. And that the loss of her mother means she is no longer a caregiver, something that had taken up most of her last eight years. By selling her mother's house, she loses the home she grew up in, the place she could always come back to when things weren't going well.

Diffuse loss

The majority of losses are concrete: you leave or lose a loved one, a house, a job, a country. Alongside these relatively identifiable losses, there are diffuse losses. These are losses that lack clarity, perhaps are unresolved in some way. Perhaps a missing person, unwanted childlessness, a parent with dementia, becoming a refugee because of war.

In 1993 Maastricht student Tanja Groen disappears as she cycles home after a party. Her parents and friends are left with a big question mark. The police soon assume she has been the victim of a crime, but there are no concrete suspects or clues. In the years that follow, there are several moments when new information arises. But, to this day, no trace of Tanja has been found.

Diffuse loss is often accompanied by conflicting emotions, and evokes feelings of fear and loneliness. These are losses that are spoken of in a limited or non-existent way, remaining to some extent invisible to the outside world. The loss turns inward, increasing the likelihood of hidden grief and/or solidified grief (see Chapter 11).

Liselotte's mother has dementia. Slowly, her mother changes from an independent woman to one with no short-term memory. She asks the same thing over and over again, goes to the supermarket three times a day to buy a pack of coffee, and then returns – not home – but to the house where she raised Liselotte. The people living there for the last 20 years are kind and know her: they bring her back to where she lives now. Liselotte feels she has lost her mother, even though she is still alive.

Cumulative losses

In our lives, we all will encounter loss again and again. Each new loss touches on previous losses in our lives. To avoid feeling the pain of loss, we unconsciously fall into survival behavior. In the short term, this shields us from the pain, but in the long term it keeps us from fully bonding with life. If you are unable to grieve and make meaning out of the losses in your life, the losses pile up.[5]

At a young age, Neeltje loses her mother after a short illness. Together with her father and sister, they try make the best of life without her. From the outside, they look like a happy family. When Neeltje is 29, her husband is killed in a car accident. After a few weeks at home, an inner 'switch' flips and she goes back to work. She immerses herself totally, steadily climbing the career ladder. At 34, she meets Pieter, and soon they are in a relationship. When he ends the relationship after a year and a half, she needs something besides her work to fill this hole in her life and seeks refuge in training for a marathon. Eight months later, she crosses the finish line in tears. But these aren't tears of joy. She's crying because she realizes that running is actually running away *and that running away is no longer an option. Later that day, she contacts a coach and explains she needs help in facing the losses that have stacked up in her life.*

The more you faced your losses and were able to integrate them into your life, the more resilience you will have when, inevitably, you lose again.

Areas of loss

With every change, planned or unplanned, wanted or unwanted, you lose someone or something. And vice versa: every loss heralds the arrival of a change. Losses typically occur in three areas: personal, professional and organizational. In Figure 10.1, we depict these symbolically: the (relative) size of the spheres might be different for everyone. As you can imagine, losses that overlap other areas have more impact on you, because they affect you in more areas of your life.

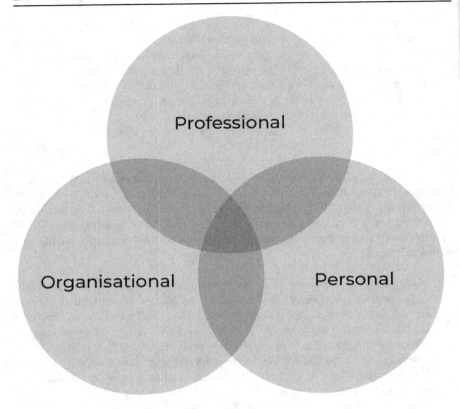

Figure 10.1 Areas where losses might occur
Source: The School for Transition and partners

Personal losses, obviously, are those that occur in your personal life: losing your health, for example, or a friendship, loved ones, your home. Professional losses are in the context of your relationship with your work: redundancy, being overlooked for promotion, your trusted manager leaving, a failed project. Loss at the organizational level affects the whole organization or a significant part of it, although the impact might again be different for each individual. Consider, for example, a name change, merger, reorganization, bankruptcy, change of direction, or the departure of a founder. It can happen that losses occur in several areas at once, or that one event causes losses in several areas.

Jan is asked to help prepare the communications around the imminent departure of the CEO who is also the founder. As the senior press officer, he has been with the company for many years and has built a warm friendship with the CEO. It saddens him to have to say goodbye to a fantastic boss, a role model from whom he was able to learn so much. In addition, they will have to shape a new friendship, in the absence of their professional connection which also meant they saw each other in the office every day.

Any change requires exploration of the losses suffered and their impacts. Even if the change is the same for everyone, the losses will be different from person to person.

Denying loss and avoiding goodbyes lead to stalled transition

Stalled transition starts when loss is not recognized or acknowledged. By denying or diminishing loss and not saying goodbye, grief solidifies and is hidden away, so to speak. Fear of the pain accompanying loss moves us away from it instead of towards it.

Stalled transition happens when loss is either not considered at all, or not considered sufficiently. Making a new beginning overrides saying goodbye to what has been lost. As a result, you don't address the loss. You take a shortcut, cutting corners so to speak. Your transition will then eventually stall, which manifests in the themes on the 'flipside' of the Transition Cycle.

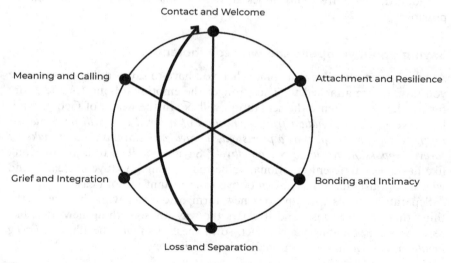

Figure 10.2 Cutting corners on the Transition Cycle leads to stalled transition

When Josefien is 16, her friendship with her best friend Tina ends due to an argument over a boyfriend. In her anger, she connects with another girl group. When her mother asks if she misses Tina, she is very clear. "No, I have ten 'Tinas' now."

Now 46, Josefien feels stuck in her job. She knows that her team members don't share important with her. When she approaches her team members, they tell her that she is closed-off and difficult. She decides she needs a coach. Together, they look back at her life-line. Josefien discovers that, when she lost Tina, at 16, she unconsciously resolved never to commit herself fully again and risk the pain of a relationship breaking up.

Pete and Kiara have been working hard on a proposal for a new client. They have high hopes for it and excitedly await the response. When the client ultimately does not choose them, they are disappointed. After a brief period of anger, they support each other with texts like "Oh well, we've got enough work without this client," "They're just one of many," "Maybe it's for the best." "Actually I didn't like them that much." Next time they are preparing a bid proposal together, they agree not to spend too much time on it.

Stalled transition continues as long as you do not acknowledge the loss and say goodbye. This can be for many years. In these cases, you might need to guide your clients in exploring the underlying losses. Go back to the places and moments of loss and pay attention to what was ignored, denied or overlooked. This frees up blocked energy and makes new movement possible.

Saying goodbye opens the way to wholeness

At some point, the time will come when you have to say goodbye to someone you love, or are attached to. The stronger the emotional bond (or the desire for it), the more intense the separation will be. In the words of George Vaillant: 'No fate, no Freudian trauma, no loss of a loved one, will be as devastating to the human spirit as a persistent, ambivalent relationship that makes it forever impossible for us to say goodbye'.[6] Saying goodbye to a job we don't like has a very different emotional value than saying goodbye to dear friend who is seriously ill. Yet saying goodbye is important in both cases.

Separation opens the way to a new form of contact with the one or the thing that has been lost, and it clears the way for something new. It is like redrafting, renegotiating the contract, so to speak, so that a healthy *continuing bond* can emerge in an emotional and symbolic sense.[7]

A beautiful funeral service celebrates the life and death of Lisa. At home, after the service, Jan is sitting at the dining table with their three children. Confronted by Lisa's empty chair, Julia is first to speak: "From now on there will be just four of us at the table, so can we choose a new seating arrangement?" Amber flinches, "Already?" Klaas looks surprised: "Can we, Dad?" Jan suggests they find out how it feels to sit in different places. The kids agree and soon they're playing 'musical chairs'. There is laughter as everyone moves from place to place. It isn't long before everyone is comfortable and they settle into their new places.

Jan and his children are facing a new reality. Wife and mother Lisa is dead and, from now on, there will be just four sitting at the family table. Accepting this new reality creates space to explore what this might mean for the future. In this case it is about the table arrangement, but when a family says goodbye, all existing patterns, agreements and habits will be challenged by, and seen through the lens of, the new reality.

Els has been ill for a long time. That she'll die sooner rather than later, is fact, but Els will not surrender to this. Until the very end, she was talking about holidays yet to be taken, as if she wasn't ill at all. After her death, Martin finds it hard to say goodbye to her things. Ten years later, her coat is still hanging in the hall and every night he lays the table for two.

Owing to the lack of a true goodbye between Els and Martin, Martin is unable to shape his life without her. His transition stalls; without Els, he is unable to reconnect with life.

When you avoid parting, you leave a lot of loose ends. Loose ends that, albeit subconsciously, clamor for attention. Giving appropriate attention to saying goodbye is about looking back, giving a permanent place in your heart to the beautiful things and really examining the painful stuff. It is important that nothing is ignored, discarded, hidden away or diminished. This allows for a full and complete parting. However painful, the truth is always better; it hurts before it heals.

Anja is furious when she is let go in the latest reorganization. When her manager suggests organizing a leaving dinner, she is absolutely against it. The manager decides to arrange a dinner anyway. He asks the team to prepare some fitting words and gifts, and he emails Anja the date and time and warmly asks her to come. She doesn't show up. In spite of this the team members say their goodbyes to Anja, honoring her and sharing how her departure feels for them. Afterwards, they agree on who will deliver the gifts and speeches to Anja.

Saying goodbye is not only for the one who leaves, but also for those who stay behind. There is loss on both sides. Therefore, it is always important to create an opportunity to say goodbye, even if the leaver is not open to it.

Separation rituals

Rituals can be really supportive when it comes to giving form and meaning to separation. Rituals help return a sense of control, which is often disrupted by loss. This 'grip' on the situation is important in, eventually, assigning meaning.[8] Rituals can be seen as symbolic acts that help mark a transition. They recognize a milestone on your life-line, reflecting the moment when, for you, everything becomes different, while the world around you seems to go on as usual. Rituals are often institutionalized, (the coronation of a new monarch for example); the practiced and defined movements providing a structure which circumscribes the emotions. They provide footing, hopefully some measure of comfort and mark important moments.[9] Smaller, but no less important, examples of separation rituals include a funeral, or a leaving dinner when you move on from your job, project or work group. The finality of marking the end opens the door to grieving, integration and the future.

> *After their divorce, Ria and Henk wanted to say a shared goodbye to their marriage. From now on, they would no longer be partners, but would still co-parent their four children. They asked two friends, a married couple, to guide them in a ritual of separation and new beginnings. Each read out a letter of thanks to the other about their marriage and expressed their wishes for the future together as parents of their children.*

Many forms of separation have no traditional ritual. However, this does leave it open for you to create your own. Rituals, whatever their origins, help. The intention with which the ritual is performed is decisive.[10] Rituals serve as homages to the past, establishing continuity between the old and the new situations.

In your day-to-day coaching, you might use symbols for the same purpose. For example, you ask people to bring something – a photo, a song, an award – that can work as a *transitional object*.[11] A transitional object, when viewed from the outside, is just a physical thing, an 'external reality'. But, for another person, it can be a symbol of a part of himself and his inner world.[12]

Rituals mainly consist of symbolic actions with symbolic objects: objects that have meaning in some way because they refer to something or someone related to (in this case) the loss. Think, for example, of an object that bears a resemblance to the person or thing being said goodbye to. This gives the object an emotional charge for the client. For example, the object could be a photograph or image of a deceased person, but it could also be a painting of a particular time period, or something that stands for a certain quality: a stone, for example, might symbolize someone's hardness. Another symbolic value might be given to something that belonged to the person who has left, was touched by them or was close to them.

According to Anselm Grün "*rituals close one door and open another.*" Only when we are able to close the door to the past, can we be fully in the present. Only then an new entrance is created. Grün adds: "*Those who never close doors are always standing in a draft.*"[13]

Rituals, besides anchoring the event in time, serve mainly to provide support from the community. David Kessler is a grief expert from the United States who worked with Elisabeth Kübler-Ross.[14] He describes how, in aboriginal villages in north Australia, on the night someone dies, everyone puts out a piece of their own furniture or some other household items. The next day, when the bereaved wake up, they see that something has changed not only for them, but for everyone in the village, because a loved one has died. The loss is made visible, the community bears witness to the fact that the loss matters.[15]

Erik was beside himself when he came to see the coach. For work reasons, during the summer holidays he had moved with the family – his wife and three children – to another city. The children were doing well at the new school, except for eight-year-old Iris. From day one, she did not want to go to school, at home there was a lot of resistance and the atmosphere was terrible. Erik told the coach he was losing his patience with her. "Did Iris say goodbye to her old class and teacher?" the coach asked. Erik looked puzzled. He and his wife hadn't been there for Iris's last school day: he had no idea. "I'd like to suggest something" says the coach. "Would you be willing to ask Iris to draw a picture for the teacher, and to make an appointment to go with her to the school? Then you, Iris and the teacher walk through the school together, saying goodbye to each other and to the school. Afterwards, of course, you go somewhere and have an ice-cream with Iris." Erik was surprised and pretty reluctant, but he agreed. Five weeks later, Erik calls the coach. "Do you believe in miracles?" he asks. "We followed your instructions exactly, and it was a heartbreaking moment. Iris handed over the drawing and they chatted together. The teacher took a cute selfie with Iris. There were tears, but it was also fun. But the most special thing is yet to come. From that moment on, she had no resistance whatsoever to going to the new school and the atmosphere at home changed as if someone had flicked a switch!"

The room where the coach holds his coaching sessions could be called a transitional space. This includes the physical space with its furnishings and decoration, and the psychic and energetic space created through music, poems, light, symbols, and ways of working. You could say that everything you use in coaching – process and language – is ritual work to foster the transition from old to new (behavior, perception, experience). So the coaching room can also be seen as a symbolic space in which you pursue change: consciously, deliberately, purposefully.

The transitional space is also a ritual space. You work with markings that act as rites of passage. You dwell on breakthroughs and new steps. You pay attention to what brings pain and doubt; you stress and celebrate new steps and successes (small and large). In this way, you and your clients mark transitions: to new insights, to new behavior, to new energy.

As clients come into your care, stay a while and leave, you can think of your coaching space as an inn where your clients find shelter. They have time and space to catch their breath and gather their strength for the rest of their journey. Emboldened, with new memories, they press on. And when they return, you look into each other's eyes and recognize that something of value happened here, something was marked.

The secure base coach at work with loss and separation

Loss and separation – Working with individuals

Aisha recently ended her marriage. She felt insecure and lonely in the relationship. She is sad about it and finds that the sadness and loneliness feel similar to previous experiences in her life. Experiences that she thought she had given meaning to. But she is stuck again. She decides to get help.

Looking along her life-line with her coach, Sietske, she talks about her chronically ill father, and how she was never really able to be close to him. Her mother was hard at work trying to take care of the family practically and financially and so had little time for her. Back then, Aisha recalls, she often felt alone and sad. Slowly, those feelings of loneliness grew and, with them, the conviction that she would have to do everything in her life on her own.

When she was 19, she met the man she would later marry, now her ex-husband. He gave her the love, attention and affection she had wanted so much from her parents. She left her parental home, married him and took care of him. After a few years, a lot changed in their marriage. He lost his job and became a very different person. From a loving and caring man to one who had no time for her and was always angry. At himself, at her, and at the world. Initially, she tried everything to be there for him, to care for him. However, he withdrew deeper and deeper into his hole. She too began to withdraw, until she could see no way out. She told him she wanted a divorce.

Looking back, Aisha realizes that leaving home and getting married so quickly was an escape. Escape from a situation in which her parents – her father due to illness, her mother due to working so hard – never established an emotional bond with her. The grief she now feels over the ending of her marriage is in reality about the loss of her parents, especially her father. She unconsciously linked her well-being and fate to his. She realizes that she did the same with her ex-husband.

And, unconsciously, this brought her into conflict at work. She realizes, in her conversation with Sietske, that there's only one thing she really wants from her manager: to be seen. Sietske works with her to understand what that means, 'being seen.' Together, they arrive at a theme that is crucial in her life. They call this theme Together and Alone. *You can lose everything in your life and feel alone as a result, but that does not automatically mean you are alone. If you want to, you can always reach out to others. Together, they look at how Aisha might do that in the future.* [16]

When clients come to you and ask you to guide them with a loss issue, chances are their story and their loss will also impact your life story. And when that happens, it's an invitation to you that you should grab with both hands. Because if you want to be a secure base for people, then you must also learn from your own experiences. Your own losses – and, for that matter, your successes – are an important resource from which you can draw. What happened to you can make you curious about your client's story. And what you learned from your experiences can help you carry the emotions your client is feeling. Again, you can only take your clients where you have been yourself.

Aisha tells Sietske about the decision to separate from her partner and the loss this meant for her. When they look together at her life-line, the bond with her parents – and especially with her father – demands attention. Aisha realizes that, early on in her life, she had to say goodbye to a bond she would have liked to build more deeply, but did not get the chance to do so due to her father's illness.

The way she dealt with that goodbye – namely, leaving the parental home as quickly as she could and in turmoil – turns out to be an important breeding ground for the way she is now shaping the separation of her relationship. She realizes that partly based on this early experience in her life, she has built up a pattern in which she has not experienced what it means to say goodbye while staying bonded. Together with Sietske, she learns to see that, as a result, she is not – or at least not sufficiently – feeling into the loss associated with the divorce. And by not taking the loss, not dwelling on it, she is now becoming stuck. It is a sign that she still has to make a connected goodbye to her parents – her father, incidentally, is no longer alive.

Sietske guides Aisha in a session where there are two empty chairs opposite Aisha. One for her mother and one for her father. First, she lets Aisha speak to her mother, the woman who gave birth to her. Aisha tells her mother what she is grateful for in their relationship. What she was able to learn from her mother and how that has made her the woman she is today. What she talks about the sweet fruits she can reap in her life from the relationship with her mother. Sietske also guides Aisha into talking about the actual moment she said goodbye – or had to say goodbye – to her parents' home. Aisha tells her mother what was on her mind at the time. What she found difficult, what she was unsure about and what she was unable to say to her mother at that time.

Aisha take a seat on her mother's chair for the first time. Aisha closes her eyes and feels what it is like to hear what Aisha said (to her) earlier from her own chair. Aisha enters into the world of her mother's thoughts and feelings. And from the heart, as mother, she shares how painful it was to see her daughter struggling with the fact that her mother was rarely at home, absent physically and emotionally. She also could see her daughter's struggle with her father's illness. The desire to be close to him and how impossible that was at the same time.

Sietske lets Aisha return to her own chair and invites her to feel into what her mother just shared. Aisha is clearly touched. Very emotionally, she starts talking about the moment she left home. How it initially felt like a liberation. Like the best choice she could make and how a burden seemed to fall from her shoulders. But that she now realizes that she did not pay enough attention to what she was leaving behind; her parents, whom she loved but who could not be there for her in the way she wanted and needed. Sietske gives Aisha all the time she needs, giving space to the feelings that are arising as she speaks.

Sietske points Aisha to her mother's chair again. Sitting there, she takes long, deep breaths. The words Aisha spoke from her own chair slowly land in her mother's body. And they touch her deeply. From her mother's heart, come these words: "I'm sorry. I would have liked to have had more attention for what was going on for you. I would have liked to have spent time together looking at the moment when you would leave home. And I wish I had been able to talk to you about the pain you felt about our relationship. But I couldn't." Again, Aisha sits down in her own chair. She lets her mother's words sink in. "What's happening?", Sietske asks her. "I see that my mother wanted to do things differently, but couldn't. And that touches me."

Sietske asks her to bring her focus onto her father's chair. The man who was chronically ill, needed care and could not be there for her for most of her childhood. Aisha's jaws tighten. "What is happening?", asks Sietske. "I am very angry." Aisha replies. As Sietske explores with Aisha what the anger is about, it becomes clear that Aisha is angry at the injustice of the situation. That whenever she was with her father, she was never allowed to feel like a child. She could never run to her father when she felt emotional about something, because she always felt she had to be there for him. And she is angry with herself. That she didn't take her space in the family. And how, as a result, she made herself the least important in almost every situation. Learned to always be there for someone else. And now she is paying the price.

"What would you like to say to your father?" asks Sietske. "That I'm angry. Angry at his illness, angry at never being in first place for him." Aisha is silent. Heavy tears roll down her cheeks. And then she says: "I missed you so much, Daddy." Sietske lets her sit in her father's place. She

closes her eyes, taking a very deep breath. "It hurts me to hear this," she says from her father's chair. He too would have wanted it, so much, to have been different.

When you can put words to the losses in your life, in the safety of a secure bases and express the stories and emotions you have created, in your head, heart and body, new space can emerge. Space in which those secure bases can encourage you to embrace new perspectives, allowing you to look more kindly and curiously at the reality you have created. The losses that have happened in your life have a lasting impact on you. But you have the power to choose whether that impact drains you or gives you energy. You decide how free you are.

Loss and separation – Working with teams

For fifteen years, Bart enjoyed working the events industry. After graduating, the boss of this company had given him the opportunity to fulfil his passion for music and festivals in a professional context. From the start, he had been given a free hand and the space to let his creativity unfold and develop. He had helped grow the company, moving up in the organization and holding various managerial positions. Partly because of his leadership, the company had gone from being a small local player to organizing some of the biggest events and festivals around the world. The company had a presence in 32 countries and was still growing.

Recently though, in fact for almost two years, Bart has been thinking about his next step. In that time, he has been developing his creativity in another area. He has started painting again and his work is being received enthusiastically. At first only by a handful of friends and acquaintances, but soon he has his first major exhibition. His particular style is bringing recognition nationally and internationally. He decides to jump in at the deep end and try to make a living from his art. It is time to say goodbye to the company and team where he literally and figuratively grew up.

Saying goodbye is emotional for everyone involved. Sometimes people are not aware of their emotions, and don't realize it's these that are deciding how they handle the situation. However, when people are aware of their emotions, during goodbyes and separations, this gives freedom to how they respond, although it might not always feel that way.

Conscious separation means giving space to the emotions that the separation evokes. It means dwelling on what is lost through the goodbye. Earlier we looked at the possible effects of not saying a conscious or real goodbye. Because emotions are not allowed to flow, there is a good chance that important things will remain unsaid. Old and new bonds are burdened by unspoken feelings, emotions, thoughts and events.

Both for those who leave and those who stay behind, it is important to mark the goodbye. In doing so, it is important not only to appreciate in a positive sense what was of value in the relationship. It is also important to 'clean' the bonds that existed and, in some cases will continue. What was painful or difficult between people is carried by them, potentially forming a barrier to really bonding with the new reality that starts unfolding the moment after parting. It can make it much harder to begin a new relationship, be it with a person, place or idea.

The owner of the company wants it to be a good leaving celebration, both for Bart and the team. He realizes that saying goodbye is important not only for Bart, but for the whole team. Earlier that year, during a leadership week, he discovered the power of rituals in a group and decides to enlist the help of a team coach to guide him and the team during a leaving ritual.

Marga is the coach. She has them make a large circle. Willem – the owner of the company – addresses the team first. He explains why it is important for him to say goodbye properly. A good goodbye not only gives Bart courage to dare, to try something different and important to him. It also helps the those left behind to play a part in Bart's departure and connect, as a group, to the new 'Life without Bart' reality. He then asks Bart to join him on the stage. He tells him how he is grateful for his enormous contribution to the company's growth and global development. He recalls old memories of when Bart, just out of university, started in the organization. Bart is visibly touched by these warm words. His eyes reflect a man who has always believed in him.

Now Marga gives the mic to Bart. He talks about the wonderful time he's had. The opportunities he was given. The creativity he could show, together with his colleagues. That he always felt he was part of something bigger than himself. And how much pleasure and strength that always gave him, how important it is. All this is making the saying of goodbye difficult, but he also feels clearly it is time to take a step forward, towards the new future that has beckoned for some time now.

Marga takes the floor. She explains that saying goodbye, and the ritual that goes with it, is a kind of door you walk through together. A door to a new reality. "Imagine," she says, "if Bart only had an hour to live – fortunately, of course, he doesn't – what would you want to say to him? What must be heard if this is the very last time you can say anything to him?"

Marga asks Willem to speak first. Willem was the only one who had time to prepare for this, but now the moment has come, it realizes it touches him more deeply than he could have imagined. He thinks back to all the lovely moments with Bart, but his attention is pulled to a painful moment when he was not there for Bart in the way he would have liked to have been. Willem wasn't really there for Bart when his mother was dying.

He'd avoided the subject with Bart about what that was like for him at the time. He can't put his finger on why he behaved that way, but it has always bothered him. Since then, he has felt it gets in the way of the relationship between him and Bart. He says this to Bart and asks him for forgiveness.

Bart is clearly touched. As are the whole group. Willem has tears running down his face. Along with all the beautiful words and memories, there was this memory. One by one, everyone says whatever they want Bart to know, given they might never see each other again. Then Bart speaks. He talks about what he is grateful for, the confidence in him and the responsibility he was given. And also about the doubt that has been ever-present since he decided to devote his creative energy to brushes, paints and canvas. He ends by saying that it is their togetherness that has made this choice possible, and that gives him the strength to take this new, big, step in his life.

By speaking out to each other, under Marga's guidance, what still needs to be said, there is not only much to dwell on, but in that dwelling a new space is opened in both Bart and all the other team members who will move on together after today. A space that is 'clean'. A space in which no one still carries anything that has remained unspoken. Meaning has been given to everything in working with Bart, allowing both Bart and the team to focus on a new future.

Exercises with your client

Exploring the life-line in the light of loss and separation

Everything that starts also ends. What we are attached to, what you have bonded with, you will lose at some point. Only when you dare to look at that loss and dare to acknowledge its impact on you, you pave the way to saying goodbye to it. Not to never look at it again, but to open the way to grief and integration. Saying goodbye properly to what you have lost is an essential part of shaping transition.

Reflection questions

- What losses have you known in your life? Which was the most painful for you? How have they shaped who you are today?
- Were you able to actually say goodbye as these losses were happening? How did you do that? What secure bases did you have or not?
- How did your parents or caregivers deal with (their) experiences of loss? What did you learn from that? How does that influence how you deal with loss?
- What risks do you avoid – personally or professionally – because you are afraid of losing something?

- How does the theme of loss play a role in your relationships, friendships and work? What exactly is its influence on your actions and those of others?
- In your eyes, are goodbyes an opportunity or a threat? How does your perspective influence your actions personally and professionally?

The Chapters of our Lives[17]

A distinction can be made between the 'event story' – the story of the loss itself – and the 'backstory', the events and the situation that preceded the loss. When rewriting the life story, reinterpreting the 'backstory', it can help to actually imagine the life story as a book with distinct chapters.

Robert Neimeyer[18]

Using the life-line, your client's life story can be divided into chapters. In this exercise, she creates a table of contents, a list of chapter titles for the book *My Life Story*. Each chapter title describes a specific period.

Reflection questions
- How are the chapters structured? Do they follow a chronological order or is there a different structure? Why did you decide to use this structure?
- How exactly did you distinguish these chapters? How did you determine where a chapter starts and ends?
- When does your story start? Is there perhaps a preface to add about where you come from, about your family of origin, your parents' relationship?
- When does the story end? How might the story continue?
- If you look at the course and development of your life story, is it gradual or are there sudden and unexpected twists? If you continue to develop in this way, where will you be in 20 years?
- Who is the author of your life story? Are there any important co-contributors who should be mentioned? Do they get some of the credit – or blame – for how your life story developed?
- In what ways might your life story be different if it were written by your father, mother or (imaginary) older self?
- For whom primarily is the book written? Which group would – or which people would – appreciate it most and who might want to adapt, rewrite or change it in some way?
- Are there deeper secrets to be unearthed in your story? Silent or hidden events not seen or heard by the reader? What price do you and your relationships possibly pay if you hold back some part your story? What would your life story look like if you included this secret part?
- What is the book's title? How would the front cover look?
- Under which genre would the book be categorized?

- What red thread can be found running through your story? Do you also recognize other threads and do they complement the red thread or not? How would your life story develop if those other threads were given more focus and weight?

Exercise
Have your client choose one chapter and go deeper into it, telling you what happens. Possible reflection questions:

- Why was this period important to you?
- What is the common thread in relation to your life story?
- What loss was hidden?
- What did you learn?

You listen attentively to your client and, at an appropriate moment, summarize the essence: "Is it true that I hear you say that ..." Ask deeper and deeper questions so that your client can discover new layers and new perspectives in their own story – especially with stories of loss. Give your client your heartfelt feedback about what touches you, about what you hear as the essence of their loss. And name what you are curious about. If desired and/or possible, explore more chapters.

Saying goodbye using the chair-switch
The chair switch can be used in numerous (loss) situations. It is one of the most powerful and also most emotional – especially when working around saying goodbye – ways of working. This exercise requires attunement and the ability of the coach to slow the process down considerably.
Before you work with the concrete situation, ask your client to tell you why he wants to do this work, with you, today. This is how you create focus.
Set two chairs facing each other. Set a chair for yourself outside of this 'system'.

- Ask him to take a seat on one of the chairs. Perhaps have him close his eyes and, for a minute or three, concentrate on his breath.
- Ask him to imagine that X is now present and is sitting on the chair opposite.
- Let him get in contact with, and feel into, his emotions.
- Ask your client (who should still have his eyes closed) to look into his heart: what still can be said? Without censorship: anger, gratitude, disappointment, lack, fear, etc.
- When he is ready and knows what he wants to say, tell him to open his eyes and say this to X, who is 'sitting' on the chair opposite.
- Guide him in such a way that he really is experiencing his emotions. Maintain your bond with him by paraphrasing and slowing him down where necessary.

- Now have him take a seat on X's chair. Eyes closed: now your client has access to X's heart. From this place, have your client say something about what he just heard.
- Now let him take his seat again in his own chair.
- Ask for a short reaction: what did he hear from X? What did he feel sitting there?
- You let the client switch places several times and work through themes around this separation: grateful memories, anger, loss, forgiveness (What do you want to forgive X for? What would you like to be forgiven for?). As coach you must follow your intuition: don't change things too quickly, but not too slowly either. Make sure that the exercise doesn't turn into a monologue. Keep the client moving back and forth. Your own attuned curiosity is a good guide. You must also be constantly alert to the fact that the client must always be talking from the 'identity' of the chair he is sitting on, and never from the other. If he strays or gets a bit confused, move him to the correct chair for what he is saying or feeling. Make sure he always speaks directly, in the first person, and that the words are addressed only to the other person.
- Ask your client, from his own chair, to imagine that this is the last time he can say anything to X. Eyes closed, heart fully open, he says what needs to be said.
- Let him sit in X's chair again. The client now has access to X's heart. If X wants, he might say something to your client.
- Now have your client say his final goodbye to X, using words and, if needed, movements and gestures. He should convey how he wants to remember the other person in the future. In this way, the language he uses increases the probability that the person to whom he is saying goodbye, becomes a secure base again, or in a different way; perhaps in a continuing bond.
- Your client takes his/her own seat again. Ask for their brief response.

Variation

You ask your client to bring a witness (friend, colleague, acquaintance, family member) who can represent the person to whom he is saying goodbye. If you use this form – which is often even more powerful – you can choose to have your client, at the end of the exercise, embrace/hug/hold the one to whom he is saying goodbye. This promotes emotional release which also has the additional effect, in the brain, of potentiating memory reconsolidation. At some point – while your client is holding the other person – ask him to speak out loud the words 'goodbye' or words with a similar meaning. Then have your client turn around and you give a name to the world to which your client is headed: *the new welcome* perhaps. Have him hold it in his mind's eye while he walks towards it. You can also do something similar during the chair switch exercise.

Comment

- The change of perspective (chair) might have to take place several times. As a coach, you have to notice this in your client: is it really complete? What is the new perspective?
- Parts of this exercise can be repeated ('must') in later sessions.

The letter in nine steps[19]

Those who encounter change on their life-line are unavoidably confronted with separation, loss and grief. We see this cyclical process of change reflected in the Transition Cycle.

When shaping (radical) change, the letter 'process' can be helpful. Your client writes a letter to something or someone to which they are, or were, attached. The letter has nine steps. Experience shows that it is an effective method *only* if the client follows all the steps from one to nine. Let your client take their time doing it. Advise them that they might experience resistance at some of the steps and at the questions that are asked. When they do encounter resistance, ask them to write about that too. Tell them to be specific, to say what needs to be said, uncensored.

The letter is not intended to be sent (if that is actually possible). However, your client will discover that reading the letter aloud to someone they trust (you), and who really listens to it, is an important step in their process.

The nine steps

1 Blame
- What are you angry about?
- How angry are you?
- Who and what do you blame?

2 Lack
- What have you lost totally (with this change)?
- What didn't you get, from the person involved or the situation?
- How did you imagine it would work out for yourself, which didn't happen that way?
- What are your disappointments?

3 Excuses
- What was your own part in it all, what did yourself do?
- What do you wish you had done (differently)?
- What do you regret, and/or feel guilty about?

4 Thanks
- What are you happy about (in retrospect)?
- What can the other person be thankful to you for?

5 Keeping/Giving back
- What positives did you take away from the other person or situation? These might include certain behaviors, attitudes, likes or dislikes, values and norms, a particular outlook.
- Which of these positives do you want to keep?
- What would you like to leave behind, what would you like to give back?

6 Reassessing convictions/beliefs
- What convictions/beliefs are no longer helpful? Think of certain *phrases* you say to yourself or that you often heard at home (e.g. "Stop complaining and get on with it" or "Asking for help is a sign of weakness.").
- How might you say each of these in a way is helpful for you?

7 Forgiveness
- What are you willing or able to forgive the other person for?
- What do you and might you forgive yourself for?

8 Moving on
- What did you learn?
- How do you want to move on with your new insights and choices?
- What goals have you set for yourself or what tasks do they bring?

9 Reconciliation
- What ritual would be appropriate for this separation, this step in your transition process?
- How do you want to mark this change?

In the next session, you can invite your client to read the letter aloud, possibly including a chair-switch exercise.

The bowl
   This exercise allows your client to share with you, without words, a recent or not so recent loss in their life. An experience they have not shared about with anyone before. A loss which brings up emotions. In the silence and vulnerability of their bond with you, this exercise gives your client space to share the loss in the safety provided by a secure base. (You will need to explain the steps of the exercise to the client before beginning).

- Connect, wordlessly, with your client.
- Have them form a bowl with their hands and imagine placing who or whatever has been lost in the bowl.
- They show the contents of their bowl to you.
- You look in the bowl and give space to whatever comes up in you.
- Intuitively follow any arising movement that concerns your client.
- Your client responds wordlessly. (They might also have no response).

Variation
Let your client make contact with a traumatic event on their life-line, where your client has been wounded.

- Connect wordlessly with your client.
- They form a bowl with their hands and imagine putting the injured part in the bowl.
- They show the contents of their bowl to you.
- You look in the bowl and give space to whatever comes up in you.
- Intuitively follow any arising movement that concerns your client.
- Your client responds wordlessly. (They might also have no response).

You then invite the client to use drawing materials to represent what he has just shown you in the bowl, the injured part.

Then look with your client at the question: How might this wound bear fruit in your life?

Exercises with the team

Exploring the team life-line in the perspective of loss and separation

Below are questions that can help you explore the themes of loss and separation with the team you are coaching. You can map out and clarify for team members the roles these themes play in a group. For example, what did people learn, in their own lives, about loss and separation, and how does that influence how they behave in the team and the organization? To what extent do these pre-existing ideas contribute to an atmosphere of learning, development and growth within the team?

Reflection questions
- What losses has this team experienced? How did you, and the team, deal with them? What did you learn and what did the team learn?
- As a team, what do you avoid for fear of losing something?
- Are there any examples of moments when you marked a goodbye or separation? How did you do that? What did it bring you as a team?
- What risks do you avoid in this group? What will no one put on the table?
- What has been the most painful loss for each of you in this team or in this organization? What made that so painful? And you are talking to your colleagues and/or your manager about it? What does the fact – that such a loss was possible here – mean to you?
- Are there times in your team's history when you have downplayed or even denied loss? What was the effect?

Loss and separation in groups

With this exercise, you get individual team members, in groups, to reflect on their experiences around loss and separation. By then having them discuss it with each other, the team gains insight into how, as a team, they might deal with these themes. *How do we, as a team, want to work with experiences of loss and how can we say goodbye to what we lose?*

Have each team member take a sheet of paper and draw several, possibly partly overlapping, circles to represent successive groups:

- The family of origin
- The larger family
- School (kindergarten, primary and secondary)
- Sports and games associations
- First time living away from home (student accommodation, shared house)
- University
- Work
- Own family

Have each team member reflect briefly on the following questions:

- What experiences around saying goodbye and not saying goodbye do you remember from being in these groups?
- What (large or small) rituals did you experience around saying goodbye?
- In each of the groups, what was the most painful experience for you around goodbyes?
- How did you say goodbye to the groups you were in? Where did you fail to do so or do insufficiently?
- What goodbye, not said, is still impacting you in the present? (Are you angry or sad about it? Do you regret it? Would you have liked to have done it differently, and so on?).

Then have the team members question each other in pairs or threes:

- How have these experiences affected you?
- How do these experiences affect how you feel and behave in this group?
- Which group, or which experience in a group, do you want to say goodbye to?
- Looking at what you needed or would have needed as a group member, what can you learn from this, that would be important for this team?
- What recent (loss) experience in this team still needs attention?

Then bring together what has been shared in the pairs and threes by asking each group the following:

- What is the essence of what you discussed?
- What did you learn about how your individual experiences in groups affect how you are and act in this group?
- What is important to you in terms of how you want to shape loss and separation in this team?
- What recent (loss) experience in this team still needs attention?

Exploring the phases of transition (William Bridges)

Change goes hand in hand with chaos – old ties are broken, new ones not yet in place. We wrote about this in Chapter 1. William Bridges' transition model shows us that shaping transition is a pendulum movement, a swinging between then and after, between separation and bonding, between grief and growth.

When a team is in transition, confronted by change, each team member goes through that transition at his own pace. It is important for teamworking and team development to be in constant dialogue with each other about where each is, what he is experiencing in that place and what he needs from his colleagues at that moment.

As a coach, you can bring extra focus to this exercise by looking at it using different themes on the Transition Cycle: Loss and Separation, Grief and Integration, Meaning and Calling, Contact and Welcome.

The team works with three positions:

- Ending, losing, releasing
- Neutral zone: the desert
- New beginning

Exploration stage: put down three floor anchors, one for each position. Ask the team members to consecutively take place at each anchor. You can also do this in sub-groups if necessary.

Reflection stage: integrating the experiences of the small groups into the overall group, the team.

During exploration, have each team member answer the following questions at each of the three places:

- What is the/your biggest challenge here?
- What feels good here?
- What is unpleasant here?
- What should you say here?
- What must you never say here?
- What are the main questions that come to mind about this place?
- What do you feel in your body when you are in this place?

- What movement wants to be made?
- What contact do you feel with the other positions?

Have team members reflect on the following questions:

- What am I learning about myself in this process?
- What am I learning about my teammates?
- What concrete action(s) would I like as a consequence of the insights gained?
- For what help will I ask my teammates?

Taking leave with and from the team

Now; ritual as exercise. Rituals are a kind of portal from an old reality to a new one. They mark a change. This marking (recognizing and accepting) gives space to everything that plays a role in the people at that moment, mentally, emotionally, physically and spiritually. This enables every participant to be a part of shaping transition. This is appropriate for individuals, groups, and teams.

This exercise will give you tools to mark a goodbye (a change) in a team. (This is just an example; many variations are possible).

Step 1. Make a large circle of chairs.

Step 2. Welcome everyone and say briefly why you are here. Also say something about the importance of saying goodbye and the power of rituals.

Step 3. You can introduce the separation ritual with music and/or by lighting a candle: but a mark of some kind is necessary.

Step 4. Explain the steps of the ritual. Everyone is invited to say something to the person saying goodbye. What each person says is a response to or interpretation of the sentence: "If this is going to be the last time I see you, I want you to know that ..."

Step 5. The leader of the team goes first, followed by each member of the team. Last to speak is the one saying goodbye.

Step 6. Check with the team if anything else needs to be said in order to end the ritual. Mark the ending clearly: music, a song, a poem, blowing out the candle.

Important points to take away

- No matter what the question a client, team or organization presents, losses suffered in the past always affect the present.
- Grieving is the price you pay for the bonds you make in your life.
- When you weave a loss, you grieve what has been lost and braid the loss into the tapestry of your life.

- There is no such thing as integration without acceptance.
- Each new loss touches on previous losses in your life.
- Loss occurs in many different forms in most areas of your life.
- Any change requires an exploration of the losses suffered and their impact then and since.
- Stalled transition starts when loss is not recognized or acknowledged, and continues as long as losses are not woven back into the fabric of one's life.
- Goodbyes are a part of our lives. Every welcome already has a goodbye in it.
- Rituals support us to shape separation(s).
- Consciously saying goodbye opens the way to grieving.

Self-reflection for the coach

- What losses have I had in my life? How do they affect my coaching?
- What did I learn from my parents/caregivers/teachers about loss? How does that help me, or not?
- In what ways have I said goodbye to losses in my life?
- What do I still have to say goodbye to? How might I benefit from doing so?
- Do I step towards or away at goodbyes? Why?
- What risks do I avoid for fear of losing something/someone?
- What does loss in groups evoke in me? How do I deal with this?
- How do I mark goodbyes with my clients and colleagues?
- How do I use rituals in my work?

Notes

1 See Chapter 7 ('From processing to interweaving'), in: Fiddelaers-Jaspers, R. (2021). *Met mijn ziel onder de arm. Tussen welkom heten en afscheid nemen (Feeling lost. Between welcoming and saying goodbye)*. Heeze: In de Wolken.
2 Van Wielink, J. and Wilhelm, L. (2015). Een nieuw begin. Over afscheid nemen in de praktijk van de professioneel begeleider (A new beginning. On saying goodbye in professional counseling practice). *Tijdschrift voor Begeleidingskunde*, 4(4): 2–13.
3 Fiddelaers-Jaspers, R. and Noten, S. (2021). *Herbergen van verlies. Thuiskomen in het Land van Rouw (Harboring loss. Coming home to the Land of Grief)*. Heeze: In de Wolken.
4 Calhoun, L. and Tedeschi, R. (1989–1990). Positive aspects of critical life problems: Recollections of grief. Omega, 20: 265–272; Calhoun, L. and Tedeschi, R. (1998). Posttraumatic growth: Future directions. In Tedeschi, R., Park, C., and Calhoun, L. (Eds), *Posttraumatic growth. Positive change in the aftermath of crisis*. Mahwah, New Jersey: Erlbaum.
5 Noten, S. (2015). *Stapeltjesverdriet. Stilstaan bij wat is. Een onderzoek naar de invloed van verlies op zeer jonge leeftijd (Stacking grief. Reflecting on what is. An investigation into the impact of loss at a very young age)*. Heeze: In de Wolken.
6 Vaillant, G. (2015). *Triumphs of Experience. The Men of the Harvard Grant Study*. Cambridge: Belknap Press.

7 Neimeyer, R., Klass, D. and Dennis, M. (2014). A Social Constructionist Account of Grief. Loss and The Narration of Meaning. *Death Studies*, 38(8): 485–498.
8 Baumeister, R. (1992). *Meanings of life*. New York: Guilford Publications.
9 Fiddelaers-Jaspers, R. (2021). *Met mijn ziel onder de arm. Tussen welkom heten en afscheid nemen (Feeling lost. Between welcoming and saying goodbye)*. Heeze: In de Wolken.
10 Norton, M. and Gino, F. (2014). Rituals Alleviate Grieving for Loved Ones, Lovers, and Lotteries. *Journal of Experimental Psychology: General*, 143(1): 266–272.
11 Winnicott, D. (1953). Transitional objects and transitional phenomena. A study of the first not–me possession. *International Journal of Psychoanalysis*, 34: 89–97.
12 Witte, H. de (1980). Over de ontwikkeling van het transitional object (On the development of the transitional object). *Tijdschrift voor Psychiatrie*, 22(5): 296–311.
13 Van Gasteren, K., Soeters, M., and Reijmerink, M. (2020). Ik bouw met woorden huizen waarin mensen zich thuisvoelen. In gesprek met Anselm Grün over leiderschap en roeping (I use words to build houses where people feel at home. In conversation with Anselm Grün on leadership and calling). *Tijdschrift voor Coaching*, 1: 50–55.
14 Kübler-Ross, E. and Kessler, D. (2014). *On Grief and Grieving. Finding the Meaning of Grief Through the Five Stages of Loss*. New York: Simon & Schuster.
15 Kessler, D. (2019). *Finding Meaning. The Sixth Stage of Grief*. New York: Scribner Book Company.
16 Van Gasteren, K., Reijmerink, M., van Wielink, J., and Wilhelm, L. (2018). Geloof je dat het ooit nog goed met me komt? De coach als bron van onvoorwaardelijke hoop door scheppende aandacht (Do you believe I'll ever be okay? The coach as a source of unconditional hope through creative attention). *Tijdschrift voor Coaching*, (3): 31–35.
17 This exercise is based on van Wielink, J., Wilhelm, L., and van Geelen-Merks, D. (2020). *Loss, Grief, and Attachment in Life Transitions. A Clinician's Guide to Secure Base Counseling*. New York: Routledge.
18 Neimeyer, R. and Thompson, B. (Ed.) (2014). *Grief and the Expressive Arts. Practices for Creative Meaning*. New York: Routledge.
19 This exercise is based on van Geelen-Merks, D. and van Wielink, J. (2015). *Met zoveel liefde heb ik van je gehouden. Woorden bij persoonlijk verlies (With so much love I have loved you. Words for personal loss)*. Antwerp: Witsand Publishers.

Chapter 11

Grief and integration

"The first weeks after Gerard left, I walked around the house numb. One question stood front and center: 'How could my husband, whom I had been happily living with for 18 years, pack his bags and leave me? What signals had I missed? Was I, in some way, not lovable? How was I supposed to move on? Was there a chance he'd realize his mistake and come back? And did I really want him to? It was so confusing.'

In retrospect, I was plunged into deep grieving and all that goes with it. But at the time all I could feel was confusion. My work was my anchor at that time; at the office everything was still the same and I was not alone. Then, months later, my manager asked me, 'Are you ready to take on a new challenge?' Then I felt: I want to move on and I can. I will pick up my life again. At that moment, I felt the energy of life again."

Marleen (45)

"From a young age, I wanted to be a plastic surgeon. I learned well, studied medicine, and specialized in my dream job. My work was my joy and my life. Whenever I was asked who I was, the first thing I would talk about was my work. At 48, I slowly started having problems with my sight. I tried to cope by taking my assistant with me everywhere. Then the day came when I stood in the operating theatre and was no longer able to use the scalpel safely or effectively. I fell to my knees and cried. This was the beginning of a long journey of anger and sadness. A journey to accepting that I am no longer a plastic surgeon."

Abdul (55)

Grieving is often called the other side of love.[1] It is the price we pay for saying goodbye to something or someone we love, to whom we are attached. But it is also the price of saying goodbye to who or what wasn't or couldn't be there for us and with whom or what we never had the bond we actually longed for. Grief opens the door to the weaving of loss back into our lives. Integrating our losses creates a new wholeness.

DOI: 10.4324/9781003424178-15

Really looking at what was lost is often accompanied by challenging emotions. Grief for example: the raw pain of no longer being bonded in the way you were bonded. And fear: not knowing how to move on now. Or guilt and shame: "If only I had ...." Not to mention those emotions we tend not to associate with grief: relief that it is finally over, or gratitude for what we did have, even if it was less than desired. Grief is as unique as the colors of your iris.

We are naturally inclined to avoid grief for shorter or longer periods of time. By not feeling the loss, by denying it, by throwing ourselves fully into something new, we might seem able to bypass grief. The reality is that, sooner or later, we need to come full circle in order to re-establish real bonds with ourselves and the world around us.[2]

In this Chapter, we explore what grieving is, how to move towards it, how to open the door to a new beginning.

Grief and integration are the gateway to healing

There is life before loss and life after loss. Grief is the onset of the feelings, sensations, thoughts and behaviors you experience as a consequence of loss. It is the visible and invisible expression of the loss you feel when you have to say goodbye to something or someone with whom you had, or wanted to have, a meaningful relationship.[3] By living in, with and through the feelings and thoughts, we gain insight into the reality that offers itself to us after the loss.

Integration means adding back into your life what you lost or have excluded. You do this by facing the loss and allowing it into your life; no longer closing yourself off to it. Integrating does not mean that you have to agree with it, but that you accept it exactly as it is. And that this loss becomes part of the new reality and helps make you who you are now. You learn to live with the new reality, even when you don't want it to be true. Marleen – in the case study at the beginning of this chapter – finally accepts that her husband chose a different path. This does not mean that she agrees with Gerard leaving, but that she chooses to relate – with the help of her manager's challenging question – to the new reality that has emerged.

Equally, you can grieve a loss that you have chosen, that you have 'created' for yourself. The divorce you felt you had to initiate, handing in your resignation at work, moving house because you want to live somewhere else. Every change, even when desired, contains loss that can come knocking at your door, just when you least expect it.

For Marieke, everything came at once when she quit her job. The competitor's offer was too good to pass up, even if she had to move house for it. There were two sides to saying goodbye to colleagues at her old employer: after many years of working together and building the business, close friendships had developed. But the fact that Marieke was moving to a competitor created problems and resentment. So the atmosphere at the leaving do was tense. And her partner did not want to move to another town with her. Faced with the choice of a long-distance relationship or no relationship, Marieke chose the latter.

She was surprised to find that, in her new home, in a new town, in a new team, for the first time in her life she felt lonely. She had never been really good at making friends, and the few friends she did have all lived some distance away. As lonely as she felt, she didn't dare to contact her former colleagues or her ex-partner. Already, during her initial three-month probationary period, she had to call in sick with fatigue: a complaint she did not understand herself. Then, when telling her story to her GP, he listened and then listed all her losses. Then the penny dropped.

Grieving is above all a learning process. By grieving, your client learns to land or re-land, as it were, in the life that stretches out before him. A life that has changed, and at the same time a life that continues. When you grieve, you return to the place where you lost something. Sometimes the client – perhaps encouraged by you – physically returns to certain places. This does not bring back what was lost, but can bring back something of the client that was left behind. A powerful question for your client can be: "What died in your heart when you lost something or someone? Often the response will include ideas like: *a piece of myself; innocence, trust,* and so on.

Everyone grieves in their own way. Both our own attachment history and the extent to which we are attached to what or who we are saying goodbye to are influential. A secure attachment provides a solid foundation for the grief process. People who are securely attached have learned 'better' to express and regulate their emotions and know they don't have to do it alone. They ask for help when they need it. People with an insecure attachment history will tend to try to do it all themselves or, on the contrary, cling completely to others. Grief invites you, as it were, to walk the fault lines of your own attachment history, repairing and healing them as you go.

Grief expresses itself in very different ways. It often evokes discomfort not only in the person who has suffered the loss, but also in those around them, and you. Especially if you don't know how to deal with another person's grief. Discomfort in dealing with another person's grief can be seen as a kind of *action inertia.* This can manifest itself in different ways. For example, by trying to avoid your own discomfort – and, in projection, that of the other person – ignoring the other person's pain by not asking about it or not being prepared to discuss it. It might also be that you find yourself looking for solutions, under the illusion that you're helping the other person move forward …

However, not everyone who is in grief – actually, hardly anyone – Is looking for comfort or solutions. Often what is sought is affirmation of their experience and recognition that it is allowed to be there, and that their dis-comfort – however it is expressed – can be present without judgment. Loss always wants its story to be heard.

The opportunity to talk about loss and the meaning of the relationship usually brings relief, because sharing is a necessary part of healing. This does not mean that talking always and at every moment in the process is neces-sary. On the contrary: there are very many ways to express grief. Yet, in the end, without language it just doesn't work.

Much of the grief that is not given space in the social environments of family, friends and colleagues, shifts to coaching and counseling. There we are then faced with a paradox. It is a great thing that more and more coa-ches – like you, the reader of this book– are developing expertise in working with loss. The downside is that 'normal' experiences, that belong in the normal societal environment are disappearing into the professional's room at an ever-increasing rate. Grief as part of life – which is quite normal – thus disappears from view. Then we risk grief being seen as not-normal or even an 'illness'. Grief, however, is an integral part of living a full life, and requires a place in society.[4] The person bearing the loss should, in turn, be allowed to feel supported by their own environment. After all, grieving is a social affair; it needs witnessing. You need a community, a tribe, in order to grieve, both personally and professionally.[5]

Clients will sometimes tell you they are afraid to go all the way into the pain or discomfort. Or they might not – yet – see the need for it. However, moving (with) your client towards grief is connected to the reason why she has come to you. It is in connecting your client's question, the goal she wants to achieve, with facing up to their grief and all the emotions that go with it, that you deliver your added value as a coach. Emotions are not a goal in them-selves, as we saw in Chapter 4. However, encapsulated within working with emotions is a beneficial learning outcome. In the encounter with your client, as coach you are the secure base, inspiring confidence that the fear of 'falling apart' can be faced and moved through. Especially if you have to walk the edge to do so. In other words, you help them to see and experience again and again, through and with grieving, that the mind's eye is no longer hostage to the painful experience evoked by the loss or separation. As a secure base you help to overcome separation anxiety – step by step.

An important new view of grief is that loss and grief do not have to be 'over'. Although a relationship changes, it also continues. Although the relationship might end physically, the bond continues. As you read in Chap-ter 2, we call this *continuing bonds*. Continuing bonds are about the lasting influence of integrating inspiring aspects of the other person into your own life and personality. In this way, so can the relationship grow alongside your continuing development. Allowing for grief is precisely what decides this.[6]

The internalization of continuing bonds is about the sustained influence of secure bases, in all their manifestations.[7] For instance, you can feel support from the continuing bond with an abandoned homeland, a previous organization or manager. This internalized support influences your ability to deal with loss, and your own ability to be a secure base for others.

Anticipatory grief

Loss does not always arrive unexpectedly. Some losses can be anticipated, especially those that are inescapable. A terminally ill family member, a parent with dementia, warning of a proposed reorganization, the latent resignation, the divorce that felt inevitable, the retirement postponed, that your children will, sooner or later, leave home, an unavoidable bankruptcy. When a future loss comes into focus, and is recognized and acknowledged, a grieving process starts. The realization that you are going to lose something or someone, is always accompanied by the feelings, physical sensations, thoughts, and behaviors of grieving. Losses present themselves in phases, so to speak. You grieve each loss as it happens, while the future losses step closer and closer.

Lisanne van Sadelhoff, journalist and 'hands-on' expert in grief, uses the term *pre-grief* for this purpose. The grief that is felt before the final goodbye. In pre-grief, feelings, thoughts and behaviors arise that are similar to those that occur during an actual separation. Pre-grief is, then, different from normal grief in that it is not yet possible to say the final goodbye. The grieving process cannot be completed.[8]

> When his mother suddenly comes to a halt in the kitchen, unable to move forward or backward, Pieter is overcome with grief. His mother, Anita, is in her mid-50s when she gets a Parkinson's diagnosis. Over the years, the trembling worsened and the list of things she can no longer do independently grows, seemingly day by day. She is now 75 and can no longer even move around independently: she is completely dependent on the people around her. Pieter realizes, as he sees her standing, trembling, in the kitchen, that the final goodbye comes ever closer.

Anticipatory grief or pre-grief does not necessarily make the grieving process easier. Although the losses have been grieved to some degree already, this does not really affect the grieving process that will come after the last goodbye.

Secondary grief

Loss never travels alone. The moment you suffer one loss, others seem to pile on top of it. When a parent dies, his or her child loses not only the parent, but also the family as it was, the parental home, expectations about things that could still be undertaken together, the hope that the parent could be present at special moments and so on. If you are laid off, there is the loss of the job, but also the possible loss of income, of colleagues, of self-confidence and so on. In the case of a sick parent, the mental or physical functions that are lost might have been farewelled at an earlier stage. However, at this later stage, these secondary losses also require a grief response.

> *"I am reminded of our first holiday with my father, my little brother and me. To the Dutch island of Ameland. We almost missed the boat because we got into a huge fight on the way, blaming each other for everything and more. But, in truth, all three of us were just very angry and unhappy because we had to go on holiday without our mother. We were together, but at the same time not complete. So I wasn't so much grieving the loss of my mother, but of this incomplete family that was the consequence. Wounded and displaced."[9]*
>
> *For Simone, her father is a true source of knowledge. If she has questions, she can always turn to him. But as he starts to suffer from dementia, she notices how what he knows is increasingly out-of-date, so to speak. She has to find other people to help her. Slowly, she says goodbye to 'wise father' and a new bond forms, in which she listens to him, sometimes correcting him, but mostly letting him be, in his new old reality.*

Hidden grief

When a loss is not (re)acknowledged, hidden grief can result: grief that is very present but neither 'seen' nor acknowledged. Perhaps you miscarried while those around you did not yet know you were pregnant, or someone is in an extramarital or secret relationship and the 'secret' partner dies. That the people around you do not or were not allowed to know about this relationship, or did not acknowledge it as meaningful, in a way denies the remaining partner the right to grief.

When the (meaning of the) relationship was not visible or overt, or when events were not (allowed to be) public, the loss remains hidden. Saying goodbye then becomes difficult, perhaps impossible. Grief expert Kenneth Doka introduced the concept of *disenfranchised grief* for this situation.[10]

Hidden or not-visible grief can refer to both tangible, but also intangible – diffuse – loss. Tangible hidden losses often involve something that cannot be shared openly or is not common, or even taboo or forbidden, in your social environment. When something has to be done secretly, it can bring give rise to shame, making it difficult to come admit to or express. For example, the death of a secret love, an unintended pregnancy, miscarriage, or abortion. But it could also be the death of a pet, losses suffered by children that go unnoticed by adults, or failed (cosmetic) surgical procedures.

Intangible losses that evoke hidden grief can trigger old losses such as the loss of childhood, ideals, dreams or confidence. Consider also – stacked or cumulative – losses that parents, of children born with disabilities, might suffer. Alongside gratitude for the child's life, there can also be great worries. In a future quite different to anticipated and hoped for, there will be many losses from events that cannot take place.

Solidified grief

If, after a loss, the grieving process has not taken place or integration of the loss has not taken place, we enter the realm of solidified grief. Without integration of the loss, no meaning can be found. Unaddressed grief stores itself in the body and often resurfaces at a later time.

The trigger is usually a new or imminent expected loss. This might walk hand in hand with a new risk that needs to be taken or an opportunity that presents itself – imagine, for example, the chance of a promotion, a job, emigrating, a holiday, a project or a new relationship. In this new moment, the original loss and associated grief, that presaged the new opportunity, are often not recognized or felt. This solidified grief can then have an amplifying effect on coping with the new loss situation. This amplification can lead to people getting stuck in a downward spiral, leading to stalled transition.[11]

> *Xavie came to Paula after losing her mother. She was overcome by emotions and could not place their origins. Losing her mother had gone in stages during her sickness. Therefore, when death occurred, Xavie was surprised and overwhelmed by the sense of helplessness she experienced. It did not feel appropriate to a situation.*
>
> *Paula invited Xavie to look back in her own history to see if there was a time when she had felt this helplessness before. She came to a time when she was 10 years old and her father died from a heart attack. She described how her mother tried to resuscitate him and how she watched, numb with fear, not knowing how to help. After her father's death, her mother fell into depression and there was no attention for Xavie's fear and grief.*

Healthy and complex grief

As a coach, you might wonder whether working with a client who is grieving is part of your job. Shouldn't they be seeing a therapist? As we stated earlier: loss is part of life. It is a process of separating that can cause intense pain. Just as you cannot remove a well-fixed plaster without some discomfort, meaningful loss is also painful. It often evokes sadness, anger, fear and despair. In their grief, your client might feel abandoned by those around them, feel lonely and exhibit searching behavior.[12] All this is normal; although your client might sometimes wonder if they are going crazy.

Recently, complex grief – in response to death – has been included in the psychiatric diagnostic manual.[13] This has advantages, such as reimbursement of treatment by health insurers, but also disadvantages. Because it suggests that grief is a disorder, whereas grief – even intense grief – is almost always a perfectly normal response. These responses cause the client suffering, and it is precisely that suffering which requires a sensitive attitude from the coach. You need to be available, present. To listen and draw out the sometimes intense emotions together with the client.

It turns out that approximately half of people who experience a loss recover well. Often with help from those closest to them. 'Expert' help can even backfire in those situations. About 40 percent have a hard time recovering and need some kind of professional help. We're not talking about intensive, process-oriented therapy here. What does help are interventions that strengthen a person's confidence in themselves, their life and future. Interventions that encourage facing up to the loss and help a person stay meaningfully engaged, says Paul Boelen, Professor of Clinical Psychology at Utrecht University and a specialist in trauma and loss.[14] In 90 percent of grievers, you can mean something to them as a coach.

Only 10 percent of losses involve complex grief.[15] These 10 percent often involve a traumatic loss such as suicide, a serious accident or murder. And even then it turns out that a complex loss does not necessarily lead to complex grief. It is not so much the event, but mainly the resilience of people – and whether or not they have experienced secure attachment – that determines whether grief becomes complex or not.

What about all those symptoms listed as the criteria of complex grief? Such as "Feeling that life has no meaning anymore." "Being unable to think of anything but the loss of your loved one." "Experiencing extreme anger or fear"[16] Belgian psychiatrist Paul Verhaeghe says: "Use common sense for a moment. These grief reactions show up in everyone who loses a loved one, especially when it happens unexpectedly. (…) Well, I propose the opposite: anyone who does not exhibit these core features of grief is seriously disturbed."[17]

Risk indicators of complex grief

Having insight into risk indicators for complex grief can help you give conscious attention to those elements when they arise in your client's life. Normalizing your client's grief reactions is especially helpful in integrating their loss. Where there might be a higher risk of additional or aggravated grief, such as accumulation or stacking, these indicators are common:

- loss coming sooner than expected
- loss under unexpected circumstances
- no social support available
- client is predominantly insecurely attached as a person
- is less resilient as a person
- meaningful but unfulfilling relationship

- *unfinished business*
- have not been able to say goodbye
- legal aftermath.

Survival by splitting-off

If the loss is (too) great, people look for a solution that makes the pain bearable. This often creates fragmentation: a splitting of your 'self' into three different kinds of parts. The *wounded* parts, which hold the painful memories, then go under lock and key behind the *survival parts* – which determine the survival strategy. The remaining *healthy* part is then allowed to control daily functioning, insofar as events are perceived as non-threatening. All parts thus have their own task and try to contribute to the goal of keeping the person afloat, despite the unbearable loss.[18] From your healthy part, you can feel the desire for wholeness and find the courage to confront your survival strategies, as they are no longer helping you to live your full potential.

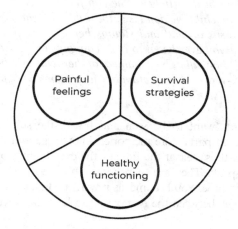

Figure 11.1 Fragmentation following loss

Certain high-impact experiences will trigger your survival parts. These parts have the job of getting you out of the painful situation as quickly as possible, by finding a way that you can manage it. In the case of major losses, the survival parts will initially dampen the experience so that it does not overwhelm you. Memories and images become blurred and feelings might temporarily withdraw. Secondary emotions might also come into play. These emotions mask the real primary feelings. Such survival behavior takes a lot of energy but makes life bearable on some level. Once there is enough security again to bear the loss, the survival parts can retreat, gently making room for the healthy part. The survival parts can manifest as follows, singly or in combinations:

- Detachment
- Avoidance
- Urge to control
- Compensatory behavior
- Making-up stories
- Downplay

The survival parts want to prevent the painful primary emotions from being seen and heard. They make sure these are put away under lock and key, where you can't feel them. Survival behavior is persistent and certain triggers will cause it to appear again and again. Different triggers can trigger different survival behaviors. And different people have different survival strategies. Survival behavior often begins in early childhood, but can also develop later in life if circumstances are difficult enough. When a person's survival behavior takes control, they are pulled back into the age where it originated.

> *Mieke is standing in the kitchen. She can feel tension building in her body as her adolescent children don't set the table, as she had asked them to. Suddenly, she turns around and stamps her feet, shouting at the boys on the sofa: "Can't you ever listen to me? You guys are always interested only in yourselves!" Immediately ashamed of her childish behavior, she sees herself as a six-year-old girl, standing in a room with parents who never had any time to listen to her.*

The wounded parts want to be seen and heard, the survival parts want the opposite. The wounded parts store memories, knowledge and facts and, crucially, the primary feelings, those felt at the time of the event. The wounded parts stand still in time, so to speak. They are snapshots. When you come into contact with them, you go back in time. You become, as it were, that child of six re-experiencing the event. The struggle between the two parts can lead to a myriad of issues.

> The father of South African Candice Mama was murdered by a death squad during apartheid. *"When I was 16, it suddenly felt like I was having a heart attack. My mother took me to the hospital, where I was kept in over-night. The next day, after many tests and examinations, the doctor gave us a chilling message: 'Your body is destroying you. If you don't change whatever it is you are doing, you will die.'* Candice Mama's stomach was full of stress-created ulcers; the heart problems turned out to be a panic attack.
> *At 18, I discovered that I had a deeper relationship with my father's killer than with my father himself."* Putting all her energy into her anger, she had immersed herself in learning all she could about her father's killer, but never into the kind of man and parent her father was. *"Holding on to traumatic experiences blocks the flow of love in our lives."*[19]

The healthy part is able to reflect on its own actions, takes responsibility for the course of life and ensures that you can function well in everyday life. You draw on this part to look at the split between the parts and see what is still asking for attention. If the wounded parts can be explored, heard and seen, by and from the healthy part, the survival parts will become less and less necessary.

Unaddressed grief leads to stalled transition

In Chapter 10, we described how stalled transition occurs when loss and separation try to move ahead to quickly. When you don't face loss and don't say goodbye, you often end up in a state where you no longer feel anything except resistance.

Resistance takes many forms, such as not accepting and going with a new situation, suspicion, sabotage behavior, forming cliques. These kinds of resistance are actually forms of not addressing the loss and not saying goodbye. To explore their resistance, you work with the client to still identify the loss and say their goodbyes. Who or what has been lost? What has not been considered? What has not been seen or heard?

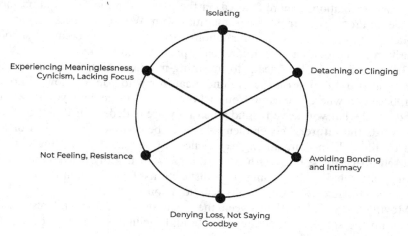

Figure 11.2 The Cycle of Stalled Transition

When Diederik joined the company, to be the team's new manager, he met with a lot of passivity. His team members made little contact with him and were unwilling to accept changes or try new things. Diederik did his best to inspire and motivate them, but he saw little improvement. When he shared his frustration with his team, he realized they were angry. Angry because he just came in and changed things that their previous manager had put in

place. Angry because he had replaced their beloved boss without explana-
tion or consultation. He discovered that his predecessor was much loved
and had been fired without notice or any apparent reason. The team was
angry and frustrated that such a thing could just happen. They had no
intention of committing to anyone new.

In some cases, unaddressed grief can lead to a situation where there is limited
or no access to the world of feelings. We already discussed the split between
the wounded parts, the survival parts, and the healthy part. When feelings
are switched off, the survival parts take over. In the short term, this strategy
helps avoid being overwhelmed by the pain the loss brings. In the long term,
however, feeling into and through the loss is necessary to live a full life.

Grieving is not a linear process

Grieving basically proceeds differently for everyone, depending on the factors we
described earlier. However, you can see grief as a pendulum or wave movement
between two orientations that are always present: loss orientation on the one
hand and restoration orientation on the other.[20] You could also see it another
way: loss orientation is more focused on the past; restoration orientation more
on the future.[21] You might see similarities with William Bridges' Transition
Model (Chapter 10). Both orientations need attention, because shaping
transition is always about connecting past, present, and future.

Grieving also looks ahead to meaning-making: discovering what the
experiences and events on the life-line mean for who you are now. Who are
you, based on where you came from, who you want to be, how you enter into
bonds, and what you leave behind when they are ended, your desire or focus
is towards the future? This challenges you to be consciously mindful of loss
and to allow the accompanying experiences to be felt. And, at times, giving
yourself space to be busy with other things, with healthy distractions. Your
brain is attracted to new things, new distractions! Grieving can be intense in
all areas: cognitive, emotional, physical, and spiritual.

Moving back and forth between the orientations of loss and restoration
opens up the space to integrate the loss and facilitates the work of making
meaning (anew) in life.

When Anne died, Pieter was only able to feel anger. He was angry at the
world, at the cancer, at the doctors, at his employer. He became obsessive about
sticking to the rituals they had developed together. He set the table for
two, made two cups of coffee in the morning and bought her favorite des-
sert every week. He sank deeper and deeper into forlorn sadness. After
three months, encouraged by his friends, he went back to the local pub for
the first time. He was surprised by the energy he got from the evening.

Shaping transition: everyday life

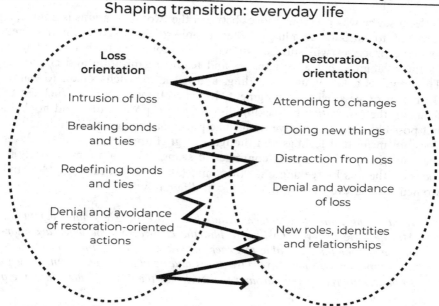

Figure 11.3 Loss and restoration orientations: a dual process
Source: Based on the Dual Process Model by Margareth Stroebe and Henk Schut (2010). The Dual Process Model of Coping with Bereavement: A Decade On. *Omega*, Vol. 61 (4). Courtesy of Sage Publications.

You could say that, in most cases shortly after a loss, the focus tends to fall on what has been lost. Pieter is still, most of the time, preoccupied with Anne. Doing 'fun' things creates an inner conflict of loyalty towards his late partner. However, these 'fun' (restoration) activities are necessary as they provide much-needed energy for grieving. As time passes, the pendulum will spend more and more time in the restoration position, but there will also be triggers that, temporarily, bring Pieter back into the loss orientation.

Janneke is on holiday and visits a small church. Standing quietly at the back, she is overcome with sadness. At home, she stopped going to church a long time ago, when as a teenager, she distanced herself from her parents when they divorced. She felt betrayed by the divorce and no longer believed in anything. Visiting the small French village church and experiencing the peace and quiet she so longed for, brings out her feelings of missing comfort. She lights two candles, one for her father and one for her mother. She has since reestablished the contact she had broken with her parents. The relationship isn't, yet, without tension, but she feels gratitude for the time they have had together.

Because the way everyone moves between the two orientations is unique, it can lead to misunderstandings. When people grieve together for a shared loss, the processes will still be different. This could be husband and wife, partners, siblings, but also manager and team, organization and employee. This requires a lot of understanding, and space for each person to follow their own process, without judgment. In general, men are more inclined to focus on the *restoration* by seeking distraction in sports, work, and hobbies, but possibly, too, in addictive things like porn, gambling, and drinking. This does not mean that feelings and thoughts of grief are not present. Whatever their activities, the pendulum continues to swing. Women are more likely to focus on the *loss* by seeking out others and talking about the loss. Men and women both grieve equally, but express it differently.[22]

As a young man of seventeen, Klaas has a dream. He wants to join the Marines. He believes it will give him the chance to experience a camaraderie that he has been able to experience at times in his life, but which he mostly misses. He will have adventures and be able to mean something to so many different people around the world. In the navy, Klaas can make a difference!

Things don't turn out as he hopes. His parents are worried about the dangers of the job. They doubt that the world of the military is the best place for him to develop his talents and fear he will be unhappy. They advise him against it and encourage him to seek his fortune closer to home: perhaps the security of a career in accountancy. He doesn't want to give up on his dream, but he feels the need wants to live up to his parents' expectations. So, he chooses a future in accountancy, just like his father.

Klaas actually quite enjoys both the studies and the student life. He meets Ellie. They go on to get married and he starts a career with an international accountancy firm. He is very successful, makes rapid strides up the ladder and is awarded a senior role at one of their branches in England.

After a few years, a feeling of boredom creeps up on him. Although he has built a successful career, something is missing. Klaas is increasingly dissatisfied. He loses pleasure in and energy for his work. Discomfort and dissatisfaction grow. On the advice of a colleague, he finds a coach. Looking back along his life-line together, the dream of joining the navy stands out. When Klaas tells his coach about the dream he gave up, he gets emotional. Talking on, he discovers that he gave up something he absolutely did not want to give up. Klaas wonders what his life would have been like if he had followed his dream. Looking back, he sees how giving up that dream fitted into a pattern of avoiding conflict, seeking harmony, complying with the expectations of others and sacrificing himself for the sake of the wishes of those around him. It is exactly this pattern that also seems to control him in his professional life.

With his coach, he reflects on his lost dream. He decides to attend a training course that will give him the chance to experience something of what life as a marine might have meant to him. Prior to that training, Klaas talks to Dennis, an ex-Marine who spent more than 20 years in the navy working around the world doing what Klaas had wanted to do. He has actually lived Klaas' dream. Dennis talks about what it gave him and what it cost him and how, over the years, he built up a kind of armor. It was needed, to protect his self and to do the dangerous work expected of him. However, it also relegated emotions to the background and closed off his heart more and more as the years passed. The armor meant that nothing could penetrate inside, but what lived inside him could not get out either. As a result, Dennis could not be the partner, the father or the friend he wanted to be. A price he was no longer willing to pay.

Klaas is touched by Dennis and the honesty in his story. He realizes that what happened to Dennis could also have happened to him. He wonders if he would have become a man with a closed heart, emotionally unreachable to himself and others. This shines a different light on the lost dreamt. He realizes that camaraderie, adventure and being meaningful to others remain very important to him. His doubts about his current career path challenge him to think about to bring these more into his life. The lost dream and the new meaning it now has, are a great inspiration.

By having a conversation with Dennis prior to the training, the training is no longer a kind of compensation for the lost dream, but rather a way to reframe a felt desire. And in that reconnection, Klaas realizes that what he values can be experienced in a different way and in a different place. By looking at both the loss and the future, Klaas is able to integrate the lost dream into his life.

Forgiveness

To make integration possible, you often have to forgive. This is one of the most difficult areas when dealing with loss and grief. Forgiving could be seen as the ultimate step in integrating your loss. Forgiveness is a step by which, in full recognition of the hurt, you give up hoping for a different past.[23]

Forgiveness starts with the conscious choice to stop being held hostage by your past or by another person. This choice starts the process, the path of forgiveness.[24] You walk this path step by step, a bit at a time. It is a matter of continual practice, picking up an aspect to look at again and again. With the encouragement of your secure bases, you can take these steps. However, walking the path of forgiveness cannot be enforced or imposed, even by yourself. It only works as a choice of free will.

The most-frequent misunderstanding about forgiveness is that you do it for someone else, or that it allows the other person to get off 'free'. However, forgiveness is something you do entirely for yourself. The other person need never know about it at all. For reconciliation you do need the other. Reconciliation is about restoring the mutual relationship with the other person in the present.[25]

Forgiveness is also taking the final step from victim (position) to liberation. Forgiveness is a gift to yourself, to speak with Edith Eva Eger[26]. It is a gift on soul level, and it is rather good for your brain. When you learn to forgive, you develop greater control over your emotions. Forgiveness changes your brain.[27] This was also the step Candice Mama was able to take when, after her encounter with her father's killer, she felt that forgiveness was the greatest gift she could give, especially to herself. The hatred she felt was making her sick. Forgiving, allowed the process of healing to start. A continuous journey that triggers old pain while makes new futures and healing possible. Her message is clear: invest in healing your own wounds. You are the protagonist in your own book, the star in your own movie. Invest in yourself. According to her, self-love is the most powerful gift you can give to yourself – and only you can give it. Self-love is very important; it is a process and takes constant practice.[28]

By choosing the path of forgiveness, you can prevent, what Kübler-Ross calls, "unfinished business."[29] Forgiving focusses your attention on potentially unfinished business, which otherwise often simmers on outside of consciousness. Perhaps you still have something to clear up with someone in your family, face guilt or shame in yourself or discuss the pain someone caused you.

The secure base coach at work with grief and integration

Grief and integration – working with individuals

Thomas can still hardly grasp it. Suddenly his fiancé, Eelke, broke off their relationship. He had completely visualized how they would marry; Eelke getting pregnant; starting a family together. They would grow old together. But Eelke made a different, her own, choice. Out of nowhere, Eelke was standing at the door with her suitcase. She walked away, leaving him sad, confused and bewildered. In the days and weeks that followed, he felt lost. The support Thomas received from friends and family was welcome, but did not help with the pain of his loss. His (ex)fiancée did not respond to his calls and messages. She seemed to have disappeared into thin air. It confused him. Of course, she could choose to break off the engagement, but it would help him so much if she could at least tell him why. As the months passed, he realized that he was not going to get even an answer, let alone an explanation. That frustrated him the most. Thomas was heartbroken: this was a great loss for him. He felt it in his body and in his heart, but his head kept trying to understand why. Alone, it exhausted him, made him angry, scared and sad. He decided to seek help. To find someone to talk to who could look with him at the impact of the loss and help him find ways to move on with it.

When someone like Thomas, someone severely impacted by a loss experience seeks help from you as a coach, he is appealing to you to listen deeply, without judgment, to his experience. Confusion, helplessness, and not knowing what to do or where to start are often where the first session(s) begins. Depending on a person's attachment history, they will find it sometimes easier, sometimes harder just to take the first step towards you. Someone who is, in the main, securely attached usually finds it easier to ask for and to accept help. Someone hampered by an insecure attachment style will either try to solve it themselves first and find a way through the loss, or they will cling to you as a companion and sometimes even expect you to take away the pain. In this sense, grieving is an attachment reaction: a person grieves for something or someone to whom they are still attached and with whom they felt a bond.

When Thomas asks coach Roel to guide him, what strikes Roel most is that Thomas wants to move on with his life, but has no idea how to. Thomas is willing to do whatever it takes to deal with the reality of life without Eelke. It is very clear that Thomas wants to move on, as soon as possible, from the pain, the discomfort and the not knowing why his fiancée broke off the relationship. Roel helps Thomas to see that the only way to move on is not to try to avoid the pain, but to move towards it, for as long as it is a part of his life.

To start with, Roel gets Thomas to recount the details of the day Eelke broke off the engagement. How had they woken up together that day? What did Thomas do that day? And Eelke? They go through the day hour by hour, sometimes minute by minute – until they come to the evening, when Eelke is standing at the door with her suitcase packed? What did she say? What was Thomas feeling? What was he thinking? What did he say? What did he do?

Thomas opens his heart to Roel, holding nothing back. He becomes increasingly emotional. Finally, all he can do is cry. He sits with his head bowed in his hands, staring at the ground. Roel sits opposite Thomas and asks him to look at him. When Thomas does, he immediately wants to look away again. "Just keep looking," Roel says gently. As Thomas does so, he slowly becomes calmer. He discovers something important: grieving is possible, but you don't have to do it alone. And that is exactly what Roel does, he walks the path with Thomas. He supports him to face his loss and the maelstrom of feelings and emotions it evokes in him. It is the start of a special journey that Thomas takes with Roel as his guide.

When you help a client to grieve, you will have to be prepared to move them towards the pain. It is essential that you help your client face not only the loss, but also the changes it inevitably brings. At some point, sooner or later, people have to address their grief. If they refuse it, and cut that corner in the Transition Cycle, at some point in their future the transition will stall. And that manifests itself in feelings like the ones we above.

As a coach, you can help people take ownership of their grief. Not only by looking at their emotions with them, but also by exploring the thoughts that take hold of them when the pain of loss is present. Also by being able to explain how the pain affects the body and can lead to physical discomfort, even illness. Making them aware of how they look at the world around them, the new world, the new reality unfolding as that older, previous reality slowly disappears. And finally also by helping the client find answers to the eternal question: "Who am I, now that I have experienced this? How does this loss, this experience, this event, change my identity?"

The secure base coach is a gatekeeper. He shows the way to the door and helps open it into the new present. Not to close it behind him, but to show the client that he can step through that door whenever he wants. It is a permanent gateway to what was, to what is and to what will be. A door that holds a promise. The promise that if you are willing to stay, time and again, with loss and the emotions it evokes, you can land in life again. That you can land in life in the new reality. Where a new, perhaps previously unimagined, future appears possible. One that exists without denying or pushing away the past.

Grieving is hard work. That's why your clients need you. A resource who supports, encourages and challenges. They need you to help them make their future more important than their past and to do whatever is necessary to achieve it.[30]

Grief and integration – Working with teams

The R&D team can't get used to the fact that, since the beginning of this year, they have been expected to work with the research department of the company that bought 'their' company, late last year. It wasn't doing well and this much larger foreign player took it over. The team members find that not only do their new colleagues have a totally different research vision and approach to work, but there are also cultural differences that, so far, make true collaboration difficult. It is leading to dissatisfaction among some colleagues and to a tense atmosphere in the (now) new team.

The manager of the team speaks sternly to everyone in a team meeting. He tells them that he expects everyone to act professionally and simply do what is necessary to make the new situation a success. After all, it was thanks to this takeover that everyone has a job at all. They all should be more grateful.

After this meeting, things rapidly go downhill. Cooperation hits rock bottom and the expected results do not materialize. The management intervenes and decides to bring in a specialist team coach.

The acquisition and the newly formed research and development team were clearly big changes for many employees. Instead of considering together what this meant for these people, the manager simply piled on the pressure and focus mainly on the future and achieving the, demanding that they achieve the targets defined in the new plans. So, precisely because he focused on making the change successful, he – and also his team – lost sight of the fact that transition is a process. The mental, emotional, and physical consequences of the change received no attention.

It was exactly about those consequences that Valerie, the team's coach, began with when she spoke with the manager and his team. Because it was not just one group of employees in the team who had to deal with change, but two groups. The people from the old company and the people from the new company were forced to work together and deliver results in a new organization. The stern, and superficial, direction of the team manager failed to address issues crucial to successful change. Even though he did so unknowingly, the result was still the same: resistance, resentment and lack of focus prevailed.

Valerie was now allowed to guide this team in shaping the transition needed to reach the level of cooperation that would achieve the desired results. She was tasked with turning this malfunctioning team into a one of excellence. She set to work and, in preparation for the first two-day session, asked each employee to write down or represent, in a form of their choosing, what had been lost personally during the takeover and what their hopes were for the future.

After everybody has checked in at the first session, each member takes their turn to show what they have written down or created. For many people in the group this is quite challenging. However, Valerie skillfully builds up their confidence through perceptive, encouraging and challenging question, Once the first one or two have bitten the bullet, saying what the change means to them, everyone is engaged and visibly curious to see and hear each other's stories. This curiosity leads them to ask questions of other team members. Towards the end of day one, the questions, combined with the shared stories and images, begin to establish bonds between all the participants. These bonds make it possible for Valerie to dive deeper and deeper into the emotions, thoughts and dreams of the team. Together with the team – and on an individual journey with the team manager – she builds a new future, one story at a time.

In team coaching, the goal-oriented energy of employees and leaders is a major obstacle to giving appropriate, and much-needed, consideration to the themes on the left side of the Transition Cycle. If you are coaching a team in transition, it can be hugely challenging to slow everything down to take the time and space processes of grief, integration, meaning-making, and calling require. Yet these very themes are essential in restoring bonding, trust and safety. As a result, healthy collaboration allows new risks to be taken that enable sustainable success.

As a team coach, you can rely on the fact that in team contexts, every person involved will fundamentally repeat their original attachment style, especially when the pressure is on. Exploring employees' attachment styles or movements is key to successful team coaching. When employees gain insight into what they learned, mostly as children, about caring and daring and how that affects their identity and their actions, individually and in groups, then they become able to talk about it (In this case with their colleagues). Understanding of, and compassion for, each other develops, enhancing bonding, cooperation, and trust. When change happens, there will be losses and gains for individuals and teams. When people experience true bonding with each other, it empowers them to dare to look at what has been lost, in the change, as individuals and as a group. Bringing light to this process together can open the gate to a new shared future.

And those who, for whatever reason, cannot or will not commit to that new future, might find greater satisfaction and fulfilment elsewhere. You can be very clear about that as a (team)coach and also as a (team)leader. Because, if you are going to be in a team, you want it to allow, not just you, but everyone, to be their best.

Exercises with your client

Exploring the life-line from the perspective of grief and integration

Shaping transition means being prepared to connect your past, present, and future. Grieving is looking at what you have lost and at the emotions, physical reactions, thoughts and questions this brings up. The client, then, together with her secure bases, can determine how to weave the loss into her life, in order that a new reality can emerge, one that recognizes and includes the old one. In fact, when the old reality embraces the loss, it might well form a new secure base for your client. A new source of inspiration.

Reflection questions

- What is the most important thing you learned about yourself at times when you were experiencing loss in your life?
- What is your first inclination when faced with loss?

- What secure bases can you call on to help you move towards the pain of loss? Are you making sufficient use of these resources?
- What losses in your life have you not (yet) grieved? Why not? What would it bring you if you did?
- Which facets of grief – emotions, physical reactions, thoughts, movements – do you pay more or less attention to? How does this effect you and those around you?
- How does grief affect the bond you have with your partner, your children, your family, your friends, your colleagues, and others?

Tension release (bodywork)

This exercise helps your client release the tension accumulated in the body through loss. Start by waking up the body by playing intense music that calls for movement, encouraging your client to let go of any concern about 'looking nice'. So you need powerful music that engages the body into full flow. Join in so that your client feels supported and encouraged.

(Music suggestion: *Watusi Warrior Drums* (live) | Slagerij Van Kampen)

After this, have your client sit on a mat and put on some music that helps your client sink back into their body. Help your client focus on their breath.

(Music suggestion: *Returning* | Jennifer Berezan)

Your client should now be lying on the mat with the soles of his feet on the floor, knees bent. Play new music.

(Music suggestion: Enigma album MCMXC a D)

As coach, you are present with your client as (one of) their secure bases. You do nothing, you are just totally present. Let your client close his eyes and feel into his body. Then encourage him to let what is in the body emerge, give it air, breathe it out. Ask your client to allow the natural movement of contraction and expansion, inhale and exhale, taking gradually deeper and deeper breaths. Ask your client to make the breath longer and connect the inhale with the exhale (this is to release something of control) so that the breathing becomes a circle without start or end. Repeat this a few times, matching the rhythm of your own breathing with your client.

Let your client give sound to what is there. Whatever kind of sound, it doesn't need to be words. Ask him to raise his hips a little and drop back to the ground; repeat this a few times. Let him again give sound to what is there: a *yes* or a *no* or a *here I am*. Give support with your presence and your voice. Make eye contact with your client if you feel it is necessary. Always let your client give sound to what is there. Be present with whatever emotions arise in either of you.

When the moment seems right, gently invite your client to bring their breath back to its usual rhythm, separating inhalation and exhalation. Stay present as he slowly returns to the now. Take plenty of time and let the client lie still for a while.

When the music ends, slowly restore full contact, and complete the exercise.

Exploration of the Dual Process Model

This exercise allows your client, under your guidance, to reflect on the loss orientation on the one hand and the restoration orientation on the other. By exploring together what happens in both orientations, new perspective can emerge about what can be discovered and learned in both places and what is needed mentally, emotionally, physically, and spiritually to keep moving back and forth between them.

- Have your client tell you briefly about a loss experience in his life.
- Put down two floor anchors, one for loss and one for restoration.
- Ask your client to stand on the loss anchor and associate out loud what comes through him.
- Do the same for the restoration anchor.
- Name and paraphrase what you see happening in body, energy, voice, posture.
- Let your client return to their own (neutral) position: what are they learning about themselves and what does this change in how they view the loss?

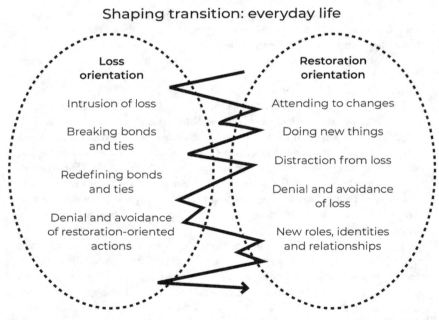

Shaping transition: everyday life

Loss orientation
- Intrusion of loss
- Breaking bonds and ties
- Redefining bonds and ties
- Denial and avoidance of restoration-oriented actions

Restoration orientation
- Attending to changes
- Doing new things
- Distraction from loss
- Denial and avoidance of loss
- New roles, identities and relationships

Figure 11.4 Based on the Dual Process Model by Margareth Stroebe and Henk Schut (2010)
Source: The Dual Process Model of Coping with Bereavement: A Decade On. Omega, Vol. 61(4). Courtesy of Sage Publications.

Stalling and streaming

With this exercise, you are helping your client to reflect on a specific loss and to experience – physically, emotionally, mentally, and spiritually – what happens when a secure base touches your heart during that process. You help your client to breathe through the loss with an open heart. Everything that rises will naturally flow away again. It is an exercise that helps the client to bear their loss. Agree with your client that they are okay with you placing your hands on them, around their breast area, during the exercise, especially if the coach is male and the client female.

- Have your client sit on a mat on the floor.
- Tell her to close her eyes.
- Ask her to think back to a loss.
- Be attentively present and pay attention to your client's breathing.
- After some time, while telling what you are going to do, place your hand on your client's heart area.
- Invite your client to feel what is happening. No words, only the experience counts.
- Now place your other hand on your client's abdominal area.
- Alternate the pressure of each hand to the rhythm of your client's breathing. Again, invite your client to feel what happens.
- Round off the exercise. Ask what this was like for your client and what (new) perspectives this experience gives her around the loss.

This exercise is very likely to bring forth strong emotions; stay completely present and make sure your client keeps breathing. By using a soft – and also somewhat lower – voice, you can, so to speak, accompany the client on their journey through their body.

Travel report[31]

With this exercise, your client maps out how they are experiencing their unplanned, unexpected, and perhaps unwanted, journey through grief and integration.

Have your client write a *trip report*. How does he look back on what was lost? Where does he stand now? And how does he envisage the future? What sources of inspiration did he encounter on his journey? How did they help him? What was missing on his journey? What will it take for the future to be more important than the past? How can he get to a situation where he can say, "I am hurting for what I lost, but I am not the pain. I am able to dream again." And then, what is his dream? What does it look like?

Ask your client to also share the report with at least two (trusted) others before the next session.

In the next session: have your client read their *trip report* to you. Ask him about his experiences.

Grieving through making a loss casket[32]

This exercise is based on the work of Riet Fiddelaers-Jaspers and also Robert Neimeyer. Ask your client to make a casket for the next session, into which he places objects associated with the loss. Decorating or adorning the inside and/or outside of the casket will make it more personal and increase its emotional weight.

The client can open and close the box whenever he wants. He learns that looking at the loss, making time and space for it, can be followed by a phase in which the loss can be put away (temporarily).

In the session you can talk to your client about the box and why it looks the way it does. You can ask about the contents. What's in it, and why? What do these objects mean to him? You can ask him what happens to him as he is opening the box and as he is closing it. What does opening and closing mean to your client? What does he feel just looking at the box in its open or closed state?

Grieving and integrating: learning from loss (memory reconsolidation)

In this exercise, you guide the client back to the moment when he realized that the loss he was experiencing was irreversible. You have him recount in detail what the situation was and what he experienced. Then, by having him connect this relived experience to the present, you widen and deepen his understanding of what he can learn from the loss he experienced.

- Ask your client to close his eyes and become aware of how it is in his body at this moment.
- Have your client go back to an experience on the life-line where there was a loss.
- "Go inside to the moment when you realized this loss was irreversible."
- Check if your client has arrived at that inner place.
- Let him speak about that moment. Where is he? What can he see? What does he feel and think?
- Paraphrase the client, focusing on the pain and emotion, you feel, hear and see in your client.
- Be curious; "What is the most painful thing for you in this situation?"
- At some point, check whether your client feels he has told everything.
- Invite him to close his eyes again and to imagine that the life-line is a slide. Ask him to slide back along the life-line to a previous moment where he had a similar loss experience.
- Ask your client to open his eyes when he arrives there.
- "Would you like to tell me where you are and what is happening 'there' for you?"
- If necessary, you let him close his eyes again and slide further back to a similar earlier experience. He travels back in search of a greater truth. You paraphrase and ask searching and daring questions.

- If you have the impression that your client has been fully in this memory, help him connect the relived memory to the present by asking the following questions (Client now has eyes open and is fully *here*):
- How do you recognize your earlier experiences now, in the present?
- How do themes belonging to this loss play a role now?
- What are you discovering now, having just told me about your memories and your losses?
- What does this give you in the present?

Exercises with the team

Exploring the team life-line in the light of grief and integration

As in people's individual lives, grief and integration also play a major role in the context of teams, departments and organizations. How prepared a group, a team, is to look at loss and at what those losses mean for working together, greatly influences the extent to which the team can excel. To excel as a team and shape transition, it is essential to consciously reflect together on what has been lost, in order to achieve sustainable results together.

Below are questions that can help you explore, with the team you are coaching, the themes of grief and integration. You can map out and clarify for team members the way these themes affect group dynamics and bonding. How have people learned to grieve in their own lives? How do they weave their losses into their lives? How do they discover a new perspective on the new reality that emerges after a loss and the changes that accompany it?

Reflection questions
- What have the members of this team learned about grief?
- How do team members support others in their grieving?
- How does this team organize support for grieving members? What secure bases does the team have?
- How does this team transition between loss and restoration? How does this team make space for the dynamics of both processes?
- What is the most painful thing that ever happened in this team? How has this affected working together?
- What dialogue(s) should this team engage in, in order to learn from the losses the team has suffered?
- What is the most important thing this team learned from those losses?
- What is the best example of a loss that is not only woven into the team's current reality, but from which team members have, in some ways, learned the most?

Experiential exploration of the Dual Process Model

Teams facing loss – and thus change – will have to shape the unavoidable transition together. In doing so, the team (members) will constantly be tossed back and forth between moments and experiences from the past on the one hand and moments and experiences occurring in the present and future on the other. As the team coach, you help the team to dialogue with each other about what the team members encounter in themselves and each other in the two different orientations (looking to the past/to the future).

- Put two place anchors on the ground: loss/past and restoration/future.
- Set some chairs away from the anchors in a neutral space.
- Discuss with the team what loss or change in the team they want to explore.
- Have team members take a seat at the loss anchor. Ask the people what they experience at that place. What do they feel? What thoughts arise? What emotions? What need does each person have? This is not yet the time to make people react to each other; you're simply gaining information and getting them used to speaking out.

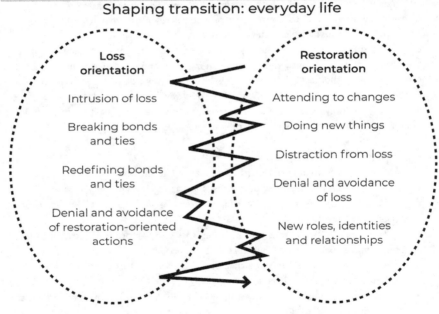

Shaping transition: everyday life

Loss orientation

Intrusion of loss

Breaking bonds and ties

Redefining bonds and ties

Denial and avoidance of restoration-oriented actions

Restoration orientation

Attending to changes

Doing new things

Distraction from loss

Denial and avoidance of loss

New roles, identities and relationships

Figure 11.5 Based on the Dual Process Model by Margareth Stroebe and Henk Schut (2010)

Source: The Dual Process Model of Coping with Bereavement: A Decade On. *Omega*, Vol. 61(4). Courtesy of Sage Publications.

- Now have team members take a seat at the restoration anchor. Ask the same questions.
- Have team members sit in the neutral place. Have each individual briefly reflect on what they discovered about this loss or change in the team.
- Now, after having explained the two orientations, let each person choose one of the two orientations, based on personal preference, and sit there. Ask: What is it like in that place? Why did you choose it? Ask colleagues to say something about their colleague's choice.
  - Let people tell what they have learned about this loss or change in the team:

  - "At this loss or change, I tend to ..."
  - "What I need in this situation is ..."
  - "What I have to offer to my colleagues in this situation is ..."
  - "My desire for us as a team is ..."

Imagining the past, present, and future

With this exercise, you enable the team to connect past, present, and future by visualizing losses, linking them to the present and asking what dream this brings for the future. You can use this exercise both during a team intervention and as preparation for a one day or multi-day training.

- Ask team members to describe, in a story or letter, the most impactful loss (or series of losses).
- Get them to focus on the event(s) themselves and the impact on them and the team.
- Have them reflect on what they learned from the loss or from all the losses.
- Have them reflect on how this loss or these losses have a place in the current, new reality in which the team functions.
- Let them speak out about their dreams with regard to the team and their own place/role in it.

Alternatively, have team members create a visual representation instead of a letter, as long as the representation (drawing, collage, painting, etc.) reveals their thoughts about the points raised.

Important points to take away

- Grief and integration are the gateway to healing.
- Grief is often called the flipside of love, but you can just as easily grieve a relationship with something or someone with whom you wanted, but never had, a love experience.
- Grief is the set of feelings, thoughts, and behaviors you experience as a result of loss.
- Grieving is learning to land in life again.
- Grief is not a linear process, but one that constantly moves back and forth between loss and restoration.
- If the loss is too great, splitting-off can occur: you can get seem to be doing well in the short term, but in the longer term you pay the price for losses that have not been looked at. You are not living, but surviving.
- The interweaving of a loss into a new reality and the grieving that goes with it is called integration.
- Grief that is not looked at and losses that are not integrated lead to resistance or a state where there is no more feeling.

Self-reflection for the coach

- In what ways do I grieve losses in my life?
- What movements have I learned to make between loss and restoration?
- What is the most important thing I have learned about loss in my life?
- To what extent do I tend to cut corners? How does that manifest in my work directly with clients?
- How does grief arise and affect my coaching?
- What rituals do I use to help me facilitate grief?
- From whom do I want to ask forgiveness and to whom should I give it? What could that bring me?

Notes

1 Hendriks, C. (2013). Rouw is de achterkant van liefde. Over Jakob van Wielink, verliesdeskundige en verliesbegeleider (Grief is the other side of love. About Jakob van Wielink, loss expert and loss coach). *Geloven onderweg*, 1.
2 See, among others, van Wielink, J. and Wilhelm, L. 'The Transition Circle' and Fiddelaers-Jaspers, R. 'The Gate of My Heart' in: Neimeyer, R. (Ed.) (2022). *New Techniques of Grief Therapy. Bereavement and Beyond*. New York: Routledge; Maes, J. and Modderman, H. (Ed.) (2014). *Handboek rouw, rouwbegeleiding, rouwtherapie. Tussen presentie en interventie (Handbook of grief, grief counseling, grief therapy. Between presence and intervention)*. Antwerp: Witsand.
3 Van Wielink, J., Fiddelaers-Jaspers, R., and Wilhelm, L. (2023). *The Language of Transition in Leadership. Your Calling as a Leader in a World of Change*. New York: Routledge.
4 Verhaeghe, P. (2022). *Intieme vreemden (Intimate strangers)*. Amsterdam: Lemniscaat.

5 Braun, D. and Kramer, J. (2018). *The Corporate Tribe. Organizational lessons from anthropology.* New York: Routledge.

6 Russac, R., Steighner, N., and Canto, A. (2002). Grief work versus continuing bonds. A call for paradigm integration or replacement? *Death Studies,* 26(6): 463–478.

7 Kosminsky, P. and Jordan, J. (2016). *Attachment-Informed Grief Therapy. The Clinician's Guide to Foundations and Applications.* New York: Routledge.

8 Van Sadelhoff, L. (2020). *Je bent jong en je rouwt wat (You are young and you grieve some).* Amsterdam: Das Mag.

9 Van Sadelhoff, L. (2020). Ik verloor niet alleen mijn moeder, maar ook onze familie zoals die was (I lost not only my mother, but our family as it was). *De Correspondent.* Accessed January 31, 2022, at https://decorrespondent.nl/11464/ ik–verloor–niet–alleen–mijn–moeder–maar–ook–onze–familie–zoals–die–was.

10 Doka, K. (1989). *Disenfranchised Grief. Recognising Hidden Sorrow.* Lanham: Lexington Books; Doka, K. (2002). *Disenfranchised Grief. New Directions, Challenges, and Strategies for Practice.* Champaign: Research Press Inc.

11 Van Wielink, J., Wilhelm, L., and van Geelen-Merks, D. (2020). *Loss, Grief, and Attachment in Life Transitions. A Clinician's Guide to Secure Base Counseling.* New York: Routledge.

12 O'Connor, M. (2022). *The Grieving Brain. The Surprising Science of How We Learn from Love and Loss.* New York: HarperOne.

13 Complex grief is listed as prolonged grief disorder in the American Psychiatric Association's Diagnostic and Statistical Manual of Mental Disorders (DSM5).

14 Boelen, P. (2020). Persisterende complexe rouwstoornis (Persistent complex grief disorder). *Impact Magazine,* (1): 4–7.

15 Keijser, J. de, Boelen, P. and Smid, G. (Ed.) (2018). *Handboek traumatische rouw. Diagnostiek en behandeling (Handbook of traumatic grief. Diagnostics and treatment).* Amsterdam: Boom.

16 Retrieved from https://rouwbehandeling.nl/rouwbehandeling/#complex, accessed April 22, 2022.

17 Vankersschaever, S. (2022). Help je rouwenden met een label (Do you help mourners with a label)? *De Standaard,* March 25.

18 Fiddelaers-Jaspers, R. and Noten, S. (2021). *Herbergen van verlies. Thuiskomen in het Land van Rouw (Harboring loss. Coming home to the Land of Grief).* Heeze: In de Wolken.

19 Van Gasteren, K., Reijmerink, M., and van Wielink, J. (2021). Je kunt je leven helen. In gesprek met Candice Mama over zelfliefde, vergeving en verzoening (You can heal your life. In conversation with Candice Mama on self–love, forgiveness and reconciliation). *Tijdschrift voor Coaching,* (2): 12–16.

20 Stroebe, M. and Schut, H. (1999). The Dual Process Model of Coping with Bereavement. Rationale and Description. *Death Studies,* 23: 197–224; Stroebe, M. and Schut, H. (2010). The Dual Process Model of Coping with Bereavement. A Decade On. *Omega,* 61(4): 273–289.

21 Gilbert, K. and Macpherson, C. (2022). Contemporary Grief Theories, in Servaty-Seib, H. and Stanton Chapple, H. (Ed.). *Handbook of Thanatology. The essential body of knowledge for the study of death, dying, and bereavement.* Association for Death Education and Counseling.

22 Fiddelaers-Jaspers, R. and Noten, S. (2021). *Herbergen van verlies. Thuiskomen in het Land van Rouw (Harboring loss. Coming home to the Land of Grief).* Heeze: In de Wolken.

23 Glaudemans, W. (2013). *Boek van vergeving. Een gids van wond naar wonder (Book of forgiveness. A guide from wound to wonder).* Utrecht: AnkhHermes.

24 Khamisa, A. (2005). *From murder to forgiveness. A Father's Journey.* Bloomington: Balboa.

25 Van Gasteren, K., Soeters, M. and Reijmerink, M. (2020). Ik bouw met woorden huizen waarin mensen zich thuisvoelen. In gesprek met Anselm Grün over leiderschap en roeping (I use words to build houses where people feel at home. In conversation with Anselm Grün on leadership and calling). *Tijdschrift voor Coaching*, 1: 50–55.
26 Eger, E. (2018). *The Choice: Embrace the Possible*. New York: Scribner Book Company.
27 Leaf, C. (2018). *Think. Learn. Succeed. Understanding and Using Your Mind to Thrive at School, the Workplace, and Life*. Michigan: Bakerbooks; Enright, R. (2012). *The Forgiving Life. A Pathway to Overcoming Resentment and Creating a Legacy of Love*. York: Maple-Vail Books.
28 Van Gasteren, K., Reijmerink, M., and van Wielink, J. (2021). Je kunt je leven helen. In gesprek met Candice Mama over zelfliefde, vergeving en verzoening (You can heal your life. In conversation with Candice Mama on self–love, forgiveness and reconciliation). *Tijdschrift voor Coaching*, (2): 12–16.
29 Paris, J. and Cummings, B. (2019). Elisabeth Kübler-Ross. A Pioneer Thinker, Influential Teacher and Contributor to Clinical Ethics. *The American Journal of Bioethics*, 19(12): 49–51.
30 Van Wielink, J., Fiddelaers-Jaspers, R., and Wilhelm, L. (2023). *The Language of Transition in Leadership. Your Calling as a Leader in a World of Change*. New York: Routledge.
31 This exercise is based on van Wielink, J., Wilhelm, L., and van Geelen-Merks, D. (2020). *Loss, Grief, and Attachment in Life Transitions. A Clinician's Guide to Secure Base Counseling*. New York: Routledge.
32 Ibid.

Chapter 12

Meaning and calling

"After a long, often very difficult, period of coming to the decision, I said goodbye to my role as a plastic surgeon. Before very long, I found myself in a state of not-knowing. Constantly, a question ran through my mind: who am I if I am no longer a surgeon? It was driving me crazy. On a long walk with a good friend, he asked, 'Who were you when you were a plastic surgeon?' I was the man who made people like their bodies again. I gave them a new face after burns or a new breast after cancer. It took me a while to turn this insight into something solid. Now, as a social worker, I help people in a Burns Center who are looking for a way to live with the aftermath of their injuries. Getting people to like their bodies again gives me a new and different kind of satisfaction."

Abdul (55)

"After 15 wonderful years, the corona crisis brought my restaurant into bankruptcy. For years, we benefitted from the same, reliable team of employees. We were very close-knit, and the team felt like family, so it was hard for me to have to let them all go, to say goodbye to them. However, and completely unexpectedly, the first weeks at home felt like a gift. Having dinner together with my family hadn't happened for years. I felt so much peace and relaxation. I discovered I was no longer prepared to miss so much of my family. After three months, I started a catering company, taking on some of my old staff. Since then I have been busy in the kitchen every day, but sitting at home at the table every evening."

Ton (38)

As the journey through this book reveals in various ways, life is not a succession of highlights, but rather a journey of peaks and valleys, bridges and fault lines, romance and horror, love and fear, longing and missing, and so on. You can think of your life journey as a search for meaning along a lemniscate that endlessly confronts you with opposing memories and experiences. Humans are intrinsically meaning-giving beings. It's a characteristic that sets us apart from other primates.

DOI: 10.4324/9781003424178-16

And it's often meaning-making that really challenges us, because it demands that we ask those big questions: Who am I?, Who do I want to be? Questions that point to the heart of your calling. And your calling is not so much about what you do, but about who you are. Everyone has a calling – arising from your unique and unblemished core. Coaching, we believe, is about helping people become who they are, who they are meant to be. That is what calling is.[1]

Your calling develops throughout your life: on the one hand, through the talents that bring your unique self to light and, on the other hand, by the impactful events in your life. Calling is the answer to the questions "Who am I?", "What do I bring to the world?", and "What is the effect on the world of who I am and what I set in motion?". Finding and living your calling is reaping the fruit of the wounds caused by the impactful events in your life. In this way, you and others in your immediate circle no longer have to suffer from that which wounded you, but can reap the fruits that result from the wounds, becoming a blessing to all.

In this chapter, we will explore what it means to live your calling. We will show that knowing your calling is not luck or luxury, but the way to a healthy and joyful life. It is a compass guiding the choices you make.

Giving meaning opens the gateway to the future

After an impactful event you are called to look anew at your life. To see who you can be in the light of this event. Who am I when you are no longer here? Who am I when I am no longer a doctor? Am I still a mother when my child has died? Who am I when I can no longer walk? Even less 'intense' changes can herald a transition that makes you question your identity: impending retirement for example, or children leaving the nest. Or the syndrome many encounter as they traverse their thirties and forties, the recurring, "Is this it? Is this all there is."

> "For a while after I became a widower last year, I no longer knew who I was. Rose and I started dating when I was 16; we grew up together. The first weeks after her death felt empty, pointless. What is left, now Rose is gone? I couldn't get out of bed, had no energy for anything. One afternoon, after six weeks or so, my mother shook me awake: 'Renzo! Are you going to stay in bed for the rest of your life? Or are you going to make something of it.' I was furious, told her to leave me alone, but the question continued to haunt me. Slowly, ideas began to form. I stopped spending the day in bed. I wanted to be there for my children, Fien and Joep, and to take the round-the-world trip together, that we had dreamed of with Rose for so long. Continue our journey together, as a family, without her. Even though her death still felt utterly pointless, it didn't mean there wasn't a good life ahead for us."

Sometimes, after an impactful event, you can't make sense of your life or know how to give it some kind of shape again. In this phase, the presence of secure bases is vital to helping you find your way again. The direct question from Renzo's mother helped him shift his focus: even though Rose is gone, he is still Fien and Joep's father. They are still a family, with dreams, goals and obligations. By giving meaning to events in your life, you release yourself from the glue of the past and open a gate to the future.

To give meaning to a life event, you begin by reflecting on the impact the event has had on your life. You explore, at the levels of head, heart and hands, how this event has shaped you. Meaning-making differs from integration in that integration is about learning to accept the new reality, so to speak. With Renzo, integration is accepting the fact that he is now a widower, the family is now three, not four, that Rose is dead and will never come back. It is accepting the consequences of loss. In meaning-making, you explore what this new reality asks of you. In Renzo's case, the loss of Rose has many consequences, and one is that he decides to take the world trip even though there's now just three of them.

Meaning-making involves connecting past, present, and future. It is a learning process. The meaning you give to a situation is unique for everyone. The way you see your parents' divorce will be different to way your brother or sister see it. This perspective determines how you give meaning to the experience. If you experienced your parents' divorce as very unpleasant, you will probably do everything to preserve your own marriage, even when it clearly isn't working. If, on the other hand, you experienced the divorce as a relief, the option of continuing as divorced parents might come more easily to mind if your marriage is struggling.

Meaningfulness does not mean that an event is meaningful in itself. The death of a loved one, a resignation, divorce: they are not meaningful as and of themselves. It is what you do with the event that determines if and what meaning you give it. For instance, Hannie gives meaning to her mother's illness and death by writing about it and making this available to others who find themselves in a similar situation.

> After the death of her mother, Hannie was keen to do something with all the knowledge she had accumulated during her mother's illness. It was a very rare form of cancer about which, even today, little information is available. It really would have been a bit easier if she could have found out more about the cancer. She decided to bring everything, she had learned and discovered, together into a book for other families facing the same disease. Just writing about all the beautiful and not-so-beautiful moments, in the journey she shared with her mother, is already a healing process for Hannie.

It is a human need to understand the world around you, to experience the meaning of life. Psychologist Emily Esfahani Smith describes four factors that contribute to a sense of meaning: feeling that you are bonded to others, having a purpose in life, the chance to share your life story with others, and the experience of being part of a bigger picture (transcendence).[2] Everyone has the need to belong and to feel bonded to others. Brené Brown describes, in her book *The Power of Vulnerability*, that bonding is the ultimate reason we are here. That the bonding we experience gives meaning and purpose to our lives.[3]

By having a purpose in your life, you are able to find direction and make choices. Having a goal is vital, as Viktor Frankl, also, describes in his book *Man's Search For Meaning*. [4] In the Nazi concentration camps where he was incarcerated during World War II, he saw that those who could find some purpose were more likely to survive. A purpose worth surviving for enabled them to bear their suffering. His own purpose was to complete his life's work, a book on *logotherapy*, an approach to finding meaning that he developed.

Making and telling stories helps to make sense of the world, to see your own place in it and make it meaningful. The last factor described by Esfahani Smith is about experiencing yourself as a small cog in a larger wheel. Transcendental experiences are experiences with a slight sense of spirituality or mystery. Examples include religious experiences, near-death experiences, but also the sense of being part of something bigger than the world.[5]

Without meaning-making, transition stalls

Finding meaning in life requires looking kindly at what is happening to you, exploring what there is to discover and learn; gently focusing on the positive. It is about answering the question "What now?" rather than the question "Why me?". The first question leads to shaping the future, the second question invites stalling. If you focus too much on "Why me?", you stop your forward movement and end up in a victim or persecutor role. Both roles prevent you from making the pendulum swing towards the restoration orientation as represented in the Dual Process Model (Chapter 11). By moving between the loss orientation and the restoration orientation the loss is integrated and it becomes possible to regain meaning in life.

Both victim and persecutor no longer take control of their own lives and put the responsibility for what happens to them onto someone else. Anger, loss, and sadness turn the attention and blame onto another. This leads to feelings of futility or resentment. Overcome by these feelings, it is almost impossible to focus on what can and wants to be learned. You no longer take responsibility for the situation you are in. Of course, it might well be that you had no influence over the initial loss, nor on the resulting situation. But what you do have influence over is how you deal with the situation.

> *When Steve was told he had not been selected for the first team, he was very angry. It had not been fair he said, he had not been given a chance, the selection committee was biased against him. Under the influence of his anger, he cancelled his membership and took his football boots to the thrift store.*

After the death of his daughter Kyra, Anton notices that he has little energy for his work. He finds everything pointless and wonders why people get so worked up over nothing.

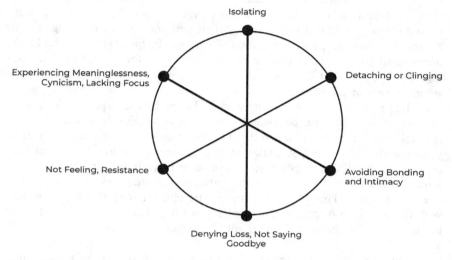

Figure 12.1 Themes on the Cycle of Stalled Transition

Stalled transition drains the joy of life away. You are no longer able to fully see and experience the beauty of life. This negative spiral stands in the way of creating or maintaining a deep bond with yourself and others. Perhaps, in the beginning, Steve's team members still ask him along to the pub. But, in time, his negativity means they just stop asking him. To break through this negative state, we needs secure bases to help us turn our focus towards what wants to be discovered and learned, so that we can reconnect with the world around us.

Everyone has a unique calling

Your life is a journey from origin to destination. While on that journey, you have an inalienable personal calling, to speak with Henri Nouwen, a unique contribution that only you can make.[6] Your calling is who you are and what you do, who you become and what you bring to this journey. A contribution that only you can make in the unique way you do. It is a coming together of who you are, all your qualities and how you use them to start something moving in the world. Your calling is the answer to three important questions: Who am I? What am I setting in motion in the world? And what is my effect on the world?

Knowing your calling is not the same as having a mission. Nowadays, the word mission is often used to denote a goal. Mission then refers to that which you want to achieve, meaningful goals you are striving towards. Examples of a personal mission include: being a good father, becoming CEO of a company, contributing to a cleaner ocean, helping people quit smoking. People can have multiple, co-existing missions throughout their lives. A mission, by definition, is finite, and this is where it differs from a calling. Your calling cannot cease to exist; it is a part of you your whole life long. In this context we also come across the idea of *purpose*. Purpose is about the larger, meaningful goals you want to realize in your life. It forms part of your calling. It is the part that follows "I am…", i.e. the part that expresses what you set in motion in the world.

Calling is a question of identity and is shaped by the experiences on your life-line. It is stable and consistent over time, remaining basically the same throughout your life. Calling refers to who you are at the deepest layer of your identity and how you make an impact on the world. Your identity is shaped by the different experiences you have in your life and the way you have learned to deal with them, the patterns and qualities you have developed as a result. This identity forms in the contact with the world around you, the people you meet and the roles you fulfil. The answer to the first of the three 'calling questions' (Who am I?) is your *being-energy*.

> When Anja was five years old, her brother Wim was born, with a clubfoot. He would never be able to walk properly. Anja made it her personal task to encourage Wim to learn new things. Like a cheerleader, she ran with him when he stumbled along upright at the age of two, dived into the water with him when he learned to swim and stood applauding him at the finish line when he ran his first race at school. In her heart, Anja is the captain of Team Wim, encouraging him to be the best he can be.

The second calling question is about the impact you want to make in the world, your *doing-energy*. This is the impact of who you are and the qualities that you exploit. Anja has made it her life's mission to encourage Wim. From an early age she has learned how to motivate others to face challenges, to see possibilities instead of impossibilities, to push boundaries. Her belief in Wim's potential encouraged her to stay by his side and challenge him to do his best in spite of his limitations.

> Anja now works as a coach at a college. When young people get stuck or are in danger of dropping out, they can go to Anja. Often she sees that they have lost self-belief, can no longer see their qualities, that they talk themselves down. Together with these students they reflect on how far they have already come, what they are good at, where and what challenges lie ahead, who they can turn to for help. She encourages them to identify what they really enjoy and what they want to get out of life. It gives her satisfaction to see them regain their self-belief and, from this position of

restored confidence, make new choices, sometimes to stay, sometimes to do something completely different.

In her role as coach, Anja uses the qualities she developed in her life with Wim, but in a different way. She encourages students to focus on what is there, to move from self-rejection to loving the self. From there, they can make choices again. The second part of Anja's calling leads to self-love: *I am the leader who encourages you to get the best out of yourself on the path to loving yourself.*

You could say we all want to contribute to a universally desired life theme. One will, therefore, in the latter part of one's calling, often come across themes like happiness, joy, health, healing, love, light, life.

Your *doing-* and *being-energy* together form your calling.

Examples of a calling are:

- *I am a friend and a father who helps people find and live their calling on the path to healing* – Jakob van Wielink
- *I am the lighthouse that illuminates the dark, making it lighter* – Klaartje van Gasteren.
- *I am a comrade who brings adventure towards surrender* – Marnix Reijmerink.
- *I am the sister who walks unknown paths to release energy on the way to healing* - Anne Verbokkem-Oerlemans.
- *I am an anchored, committed woman, a landmark that gives support in weaving back together the fault lines of life* – Riet Fiddelaers-Jaspers.
- *As a guide, I accompany you to the top of your mountain so that you can experience, celebrate and share your success* – Leo Wilhelm.

To find the words that reflect your calling, you will often create a 'first' version. Then it is useful to let it sit in you for a while, letting it rise and fall in your consciousness, changing it slightly or wholly until it begins to find its real shape. You feel if the words are right, hone them, and continue until you feel you are there. If you are willing to embark on this journey, the fruits will be sweet. Living from your calling provides the clarity, focus and confidence necessary to make choices. It is like a compass that points the way. More and more, in small and big ways – in interactions and encounters in the present and in larger choices – you will ask yourself the question: Does what I am doing, saying, avoiding or setting in motion, take me towards my calling or away from it?

The second mountain

From the moment we are born, we are making our way in the world: origin to destination. Experiences, positive and negative, shape us, and through these we build our identity. This process shapes the core of who we are. You can think of this journey as the first mountain you climb in the development of your personal leadership style.[7]

The first mountain is about self-actualization – developing your healthy ego – and achieving goals. This mountain is characterized by engaging in competition, realizing success and peak moments, and developing competences. Seeking or avoiding competition says different things about who we are and what we value. You will be more inclined to compete for things that are close to your heart than for things that are not so valuable to you.

Engaging in competition is a driver of growth and development. Here you should not confuse competition with battle. Competition here is about growing together by challenging each other. In sports, we see this reflected by measuring yourself against your competitors and challenging yourself to become as good as or better than the other. If you are by far the best in a sport, there is less challenge to maintain the motivation to keep improving. In organizations, we see this when *peers push each other* moving towards a desired promotion.

This is also the mountain on which goals are achieved, such as getting a degree, your first job, buying a house, having children. The basic needs of a happy life are made real here. Through experiences on the first mountain, beautiful and not, our capabilities develop. The things we are good at.

> *Cedric stands in the driveway of his villa. He looks around, sees his house, beloved cars, beautifully landscaped garden. In recent years, he has worked hard to make this happen. Every success he achieved, he learned to convert into something material. His collection of cars reflects all his successes, so to speak. But where he used to dream of a big house and beautiful cars, he now feels empty and sad inside.*

There is also a second mountain. The mountain of moral dedication. This mountain too is characterized by three themes: calling, joy and service. On this mountain the focus shifts from I to the other. It is no longer about experiencing even more moments of happiness on the first mountain, but about putting what you have to bring to the world at the service of others – and getting your joy from that.

> *At dinner in the evening, he tells his wife that he feels empty. She is surprised. She had not seen it coming. She had never felt that the life they had built together would one day no longer be enough for him. She asks him if he would like to join her, tomorrow, at the day care center where she has been a volunteer for many years. She sees how he enjoys helping everyone. When they get back home, he is energetic and determined to find out what really makes him happy and how he can find a new way to make that real in his life.*

Moving from the first mountain to the second can be done in different ways. There comes a point when peak moments on the first mountain such as an extra degree, a bigger house, a new car, are no longer satisfying. Then the question might arise: 'Is this all?' It is also possible that an impactful event such as a loss, redundancy, illness or some personal crisis calls you to look at your life anew.

When we reach the point where the first mountain no longer has the answers to the questions we ask ourselves, we are now down in the valley between the first and second mountains. Here we have to discover how to climb the second mountain. However, not everyone arrives at the foot of the second mountain. Some people will never enter the valley, and never see the second mountain. Others will look up from the valley but not find the courage to climb the second mountain. Living your calling means, after all, making firm and deliberate choices, saying goodbye to that which no longer serves you, to people who do not really empower you to bring your gifts into the world by living your calling.

Calling as the fruit of our wounds

Throughout our lives, we sustain injuries. Injuries caused by impactful events that challenge us to respond to the pain. Not infrequently, we develop qualities and patterns as a result of that pain, and we call these the *wound response*.

> *As a little girl, Eri is often bullied at school. To avoid being the target of the bullying every time, Eri learns to 'go with the flow', to do as the others do. She learns to keep her mouth shut and adapt.*

Eri's adaptability serves her well later in her life. She becomes very good at adjusting to a situation and avoiding conflict. This adaptability is her *wound response*. The qualities we develop in healing our wounds form the basis of our calling.

> *Years later, when Eri faces petty harassment at work, she is overcome with emotion. She seeks out her manager and shares her story with him. He invites her to share the impact of the teasing with her colleagues at the next meeting. In the presence of her manager, she tells her story. The reactions she receives surprise and encourage her. Her colleagues apologize and Eri feels how, by telling her story, she is welcoming herself rather than shying away.*

Not infrequently, the *wound response* is confused with the fruit response. Through Eri's new experience – of speaking out what she feels – she discovers that, for a long time, her adaptability has also kept her away from actually bringing herself into contact with others. This experience forms the basis of her *fruit response*, that of 'speaking out for herself.'

Calling in organizations

Teams and organizations also have a calling.[8] More and more organizations are communicating their purpose: what they want to contribute to the world. For example, Tony's Chocolonely's purpose is *100% slave-free chocolate,*[9] ING's is *Empowering people to stay a step ahead in life and in business.*[10] An organization's calling combines their purpose with their identity.

The basis and the starting point lie in the founder's calling. An organization starts because one or more people (the founders) have an idea they want to bring into the world and the impact they want to achieve through doing so. Leaders (agree) to accept and carry this calling, in order to inspire and engage their employees and customers.

In organizations, the calling can be found at different levels: the organization, the department or team, and the individual. The more these are aligned, the better employee engagement will be, and the greater the focus on the desired outcome.

Calling and roles

Knowing your calling is just the first step. Actually living your calling is another. As already mentioned, everyone has their unique calling. It will be reflected in the different roles you fulfil in your life. So a calling is never just one role; however, a role is a form in which you can express your calling. We all have many different roles in our lives. These roles can be divided into four categories:

- Personal
- Organizational
- Social
- Professional[11]

Kiki is an energetic 38-year-old woman. A marketing manager at a health insurance company four days a week, she runs a yoga studio in the evenings and is a senior hockey coach on Sundays. She really enjoys guiding her employees in their development, but feels more and more resistance to her daily duties.

She gets herself a coach. Together, they explore her life-line and see impactful childhood experiences, moments of success and failure, and patterns she has developed. One event jumps out immediately for Kiki. It is the arrival of a puppy in the family when Kiki is seven. The tiny puppy can do hardly anything for itself when it comes into their home. Kiki enjoys teaching the puppy new things and seeing it grow and develop. Looking further down her life-line, Kiki discovers that many of the times she felt happiness were when she was helping someone else to grow. She realizes that her calling is to be a kind of earth-mother, encouraging and challenging others to develop their full potential. Kiki talks to her manager about this and together they conclude that a role in HR would be a great next step. Not much later, a position becomes available as HR manager within another division.

Figure 12.2 Window of leadership and calling

Partly of the switching of roles, Kiki is free to express her calling across all her roles: as a mother and wife (personal), as a businesswoman who own her yoga studio (organizational), a hockey coach (social) and as an HR manager (professional). The different roles fit her vision and values, and provide the space to achieve her goals. The moment you occupy roles that do not fit your calling or there is not a good balance between all your different roles, this will inevitably lead to problems. These can manifest as battle, under-performance, dissatisfaction, or, in more extreme cases, health issues such as illness, loneliness, or burnout.

Should you not yet be clear about your calling, the roles you already fill can also give clues to help you formulate your calling. We already know that living your calling is not an easy path, that it requires making choices, say goodbye to certain things, ideas, even people, and it asks for focus. Research shows that knowing your calling but not giving it form has a more detrimental effect on well-being than not having a calling at all.[12]

The secure base coach at work with meaning and calling

Meaning and calling – Working with individuals

Marcel looks at Anna, his coach for the last few months. "I didn't think I could do it," he says. A year and a half ago, he lost control of the car – with his wife alongside him and his 13-year-old daughter in the back seat – and crashed into a tree. He was okay, but his wife and daughter died instantly. A single-vehicle accident and a tragedy on a dark, slippery road.

"What did you think you couldn't do?" asks Anna, "To be able to live without them and to feel that there is still some meaning in my life." Marcel had obviously struggled with the loss of his wife and daughter. He felt tremendous guilt and found it hard to accept that he had survived and they hadn't. Why him and not them? And what had they done to deserve to die? There must have been something he could have done to prevent it? How was he supposed to continue alone, without them? Did his life still have meaning? Would he ever forgive himself?

He came into contact with Anna through a friend. He talked to her about the night of the crash and about the questions that he couldn't escape from. He was sleeping badly, on sick leave from his work and was weighed down by a blanket of hopelessness. Now, many months later, he could see some light at the end of the tunnel. The conversations with Anna had opened a new space within him. A space in which he could give meaning to the moments when thoughts and emotions unexpectedly overwhelmed him. He could feel that he had suffered this tragic loss, but that he did not have to be the loss or live the tragedy.

Anna had seen and felt his despair when they first met. Marcel's story touched her immensely. She could hardly imagine how it must have felt for him to have lost his wife and daughter. She thought of how she could help Marcel find meaning in his loss. Of course, the accident was not meaningful in itself. She would begin a process in which she would have to search with Marcel for what this experience evoked in him. An inventory of thoughts, emotions, physical and spiritual experiences which she hoped would enable him to answer the questions: "Who am I now after this experience?" and "How do I create a future for myself."

This process of meaning-making required examining and weighing-up the event. Anna kept in mind Marcel's desire for a new and meaningful future for himself. His desire to find a new direction would prove decisive in their conversations. Step by step, Anna and Marcel picked up the pieces of his shattered life and put them back together. They looked for what matched, and stuck these together, as it were, bit by bit. The aim was not to make a perfect 'vase' that could symbolize his life as if nothing had happened, but a vase with visible cracks, fracture lines, signs of having once been broken.

In their conversations, the theme of forgiveness formed an essential part of the coaching sessions. Anna spoke intensively with Marcel about the guilt and also the shame he felt about his wife and daughter and also around family and friends. For a long time he did not dare to face these people. Unable to break through the feelings of guilt and shame, he began to shun contact with others. This didn't work: he felt increasingly lonely and increasingly guilty and ashamed. A typical example of a self-fulfilling prophecy: he was getting exactly what he was trying to avoid.

Marcel's shame was toxic. The root of the toxicity was the feeling of no longer being worthy. As a human being, as a partner, as a father, as a son, as a friend – as anything that anyone might need or expect from him. This feeling was not so much fueled by explicit or implicit messages from others, but was mainly driven by the endless self-condemnation arising in Marcel's mind. He was hard with himself on many levels; in fact he went a bit overboard with this. In the conversations with Anna, for instance, he discovered that the extreme exercise and diet regime he followed, was a way of punishing himself for what happened. The physical pain he felt after exercising and the intense hunger pangs were nothing compared to the heartbreaking pain of missing his wife and daughter. Marcel was continually confronted by the trio of shame: denial, avoidance, and forgetting. Extreme sports and diet were his attempts to rid himself of the guilt and shame.

But this was a waste of his time and life. He was totally exhausted himself and the pain simply got worse and worse. In his sessions with Anna, he learned that there was a way to break through the shame and guilt: sharing his story, in detail, with all the pain, emotion, and uncertainty; with all the guilt and shame. Beside the feeling of rejection and being unworthy, he told Anna everything that concerned him. Everything that he felt imprisoned by. Finally finding the will to share his story, he discovered he also had the will to forgive himself.

That is how forgiveness starts. An active decision. One you consciously make to no longer be held hostage. But the will for forgiveness is not the end point. Forgiveness is a process, not an action.[13]

Through the conversations with Anna and the discoveries he made there, Marcel slowly allowed himself permission to stop feeling guilty. By acknowledging his wounds and giving up the desire and hope that it just hadn't happened, he no longer felt like a victim. He could feel himself slowly letting go of the hostage feelings of shame and guilt. he began to experience greater control over his emotions and turned less and less to his escapist diet and exercise regime.

Anna guided Marcel around the themes of the Transition Cycle over the course of many months. They dwelled on each theme. In doing so, she also noticed that for both her and Marcel multiple themes often were intertwined. Meaning-making, for example, was continually present because of Marcel's presenting issue when he first approached Anna, but themes like welcome (How do I welcome someone with all that is present?, and How am I welcomed with all that is present?) and bonding (How do I overcome my shame enough to trust myself to someone I don't know?) were constantly influencing the primary theme with which they were working.

And so, as a secure base coach, you are invited and challenged to develop a client-perspective that is, simultaneously, pin-point focused and zoomed out. This is the burden and the beauty of your profession. For you are also searching within yourself and with the other for ways not to get lost in the labyrinth of your client's quest. At the same time, you have the task of keeping the greater arc of someone's journey (and your own) in mind. For Anna, it reminded her that, as a coach, you need to have your own sources of inspiration in place. For Anna, her own supervisor was an important source. Guiding a person through their transitions is a task that shouldn't just touch the client, it should touch you deeply too.

Meaning and calling – Working with teams

In the coaching session with the team, the air is thick with tension. Aron, the coach, is standing in front of the group and he is enjoying it: this tension feels like what the team members had told him about in the introductory interviews. Like pressure building in a volcano; an eruption could happen at any moment, but it doesn't have to. Aron had hoped this tension would manifest in the session, so that he could discuss it with the team. Something they have been unable to do themselves. This team is struggling to work together at all, let alone effectively. Aron suspects this is because it has been formed by merging three separate teams.

Aron begins by checking out his hunch: he mentions the tension he is feeling and asks if anyone else feels something similar. Several hands go up. He invites each 'hand' to say what's going on for them. Via Aron's skillful paraphrasing and questioning, several team members make new discoveries. AS they speak from their new perspectives, others who did not raise their hands earlier, do so now. It becomes clear that the merger has triggered a lot in most of the team.

After exploring and deepening what has been revealed, in the group, Aron decides to let the team members dialogue with each other about the merger. Not about the merger, because that is simply a fact; it cannot be changed. But about what the merger meant and still means for individual team members. What did you lose through the merger? Had to say goodbye to? How has it affected your day-to-day work? What is its impact on how much you enjoy your work? And collaboration with your colleagues – old and new?

In several dialogue rounds, team members explore these and other questions in threes – one from each of the pre-merger teams. When the dialogues are complete, Aron instructs each team member to take two minutes, standing in front of the group, to answer the question: Who am I as a team member in the new team and what do I want for it?

When team members face change, it evokes – as we have learned – mental, emotional, physical, and spiritual reactions. At the level of the individual level and of the team. Whereas it might seem obvious that it's important for individuals to reflect on how change changes them, it might not be so clear that it is exactly the same for the team. When impact and meaning is made visible, tangible and audible – per individual – it opens up space for the team's search for answers to questions such as "So who are we as a team now? What do we want to set in motion in the world? What impact do we want to make?".

After everyone had spoken, it was absolutely evident to the group what the impact of the change was and is for each team member and what wishes exist in the group for the future. Some of the wishes are individually oriented, while others are about the impact the team as a whole can make. Impact on both the organization and the world beyond.

As we described earlier in this Chapter, everyone has a unique calling. A unique response to the question of identity and the particular impact that identity is driven to make. Teams too have a unique calling, a conflation of individual callings linked to the organization, the *corporate story*: a meaningful narrative that makes the company stand out in the world.[14] The corporate story represents the soul of the organization and is kept alive by dialogue: the essential conversations that everyone involved in the organization have together.

Aron coaches the team in a process of identifying their individual wishes to formulate each individual calling. Under his guidance, everyone finds and formulates an initial calling. Together they gather the elements of each calling and Aron guides them to finding and formulate their team's calling.

Organizations which incorporate callings-dialogue at individual, team and organizational level alike, use their full potential, achieving set goals, and often achieving growth that they did not previously think possible. Employees who live their individual calling and feel it is aligned with the calling of the organization where they work, act from a mindset of excelling. They experience more joy and energy, they bring more focus to their work, and derive more satisfaction from being in contact with themselves and collaborating with others.

Exercises with your client

Exploring the life-line in the light of meaning-making and calling

A new beginning becomes possible when we are willing to investigate within: "Who am I after this experience(s)?" And: "What does this loss mean for the larger arc of my life?" Shaping transition starts and ends with knowing and living your calling. In your life, somewhere in every day, you will be challenged to reflect on your identity, on who you are at the deepest level, and who you are meant to be. When you can find an answer to this based on all the positive and negative experiences on your life-line – and in bonding with secure bases – the question of what you want to set in motion in the world from that identity also arises. Linked to that is the question of how to be of service to others. After all, few humans really live just for themselves.

Reflection questions

- What capabilities have you developed in your life? What are you good at?
- In what ways have you developed and your talents and allowed them to flourish?
- In what ways have you faced-up to competition in your life and where have you avoided it?
- How are you in service of others? How are you, perhaps, not that?
- At what moments/situations do you experience joy in your life?
- What is the balance between the different roles you play in your life? How are the personal, professional, organizational and social roles connected?
- What is your calling and how does it help you shape transition in your own life and the lives of others?
- What meaning have transitions acquired in your life? How has this meaning developed over the course of your life?

Signals on the path to your calling

We need others in our lives to give meaning to change. In dialogue, we explore what inspires and moves us, and keeps us moving: our drives and passions. This investigation helps us get closer to our calling.

In this exercise, you question your client. For example, start with a question like: 'What is an important question about your calling?" Listen carefully to the answer. Then select at least four of the following themes and have a dialogue (in open curiosity) about each one. Reflect on each theme for not less than five minutes. During the dialogue, make a note of at least three responses per theme, i.e. three role models, three favorite books/magazines/television series, and so on.

1. Role models

What people and characters, real or fictional, did you admire when you were growing up? Why? Tell us about them. What qualities did they have? How were they similar to you? How were they different from you? How did they influence your life? What attracted you to them?

2. Books

As a child or adolescent, what were your favorite books?

3. Magazines

What magazines do you/did you read regularly? Why?

4. Television series

What series do you/did you watch regularly?

5. Mottoes

Your three favorite mottoes.

6. Leisure

What do you like to do in your free time? What are your hobbies? What makes these hobbies so enjoyable for you?

7. School

What were your three favorite subjects at school? Why? Which subjects did you hate? Why?

8. Early memories

What are your earliest memories? I would like to hear stories you remember from when you were three to six years old.

Points to note during this exercise

- Really connect with your client before you begin.
- Pay attention to physical expressions and emotions. Allow silences. Observe all the signals your client gives: words, gestures, silences, and behaviors.
- Ask searching questions.
- Make short notes on each theme. Write down the essence of what the other person says on each theme.
- How did their role models provide clues or directions relevant to the challenge your client faces today?
- At the end, show your client the structure of his story by giving back the key phrases and solutions you heard (and wrote down).
- Be curious: don't think you know anything for certain. Your client is an expert on his own life. So be cautious with interpretations and suggestions.
- At the end, when you have shared your observations, ask the other person how they look back on this session and what they learned.

Finding and formulating your calling

With this exercise, you facilitate your client in doing an initial exploration around their calling. It is a way of gathering an initial feeling for what makes up their calling. A feeling about the two core energies of their calling: their being energy and their doing energy.

The first part of a calling is about who a person is at the deepest layer of their identity. The second part is about what they want to set in motion in the world from that identity. For example, a formulated calling might look like this:

I am a guide who prepares the way so that new perspectives become visible.

I am a comrade who brings adventure towards surrender.

I am the lighthouse that shines when the road gets dark, making it light.

Ask your client to go through the following steps and to write something about them:

Step 1

Describe two or three special/magical moments from your childhood. What specifically stands out? What emotions did you feel at those moments?

Step 2

Describe what sources of inspiration you had earlier in your life. What got you excited? What inspired you? What/who were these people, activities, pursuits, elements or objects? And what do you draw inspiration from now? What energy and emotions does being in touch with these sources give/bring up in you?

Step 3

Describe two or three key moments in your life. Transition moments where (looking back now) your life took a significant turn, or moments that were impactful in positive or negative ways. What were the tests and challenges you met? What helped you through them and what 'gifts' did you receive?

Step 4

What are your passions in life? What do you enjoy doing? And what gives you energy? Give examples of all three answers.

Step 5

Reread everything you wrote down in steps 1 to 3. What put a smile on your face? Which words and elements jump out at the different steps? Write down these words. Let the words and elements pass through your mind, feel them in your body, and try to capture the essence in a sentence or statement.

The hero's journey

Here, your client uses the themes of the Transition Cycle to shape real transition. The aim is to find his answers, on his journey of transition, about what those themes ask of him. This journey needs courage!

Looking back on his journey – made partly with your guidance – you help him to recognize in it the elements of a hero's journey: he embarked on a journey, with a goal, he encountered setbacks, these were overcome and he (we hope) came out wiser and stronger.

How does his story go? What or with whom from his story does he feel most bonded? And the least?

Ask your client to write a travel story with the following ingredients:

What is your heroic story, how would you describe it?

- Once upon a time ...
- The setback I met is ...
- I dealt with adversity by ...
- I grew and learned that ...
- What I know now is ...
- And that every day I ...
- This means that I ...

When he's describing the story, he should pay attention to at least:

- the messenger, who summons the hero to set out on his quest/adventure
- the wise (old) man or woman (the secure bases), who give the hero advice and/or (magical) gifts
- the shadow figure, the hero's enemy
- the shadow figure's sidekicks, who antagonize the hero
- the rogue, of whom it is unclear whether he is for or against the hero
- The hero's friend(s), who assists the hero on the journey
- other secure bases.

What do these experiences mean for how you continue your journey?

Let your client read the story aloud to you. Don't interrupt. When he's finished reading, tell your client what touched you in his hero story.

Exercises with the team

Exploring the team life-line in the light of meaning-making and calling
As in people's individual lives, meaning and calling also play a major role in the context of the team and organization. How does the team give meaning to the losses and changes it encounters? And in what way does intra-team dialogue about this create more psychological safety? Which rituals help with this?

Reflection questions
- How do the impactful events in this team affect collaboration, team identity, and the impact the team makes on the world around it?

- What is the team's identity and what is its higher purpose?
- How is everyone's individual calling reflected in the team's calling?
- How does reflecting on the impact of events that happened to and in this team affect the level of bonding you feel to the team?
- How well do individual team members subordinate themselves to the higher purpose of the team?
- Is the team bonded to the organization's purpose and the larger corporate story? If yes, how? If not, how does this affect group dynamics and achieving targets?

The calling of the team

Like any individual, a team also has a calling. That calling is an amalgam of the individual identities and of the various individual higher purposes. The questions asked in the team calling are: "Who are we?" and "What do we, as a team, want to set in motion in the world?"

The search for the team calling is a valuable process in which interconnectedness can grow through answering the central question of whether everyone can and wants to commit to the team. Once the team has formulated their team calling, they can explore together how this calling connects to the corporate story and the organization's calling. Lead team members through the following steps.

Step 1

Individually complete the exercise *Finding and shaping your calling*.

Step 2

Have team members discuss Step 1 in pairs or threes. Where can they challenge and/or complement each other? By the end of this step, everyone should have formulated their calling in a single *I am* sentence.

Step 3

In front of the group, have everyone speak their calling out loud. Invite the other team members to respond from their hearts and share whether this calling touches them and resonates in some way.

Step 4

Have everyone in the team write down three words on three A4 sheets (one word on each sheet): a word that is at the heart of individual *being* energy, individual *doing* energy, and the impact that this *being and doing* has on the world.

Examples

The calling *"I am a comrade who brings adventure towards surrender"* yields these three words (and thus three pages): Comrade, Adventure, Surrender.

The calling *"I am the lighthouse that shines when the road gets dark, making it light"* yields these three words: Lighthouse, Shines, Light.

Step 5

Place all the pages about *identity* (being-energy) on the ground below each other in a single pile. Do the same for the pages about everyone's *purpose* (doing energy) and about their *impact* on the world. So there are now three columns next to each other in the space on the floor containing everybody's three pages.

Step 6

Together with the team members, find the thread that connects each pile. What words appear on that thread? How then can the team's identity (being-energy) be formulated? How can the purpose (doing-energy) be formulated? Based on the third column, how can the team's impact on the world be formulated? What team calling does this produce?

Individual callings:

- *I am the lighthouse that illuminates the dark, making it lighter.*
- *I am a comrade who brings adventure towards surrender.*
- *I am a friend and father who helps people find and live their calling on the path to healing.*
- *I am the sister who walks unfamiliar paths to release energy on the way to healing.*
- *As a guide, I accompany you to the top of your mountain so that you can experience, celebrate and share your success.*
- *I am an anchored, committed woman, a landmark that gives support in weaving back together the fault lines of life.*

Team calling:

- *We are a secure base for people and organizations who want to shape real change.*

Important points to take away

- After an impactful event, you are called to look again at your life; this is the process of meaning-making.
- Giving meaning to events in your life does not keep you stuck in the past, but opens a gateway to the future.
- Meaning-making involves connecting past, present, and future.
- One's calling is the answer to the questions "Who am I?", "What am I here to set in motion in the world?", and "What is my effect on the world?".
- Your life is your journey from origin to destination. On that journey you have a unique calling.
- Calling is about your identity and is shaped by the experiences on your life-line.
- The first mountain is about developing a healthy ego (competence, competition and happiness). The second mountain is about the path to service, calling, and joy.

- Calling is the fruit of a wound what you learned and developed in the process of healing from that wound.
- Calling brings focus, pleasure, energy, and fulfilment.
- Teams and organizations have a calling.

Self-reflection for the coach

- What talents and capabilities have I developed in my life?
- Where did I face competition and avoid it? What has this brought me?
- In what ways have I given meaning to impactful moments in my life?
- How do I help clients with meaning-making?
- How do I find meaning in the different roles in my life?
- Who am I, what do I want to set in motion in the world and what effect do I want to have by doing so?
- Am I serving others? How?
- At what moments did I experience joy in my life?
- How does my calling manifest in and direct my various roles?
- How is my calling reflected in my coaching?
- What sacrifices am I willing to make to fully live my calling?

Poem written for The School for Transition on the occasion of its fifth anniversary at the presentation of the calling stone placed in the monastery garden in Huissen:

here at your feet I lie
from origin to destination
worn, broken and softened
stay awhile with me
so together we feel
what brought you to me

hear the wind and the trees
and further the sun and rain
the silence in your heart
feel the cracks and the wholeness
your true being
is never lost or confused

in the deepest silence
clear and powerful
the voice that says it all
without doubt or reserve
speaks your source and your movement
pure and sincere

here at your feet I lie
you don't have to give me anything
I am, do and trust
that you will experience
what is calling you?

Floortje Agema

Notes

1 Van Wielink, J. and Wilhelm, L. (2020). De roeping van de begeleider om transitie te helpen vormgeven. Een vervolg (The coach's calling to help shape transition. A sequel). *Tijdchrift voor Begeleidingskunde*, (9): 38–43.
2 Esfahani Smith, E. (2017). *The Power of Meaning. The true route to happiness.* London: Rider & Co.
3 Brown, B. (2015). *Daring Greatly. How the Courage to Be Vulnerable Transforms the Way We Live, Love, Parent, and Lead.* New York: Penguin.
4 Frankl, V. (2008). *Man's Search For Meaning. The classic tribute to hope from the Holocaust.* London: Ebury Publishing.
5 Van Wielink, J., Fiddelaers-Jaspers, R., and Wilhelm, L. (2023). *The Language of Transition in Leadership. Your Calling as a Leader in a World of Change.* New York: Routledge.
6 Nouwen, H. (2017). *You Are the Beloved: 365 Daily Readings and Meditations for Spiritual Living: A Devotional.* Veghel: Image.
7 Brooks, D. (2019). *The Second Mountain. The Quest for a Moral Life.* London: Random House.
8 Laloux, F. (2014). *Reinventing Organizations: A Guide to Creating Organizations Inspired by the Next Stage of Human Consciousness.* Millis: Nelson Parker.
9 On https://tonyschocolonely.com/be/nl/ons-verhaal, accessed October 8, 2023.
10 On www.ing.jobs/nederland/over-ing/duurzaam-en-betrokken.htm, accessed October 8, 2023.
11 Van Wielink, J. and Wilhelm, L. (2020). (Re)discovering your calling through secure bases at loss. *Psychosocial Digital*, 2: 42–47.
12 Hirschi, A., Keller, A., and Spurk, D. (2018). Living one's calling. Job resources as a link between having and living a calling. *Journal of Vocational Behavior*, 106: 1–10.
13 Kahmisa, A. (2005). *From murder to forgiveness. A Father's Journey.* Bloomington: Balboa.
14 Forman, J. (2013). *Storytelling in Business. The authentic and Fluent Organization.* Redwood City: Stanford Business Books.

Reflection and feedback tool

In this concluding piece, we want to offer you a feedback tool. Learning and growing doesn't happen without feedback. Coaching is always dynamic, a moving process, and, as you also learned in this book, develops in bonding with others: colleagues, managers, friends, family, clients, and so on. Through living, practicing, and regularly asking for feedback, your coaching becomes stronger.

How does the tool work?

Its purpose is to help you to reflect on your own or someone else's coaching, for example as a part of intervision and supervision. However, you can also use the tool in a coaching process with a client. It enables you to get a clearer view of the person effect you read about in Chapter 6.

At each station on the Transition Cycle there are statements. In the explanation that follows, you will find a mini summary, as it were, of the concepts at the stations and an explanation of the questions.

Reflect on each of the statements and give each a mark from 1 to 5. You do this by coloring in the boxes next to each question.

1 ALMOST NEVER
2 SELDOM
3 SOMETIMES
4 USUALLY
5 ALMOST ALWAYS

Asking for feedback

If you use this tool to gain insight into your own coaching, ask people close to you to complete the tool for you. When doing so, give them a copy of this document.

You can download a digital version of the document at: www.deschoolvoortransitie.nl/feedbacktool-en.

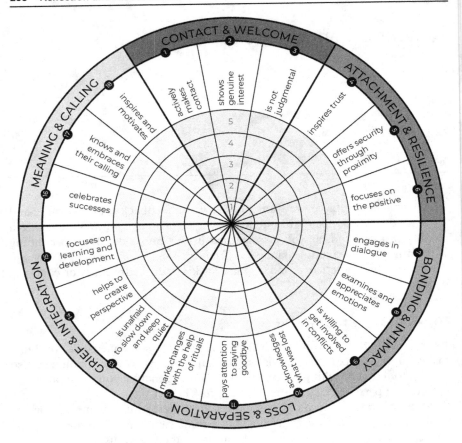

1 = almost never | 2 = rarely | 3 = sometimes | 4 = often | 5 = almost always

Figure A1.1 Reflection and feedback tool

To get a complete picture, we recommend asking for feedback from people from the different roles in your life, e.g.:

- *Personal*: your partner, an (almost) adult child, a parent, sibling, a friend.
- *Professional*: colleague (team member), direct-report (someone you manage), own coach.
- *Social*: someone from a club/charity/society where you are active, for example.

Ask people to write a short comment at the end.

To get a better view of the feedback received, you can have a dialogue with the feedback giver. The dialogue will help you firm up your understanding of what you are doing or failing to do. Questions that can help you with this include:

- What is a defining example for this score?
- What do I do in these situations? And what do I avoid doing?
- What effect does that have on you?

Explanation of Transition Cycle themes

Below is a brief explanation of each theme on the Transition Cycle. In addition, a number of behaviors are included for each statement to give you an idea.

Theme 1: Contact and Welcome

Welcoming and feeling welcome are the basis of any relationship, and therefore any collaboration. Without welcome no contact, without contact no welcome. Every new contact you make evokes previous experiences of making first contact. And every welcome refers to previous experiences of welcoming and being welcomed.

Statement 1 – Actively makes contact

- Takes initiative in making contact
- Devotes conscious attention to creating an environment where people feel welcome

Statement 2 – Shows genuine interest

- Is sufficiently focused on the other person during contact
- Is intrinsically motivated to get to know the other person

Statement 3 – Is not judgmental

- Is willing to delay his responses and listen to what wants to be said
- Makes acceptance of the other person clear

Theme 2: Attachment and Resilience

Attachment is the natural and unconscious behavior by which proximity to another person is sought. Good, secure attachment allows people to grow. Attachment is linked to the development of resilience, your ability to cope with setbacks and disappointments.

Statement 4 – Inspires confidence

- Is able to manage stress and exude calmness
- Takes an open attitude in meetings
- Uses language that instills hope

Statement 5 – Offers security out of proximity

- Exudes availability
- Keeps agreements
- Shows warmth and empathy

Statement 6– Focuses on the positive

- Is focused on learning and development in all contexts
- Has a positive basic attitude, even when giving negative feedback or bad news

Theme 3: Bonding and Intimacy

Bonding is about your conscious choice to deepen relationships by allowing vulnerability to be present. Intimacy is your ability to truly bond and entrust yourself to another. Intimacy is needed to learn and develop, to address conflict, and experience psychological safety together.

Statement 7 – Engages in dialogue

- Paraphrases; gives the other person back what is heard and perceived before asking further
- Engages in conversation out of curiosity, without wanting to defend/ explain himself
- Is willing to accept/look for new insights

Statement 8 – Examines and values emotions

- Welcomes emotions, giving space to anger, sadness, and fear, as well as joy
- Explores the information hidden behind the emotions

Statement 9 – Is willing to get into conflict

- Is able to appreciate differences of opinion, experience, and thinking
- Actively seeks tension to strengthen bonding
- Sees conflict as an opportunity to learn and grow

Theme 4: Loss and separation

Loss and separation are part of relationships and test your ability to (re) connect. Loss can include goals, workplaces, people, health, meaningful projects, and dreams. Your behavior at work and beyond is determined, to a very large extent, by your fear of losing or by previous losses you experienced. Acknowledging, recognizing, and exploring loss and saying goodbye properly are necessary to welcome and be welcomed again.

Statement 10 – Acknowledges what has been lost

- Has an eye for the losses people face
- Honors the history of the organization and the people who contributed to it

Statement 11 – Has attention for separations

- Creates space to actively say goodbye
- Is present at key moments of separation
- Speaks words of bonding during moments of separation

Statement 12 – Uses rituals to mark transitions

- Brings people together to mark important moments
- Actively involves others in the interpretation of rituals
- Leads the way in creating meaningful memories

Theme 5: Grief and Integration

Grieving is essentially a learning process on the way to different, new or changed bonds. It is about the discomfort, the pain, the difficulty, and the inconvenience you might experience around saying goodbye. It has a double movement of being engaged with the past – that which has been lost – and with the future – that which is unknown. It invites you to put the puzzle back together again.

Statement 13 – Dares to slow down and be still

- Harnesses the power of silence during painful and uncomfortable emotions
- Dares to go beyond his own discomfort and continue asking
- Doesn't get lost in unsolicited advice and platitudes

Statement 14 – Helps create perspective

- Helps create calm when change evokes uncertainty and loss of control

- Is willing to contribute own experience to provide inspiration and recognition
- Helps look to the future

Statement 15 – Focuses on learning and development

- Supports exploring options and making choices
- Invites the taking of responsibility

Theme 6: Meaning and Calling

Meaning-making is being able to see how events and experiences have helped make you who you are. Meaning-making creates new perspectives. "Who am I, Who are we, after this loss?" It leads the way into the question of calling. "Who are you at the level of your identity? What are your bigger goals in life and how are you making them real?"

Statement 16 – Celebrates success

- Proud of their own successes
- Actively seeks success experiences and moments, large or small
- Celebrates successes of self and others with whom they have bonded

Statement 17 – Knows and lives their calling

- Knows their own calling and lives it
- Helps others find and live their calling
- Is focused on development talents, theirs and others

Statement 18 – Inspires, and sets things in motion

- Knows how to engage people
- Encourages others to see unknown possibilities and to dream big
- Radiates joy

Appendix 2

Ethics and Code of Conduct of The School for Transition

The School for Transition is passionate about being transparent in its ethics and the fundamentals of the behavior of its own staff and those with whom it works. At the heart of The School for Transition, and thus the basis of our work, the encounters we advocate and the contributions we want to make, are the themes on the Transition Cycle.

The School for Transition is committed to being there for people who want to shape real change. We believe that the development of employees, leadership, and organizations comes about in the bonds between people. That is why The School for Transition is dedicated to clearly and unambiguously expressing these *raisons d'être*. The following sections discuss our basic values, the code of conduct and their concrete implementation.

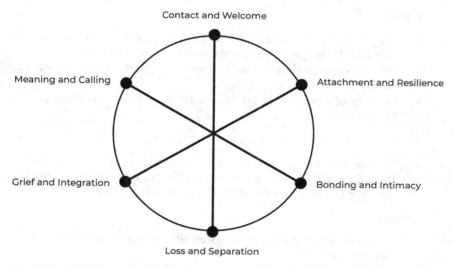

Figure A2.1 Transition Cycle

Basic Principles

Love: every person is unique and worthwhile, regardless of gender, position, belief, origin, health, or orientation.

Autonomy: every human being has the freedom, regardless of circumstances, to make their own choices and thereby shape their future. In doing so, they are responsible for ensuring their freedom and that of others.

Balance: every human being has the right to physical, emotional, mental, and spiritual stability and growth.

Base: every human being is entitled to a safe environment in which to grow and develop.

Leadership: every human being is called to take leadership and place themselves in a context from which they tap into their source to take agency and give direction to their life. Thus, in bonding with themselves and others, they create inspiration for themselves and others and shape their singular destiny.

Behavior

The code of conduct is based on our core values and ethical principles. The code meets our need to know how to act ethically. It is a common framework that guides our behavior and helps us do the right thing. We support each other in this and work together in all areas.

The code of conduct has seven elements, detailed below in terms of specific behavior:

1   *Caring*

   - We welcome the other and ourselves in every contact and we consciously say goodbye at the conclusion of each contact.
   - We are curious about what is important to the other person and willing to defer our own judgment.
   - We help others grow in safety and trust, in ways that bring out the best in them.

2   *Daring*

   - We innovate, experiment, and take risks and invite others to do so.
   - We acknowledge mistakes and the pain they bring, carry this into dialogue to learn and develop, and invite others to do so too.

3   *Integrity*

   - We speak out and act on what we think is right, even when we find this difficult.
   - We expect and deliver results of the highest quality we can offer.
   - We do the right thing even when no one can see us.

4   *Dialogue*

- In every contact, we are willing to search for a greater truth than the one we know. Therefore, we are curious and willing to be vulnerable and empathetic.
- We are prepared to *put the fish on the table*. That is, we bring into the contact anything that potentially stands in the way of bonding.
- We are willing to go into conflict, based on the belief that it leads to growth.
- We actively give and solicit feedback, aiming at growth.

5   *Transparency*

- We are prepared to be held accountable, whether expected to or not, for the choices we make as professionals.
- We actively discuss our core values and ethics.
- We take responsibility for voicing our concerns in an honest and professional manner. In doing so, we actively contribute to ensuring that every perspective is given space.

6   *Fun*

- We collaborate and share relationships, ideas, and knowledge.
- Our work aims to foster an atmosphere of playfulness, relaxation, and learning.

7   *Confidentiality*

- We respect all applicable laws and regulations regarding privacy, confidentiality, and personal data.
- We are able to safeguard the confidentiality of information that becomes available to us in the exercise of our craft.

Index

Printed in the United States
by Baker & Taylor Publisher Services